Corporate Recovery

Corporate Recovery

Managing Companies in Distress

by Stuart Slatter and David Lovett

BeardBooks
Washington, D.C.

To Clare and Sue

Contents

List of Figures

Acknowledgements

This book started as a project to revise an earlier book on turnaround management written by one of us in the early 1980s. The book, *Corporate Recovery – A Guide to Turnaround Management* by Stuart Slatter has been widely used by managers and students of management, both in the UK and overseas. Once we started on the project to update the book we realized that while the basic concepts and approach of the earlier book are as applicable today as they were fifteen years ago, we wanted to include a lot of new ideas and material that we have developed in recent years. Only Chapters 2 and 3 have much in common with *Corporate Recovery*, and so very quickly the project became a new book with a new title.

We would like to acknowledge a number of people who have contributed substantially to the production of this book. In particular we would like to thank Julian Cooper, an Arthur Andersen partner who is now based in Bangkok. His very analytical and structured approach enabled us to clearly communicate our thoughts and concepts. We would also like to thank Laura Barlow, who did much of the work towards capturing our views on the critical areas of developing turnaround plans and signposting the way out of the maze. Adrian Wolsterhome captured much of the importance of tight working capital and cash management, and Derek Elliott project-managed the input from these and other members of the Arthur Andersen turnaround team. This is not an easy task, and we are grateful to Derek for applying his usual unflappable style to a project that could on occasions be like herding cats. We would particularly like to thank Julian Gething, who is a Director in the Arthur Andersen Global Corporate Finance practice.

He took an unpaid year out to obtain an MBA at London Business School, during which he researched the key success factors in achieving turnaround. Many other Arthur Andersen staff contributed to this book, including Wolf Waschkuhn, John Leahy, Greg Tate, Russell Pope, Chris Lawton, and David Turver. We are grateful to them all; but the views expressed in this book are the views of the authors alone.

Many business practitioners have reviewed this book and shared with us their insights on implementing turnaround plans. We are very grateful for the time freely given and hope that we have adequately reflected their observations in our book.

The development of any book takes a great deal of commitment and support, and since both authors have a pretty hectic professional life, three secretaries have had to take the brunt of our often extreme demands. We are both fortunate in having these excellent allies and we would like to thank Nancy Earl, Jenny Drew, and Carol Goodall who patiently kept us to the task in hand.

Preface

Turnaround is big business. Consider just some of the financial headlines from around the world on one day in September 1997:

Ssangyong: renewed rumours of serious cashflow and other financial problems at South Korea's sixth largest conglomerate. This follows persistent rumours about the possible collapse of the Kia Motor Group and the insolvency earlier this year of three other large conglomerates, including the collapse of Hanbo Steel.

Sears: UK retailing group tumbled £98 million into the red as newly appointed company doctor David James commences turnaround with £80 million provision against future restructuring costs.

Philippines: rumours of serious cash-flow problems at Philippines' largest food producer sent stock plummeting.

Laura Ashley: troubled UK retailer warns of further losses more than two and a half years after the appointment of company doctor, Anne Iverson.

Other main stories in 1997 included the financial crisis in Thailand which resulted in the suspension of fifty-four troubled financial institutions; the IMF rescue package for South Korea and Indonesia; and the Communist Party of China's three-year initiative to sort out inefficient or loss-making state enterprises. Whereas turnaround management was a relatively obscure subject when this book's predecessor, *Corporate Recovery*, was published, today it represents a global phenomenon.

This book is written for those directly involved in turnaround situations. It is particularly relevant for chief executives who find themselves having to lead a turnaround, but will also be useful for any other member of the management team (chairman, non-executive director, etc.) of a troubled enterprise. Investors are the second major group for whom the book is written. Venture capitalists, bankers and other finance providers who are involved with troubled companies may find it helpful as a checklist against which they can evaluate the rescue plans of the management teams they are being asked to back. And finally we hope it will help advisors of troubled companies – merchant bankers, management consultants, and others.

We subscribe to the view that turnaround management is everyday management. Although the approach and techniques set out in this book are specifically directed at turnaround situations, they can have broader application. Many companies at an early stage of decline would benefit from a mild dose of turnaround medicine. Equally, companies that have just been acquired usually need 'sorting out'. Turnaround management involves applying traditional management techniques in a rather unusual environment. The patient is seriously ill, both cash and time are in short supply, and rapid recovery is required. The book should therefore also be of interest to any general manager who wants to improve the short-term financial performance of his/her business. However, it would be a mistake to push this point too far. We strongly believe that organizations at different stages of the corporate life cyle require quite different management approaches. For example, start-ups and high-growth companies require a 'looser', more entrepreneurial management approach, whereas the early stages of a turnaround require more 'command and control'.

This book aims to be a practical reference guide for turnaround management. It is written by people who have been at the 'coalface' of turnaround management. It is based on a mixture of practical experience and academic research, and reflects our view of best practice in the field of turnaround management. It describes *what* must be done and *how* to do it.

1 Turnaround Management

What Is a Turnaround Situation?

There is no hard-and-fast definition of what constitutes a turnaround situation. We use the term here to refer to those firms or operating units (the latter will be included under the generic term 'firm' or 'company' from now on) whose financial performance indicates that the firm will fail in the foreseeable future unless short-term corrective action is taken. The profit performance of such firms, as measured by return on capital employed, is likely to be considerably below what one would expect for the type of business in which it is engaged. Our definition includes firms that do not have a current cash crisis, and is therefore a wider definition than that used by some writers who equate turnaround situations with the existence of a cash crisis. Certainly, whenever there is a cash crisis there is a turnaround situation but, under the definition used in this book, a turnaround situation may exist without a cash crisis. A broad definition of what constitutes a turnaround situation recognizes that firms often exhibit symptoms of failure long before any crisis begins. Such firms are often stagnant businesses with under-utilized assets and ineffective management. Many such firms have survived over the years *in spite of* their poor management. If a stagnant business is not turned around, a crisis situation will eventually ensue because the management is unlikely to be taking the necessary steps to adapt to the changing product-market environment in which the firm is operating. Stagnant businesses are often in stable and mature industries with a competitive advantage that exists for largely historical reasons (due to location, for example). They are often businesses which

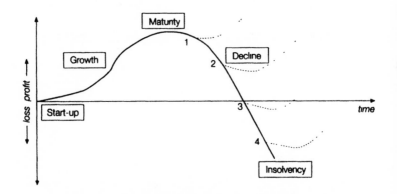

Figure 1.1: **Corporate Life Cycle**

are family-controlled or controlled by the board of directors. By adopting turnaround strategies early enough, recovery can take place without the traumas usually associated with a crisis situation.

Profitability alone is not a reliable measure of the existence of a turnaround situation. A growth-oriented firm that has grown too fast may continue to be quite profitable while at the same time being in a severe cash-flow crisis. Alternatively, the fact that a firm reports a loss in a single year does not itself indicate a turnaround situation. There may, for example, have been an extraordinary write-off of assets during the financial year, while the rest of the business remained reasonably healthy. On the other hand, a large loss in just one year in one operating unit can place the whole firm in jeopardy. The profit picture of the typical turnaround situation is several years of successively lower profits culminating in a loss situation and a cash-flow crisis.

If no corrective management action is taken in a turnaround situation, the firm becomes insolvent, since external events can only postpone insolvency, not avert it. Where specific corrective action is taken by management, the outcome can be either successful or unsuccessful, in which case the firm becomes insolvent and falls into receivership or liquidation.

Figure 1.1 shows four different points of financial decline during a typical corporate life cycle. Not all companies follow such a life cycle, since organizations can be 'reborn' or transformed at any time. However, the model provides a useful illustration of what we mean by a turnaround situation. All points of decline with the exception of Point 1 are likely to be candidates for the approach to turnaround management discussed in this book.

Sustainable Recovery

The aim of this book is to describe the corrective actions management needs to take to achieve recovery in a turnaround situation. However, just as it is difficult to give a precise definition of a turnaround situation, so it is difficult to define what we mean by corporate recovery. There is no absolute measure, but it is worth distinguishing between firms which survive but never make an adequate return on capital employed, or survive only in the short term and then become insolvent, and those which achieve what we call *sustainable* recovery. Sustainable recovery involves achieving a viable and defensible business strategy, supported by an adequate organization and control structure. It means that the firm has fully recovered, is making 'good' profits and is unlikely to face another crisis in the foreseeable future. The corrective action described in this book is aimed at assisting management to achieve sustainable recovery, although it is important to realize at the outset that many turnaround situations can never attain such a position.

Sustainable recovery requires the firm to develop sustainable competitive advantage. This is an important concept and is the basis of developing a viable and defensible business strategy. We know from basic economics that the firm can only make above-average profits ('economic rents', in economists' jargon) if the market in which it operates is imperfect. The process by which firms develop and exploit these market imperfections is the basis of competitive business strategy. There are three main sources of competitive advantage for the firm to exploit – economic factors; organizational factors; and political and legal factors.

Economic factors provide the firm with three possible sources of sustainable competitive advantage: absolute cost advantage over competitors because the firm has control of or access to cheaper sources of raw material, cheaper labour, or proprietary production know-how; relative cost advantage due to the presence of economies of scale; and product differentiation advantages (for example, brand name, control or access to distribution channels, superior product technology and superior service levels).

Organizational factors relate to the quality and expertise of management, which in turn affect the quality of strategy implementation. Good implementation can be a major source of competitive advantage if the firm's 'economic' strategy is sound, but good implementation of a poor strategy is wasteful and ineffective.

Political and legal factors may also give the firm a competitive advantage, for instance when government purchasing departments favour domestic (rather than foreign) manufacturers.

The mere existence of any of these factors does not imply competitive advantage, since competitive advantage is a relative concept. Thus, for example, a firm may have a good brand name and proprietary technology but be at a competitive disadvantage because, although competitors may lack proprietary technology, they have an even stronger brand name and can take advantage of economies of scale due to their larger size.

Firms that are unable to develop any competitive advantage may recover, but their profits will be unexciting and they will be highly susceptible to further crisis in the future. Other firms in a turnaround situation may be at such a significant competitive disadvantage that they will become insolvent despite the best efforts of the most able management.

Turnaround Management

It is a commonly held but mistaken view that the primary role of a turnaround leader is short-term cost reduction. The media have fuelled this myth by promoting the company doctor as some sort of corporate commando on a 'seek and destroy' mission. Perhaps the best known illustrations of this are the nicknames the media have given to two American CEOs of modern times, Jack 'Neutron' Welch and Al 'Chainsaw' Dunlap.

One of our fundamental propositions is that turnaround management is *holistic*. Successful turnarounds are based on addressing both strategic and operational issues. Rescue plans seek to cut costs and grow revenues. The perspective is both short and long term. The CEO must tackle both the soft and hard elements of an organization. Only by taking this broader view can the four key objectives of most turnaround situations be addressed. These are:

- take control and manage the immediate crisis
- rebuild stakeholder support
- fix the business
- resolve future funding.

We have identified seven essential ingredients which address these objectives, and which for us make up the discipline known as turnaround management. Figure 1.2 shows how the seven ingredients support the four objectives.

Another way of thinking about the scope of turnaround management is to consider the phases of the turnaround process:

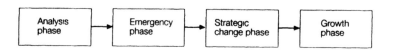

A narrow definition might seek to restrict the process to the analysis and emergency phases. However, in our experience, the implementation of

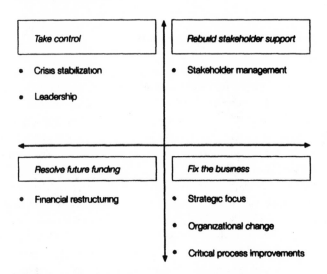

Figure 1.2: **Key Objectives and Their Essential Ingredients**

many generic turnaround strategies involve significant strategic change. Although there is generally considerable overlap between the phases, the linear sequence remains typical of most situations. It is unlikely that a substantially underperforming company that is close to insolvency can be restored to sustainable viability within twelve months. In our experience the journey through the first three phases usually takes from eighteen months to two years. Once the turnaround moves into the growth phase, classic turnaround management is complete.

Turnaround or Workout?

Turnaround can be compared with other forms of process applied to troubled companies.

Business Transformation

Transformation generally describes an enterprise-wide performance improvement programme for companies that are moderately, rather than substantially, underperforming. The organization may be seeking to achieve world leadership; or, if it is a mature business, trying to regenerate growth; if in decline, seeking to reverse the trend.

Business transformation therefore tends to apply to companies at an earlier stage of the corporate life cycle. Although both turnaround and transformation aim to achieve a quantum leap in performance, the speed of recovery and desired end-state differ. Transformation projects aim to achieve a high level of absolute and relative performance improvement over the medium term; turnarounds are seeking to achieve sustained viability fast. The differences are illustrated in Figure 1.3. The turnaround performance improvement line starts lower and climbs at a steeper gradient, but finishes well below the transformation curve.

The final difference relates to the scope of the change programme. Business transformation projects are generally restricted to business improvement and do not encompass crisis management, capital restructuring or dealing with stakeholders.

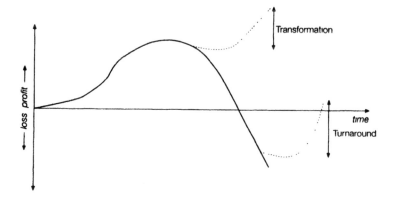

Figure 1.3: **Transformation Versus Turnaround**

Workout

Workout is usually used to describe a creditor-led rather than debtor-led process which has as its objective the reduction of an organization's indebtedness via the disposal of its assets, but avoiding insolvency. The process of dealing with a troubled business may be initiated and controlled either by the company's management or by its creditors. In the UK (and other jurisdictions) corporate debt is typically secured and therefore in a default situation a secured lender has considerable influence in determining how the problem is handled. In many cases the appropriate solution is de facto controlled by the creditors, and is therefore referred to as 'creditor-led'. By contrast, where management has retained the initiative and is in control of the solution, it is debtor-led.

In general, creditor-led solutions involve either a workout or formal insolvency. The objective of both processes is the same: the company's assets are realized to repay debt, although in the case of a workout the management is notionally in charge, whereas insolvency involves the appointment of a receiver or administrator to carry out the task. A workout typically involves a heavy emphasis on crisis management and financial restructuring; business improvement is not a priority because the objective is not necessarily to retain and fix the troubled businesses.

By contrast, a turnaround is usually debtor-led and involves a greater emphasis on business improvement. It is debtor-led because only management can lead the rescue of a troubled company; investors and debt providers can help and be supportive but they cannot lead the process. It involves business improvement because the objective is the rescue of the company, not its liquidation.

Insolvency

There are two basic insolvency procedures. One provides a limited period of protection for a company from its creditors to allow it to develop a rescue plan which will allow both the company and its business to emerge from formal insolvency proceedings. The other provides for the realization of a company's assets and the distribution of the proceeds to its creditors. This latter form generally does not involve the survival of the company, although the business carried out by the company may survive and be sold as a going concern. The American Chapter 11 process is an example of the former 'protection' process. The rescue of the company via Chapter 11 may involve a comprehensive turnaround with crisis management, business improvement, financial restructuring and stakeholder management, although the process is often heavily oriented towards financial restructuring. In this, it is similar to the UK receivership process: the work of a receiver is heavily biased towards crisis management and the realization of assets. Increasingly, receivers are trying to improve the quality of the assets prior to sale, but this process is substantially different from a turnaround, even though the 'commander' style of management in the early days may be very similar.

The Demand for Turnaround Management

The size of the turnaround market is dependent upon three key drivers: macro-economic health, industry competition, and political changes.

At the macro-economic level, the overall health of the economy has a major impact on the number of ailing companies. Economies in recession generally have a relatively high incidence of corporate distress, resulting primarily from weak demand, asset price deflation and high interest rates. At the time of writing, the economies of the UK and the US are slowing down but the current level of corporate failure is still relatively low. In comparison, many of the newly developed economies of Asia have considerable macro-economic problems, and in consequence many large companies in the region are experiencing serious financial problems. However, even in the relatively healthy economic climate of the United Kingdom, we can expect the number of companies in distress to increase. Corporate debt is now higher than in the late 1980s, the number of profit warnings is increasing, and leading economic indicators point to a slowing-down in the economy.

Another significant factor is the relative health of various industries. Michael Porter's 'five forces model' provides a way of determining the relative profit potential of an industry.[1] He identified unattractive industries such as steel and tyres where no company earned high returns; equally he noted that there were attractive industries such as toiletries and soft drinks where high returns are possible. It is now nearly twenty years since Porter published his thinking. Perhaps the biggest change since then is the substantial capacity growth that has occurred in many industries. The *Financial Times* in September 1997 quoted General Electric's Jack Welch as saying, 'There is excess global capacity in almost every industry.'

The globalization of competition within many industries, the impact of new technology, and the pervasive nature of change have radically increased the hostility of most business environments. The days when even the laggards within an industry could enjoy a comfortable existence have long since gone in most sectors. Consequently, even in a benign macro-economic climate, most industries offer substantial turnaround opportunities.

Radical political change has created a massive demand for turnaround management in the transitional economies of Eastern Europe and China. The move towards a market economy and mass privatization have put substantial pressure on formerly state-owned enterprises to reform or die. In many cases the scale and urgency of the restructuring required mean that the change programmes are genuine turnarounds rather than business transformations. To a lesser extent, similar reforms are apparent even in the economies of Western Europe. More and more state enterprises are being privatized, and those that remain in the public sector are finding it increasingly hard to procure state subsidies.

The nature of these three drivers – macro-economic health, industry competition and political change – tend to suggest that ailing companies will be a continuing feature of the global business landscape.

Availability of Funding and Management

There has been a substantial growth in specialist investors in turnaround situations during the past decade. Various classes of investor, who specifically target underperforming situations, have emerged from the capital markets. The acquisitive conglomerates such as Hanson developed a business system based on hunting, acquiring and turning around troubled and underperforming companies. More recently, rival 'corporate predator' competitors in the form of leveraged buyout (LBO) funds have emerged. Initially these LBO funds were general, but the latest generation include highly specialist debt and equity funds focused solely on troubled situations. All these are relatively long-term 'hands on' financial investors; their objective is to invest in under-performing businesses, proactively drive the turnaround, and realize a capital gain from the improved value of business.

The increased flow of capital into the turnaround market has been accompanied by the emergence of a growing number of company doctors and turnaround practitioners. The popularity of Sir John Harvey-Jones' *Troubleshooter* television series in the United Kingdom is the most visible example of the heightened profile of company doctors. A growing number of corporate troubleshooters are being brought in by institutional investors to turn around ailing public companies. These serial turnaround leaders move from one assignment to the next, each one typically lasting a couple of years. Their rewards can be substantial, as generous stock option schemes offer the opportunity of making a major capital gain for the successful practitioner.

There is also a growing number of specialized turnaround consulting firms, ranging from the small boutique to firms as large as Arthur Andersen and Pricewaterhouse Coopers. Their entry into this emerging market means we can probably conclude that the turnaround industry has truly come of age.

Structure of the Book

Business books are rarely read from cover to cover, and we doubt if this one will be any different! Chapter 4 provides the basic framework for turnaround management, outlining the seven essential ingredients for a successful turnaround and the key implementation tasks which need to be undertaken. If the reader wants to understand why companies get into trouble and what happens in the ensuing crisis, they should also read Chapters 2 and 3. Before any turnaround can be considered, a diagnostic review needs to be carried out, and we discuss how to do this in Chapter 5.

The rest of the book devotes a chapter to each of the seven essential ingredients. Chapters 6, 7 and 8 describe crisis stabilization, leadership and stakeholder management, all of which must start more or less simultaneously on day one of the turnaround. Chapter 9 describes how to develop a business plan to fix the business, which will consist of three of the seven key ingredients: strategic focus (Chapter 10). organizational change (Chapter 11) and critical process improvements (Chapter 12). Chapter 13 provides suggestions for how to implement the business plan. Chapter 14 is only relevant to those likely to be involved in obtaining additional finance or reorganizing the capital structure of the firm.

Note

1. M. Porter, *Competitive Strategy* (Free Press, New York, 1980).

2 Symptoms and Causes of Decline

Before we can start to talk sensibly about turnaround strategies, we need to have a good understanding of just how and why firms find themselves in a crisis situation. This is an enormously large topic, since each major cause of decline is a potential book in itself. The aim of this chapter therefore is only to summarize the causes and symptoms of corporate decline.

When analysing a firm's decline, the reader should be careful to distinguish between symptoms and causes of failure. Symptoms are merely tell-tale signs – danger signals, if you like – which a perceptive analyst outside the firm can discern. Symptoms give clues as to what *might* be wrong with the firm, but they do not provide a guideline for management action. What is important if we are to help the sick firm to recover is to find out the root causes of the firm's problems. The medical analogy is commonly used: a headache and temperature are symptoms of an illness, not its cause, and the doctor who treats merely the symptoms may well find himself with a dead patient. So it is with a firm in crisis. One critical difference, though, between a patient and a dying company is that the company requires the support of the stakeholders around it to survive. Therefore, in some circumstances, it may be necessary for the company doctor to treat the publicly visible symptoms so as to repair third-party confidence and allow the company to receive support.

Symptoms of Decline

There are numerous symptoms indicating that a company may be entering decline. Depending on the observer's perspective, though, some are easier to see than others. Those closest to the company (i.e., its management and employees) are usually able to see the onset of problems before outsiders, who tend to rely on publicly available financial information to analyse the company's performance. However, there is usually a lengthy time lag with financial information and there are many other alternative and non-financial symptoms of decline which can act as important warning signs. In many instances, it is critical that these non-financial indicators are identified and acted on early, because by the time the financial impact of the causes of decline show through it may be too late to save the company.

Figure 2.1 identifies some of the more common symptoms of decline from different observer perspectives. This is by no means an exhaustive list of symptoms, and of course many of these symptoms exist in healthy companies. An alert observer will note a trend over time, and a cocktail of symptoms should warn management, outside observers and stakeholders of impending problems.

It is curious how often the recognition that a company is in trouble comes as a surprise. However, the attentive observer will not be so surprised because s/he will note the build-up of the symptoms. Unfortunately management often deny or suppress the symptoms, to the extent that they also express surprise when a crisis suddenly erupts.

One is reminded of the story of the frog and the boiling water. If a live frog is put into cold water which is slowly heated, it will end up boiled alive, having not recognized the severity of the impending crisis. But if a frog lands in boiling water, it will react and jump out. The frog, like many observers and stakeholders, can recognize a crisis when it occurs but fails to recognize the trends leading to the crisis.

Predicting Company Failure

Most external observers rely on financial indicators to predict decline. Analysing empirical evidence from firms which have failed has led to the development of 'z-scores'. These began with the work of Edward Altman, who used five financial ratios and a statistical technique known as linear discriminant analysis to classify firms as solvent or insolvent.[1] Altman calculated an index, which he called a Z-score, as follows:

$$Z = 1.2\, x_1 + 1.4\, x_2 + 3.3\, x_3 + 0.6\, x_4 + 1.0\, x_5$$
where
x_1 = working capital/total assets
x_2 = retained earnings/total assets
x_3 = earnings before interest and tax/total assets
x_4 = market value of equity and preferred stock/total liabilities
x_5 = sales/total assets

Z-scores were used to classify firms as either bankrupt or non-bankrupt. Where the score was below 1.81, the firm was considered to be failing; where it was above 2.99 it was healthy. Altman's results were 95 per cent accurate one year prior to bankruptcy, and 72 per cent accurate two years prior to bankruptcy. The Z-score has been found not to be a good predictor for longer than two years before bankruptcy which, it could be claimed, is not much use since most investors and banks know (or should know) from more conventional analysis that a firm is headed for insolvency two years before it actually happens.

Altman's work has been applied to UK financial data by Argenti[2] and Taffler.[3] Taffler's study concluded that financial gearing and profitability measures were the most significant ratios in predicting failure, and that liquidity ratios are of less importance than the more fundamental aspects of a firm's structure, such as its earnings ability and the size of its liabilities. Both Argenti and Taffler recognized that the Z-scores used by Altman as cut-offs will be different in the UK, will differ by industry, and will change over time as economic conditions change. Great care

Figure 2.1: **Common Symptoms of Decline**

Observer	Business	Capital Market	Financial Information
'Man in the street'	• Subject of takeover bid. • Embarrassing loss of CEO. • Major disaster (e.g., Eurotunnel fire). • Obsolete or hopeless products.	• Very public refinancing deals (e.g., Queens Moat).	• Stunningly poor financial results. • Serious profits warning.

Informed reader/shareholder	• Rapid senior management turnover.
	• Repeated failure of new product launches.
	• Public disagreements among directors over strategy.
	• Post-acquisition integration failing to reap benefits.
		• Raising of new funds – debt or equity – to fund losses.
		• Vulture funds trading in debt.
			• Declining:
			  – share price
			  – profits
			  – market share
			  – credit score
			  – liquidity
			  – dividends
			  – sales volume
			    (at constant prices)
			  – equity-to-debt ratio.
			• Delays in publishing accounts.
			• Qualification of accounts by auditors.

City analyst	• Lack of strategy or ability to implement it. • Loss of key staff. • Concealed Main Board conflict and fear.	• Breach of banking covenants. • Discussion of financial restructuring plans.	• Destruction of shareholder value. • Share performance significantly worse than sector average.

	• Lack of investment in new technology, people, capital. • 'Big projects will save the day' – white elephants. • Loss of key customers and contracts. • Low morale.	
Suppliers and customers	• Worsening terms of trade. • Late payment of supplier invoices. • Factoring customer invoices. • Declining customer service. • Increased supplier disputes leading to supplies 'on stop'. • Raising of credit notes after year-end. • Low staff morale pervasive throughout business. • Start-up problems with new IT systems.	• Negotiations by suppliers with company bankers to support a difficult restructuring plan.

Figure 2.1: **Common Symptoms of Decline** (Continued)

Observer	Business	Capital Market	Financial Information
Investigating accountant	• Lack of leadership. • Loss of credibility of senior management. • Poor working capital management. • Operational objectives not aligned with any strategy or being implemented. • 'Analysis paralysis'. • No sense of urgency. • Litigation matters pending.	• Worsening bank security against company requirement for increased borrowings.	• Creative accounting practices. • Declining performance in management accounts – large negative variances of actual performance to budget.
Employees	• Major management issues can often only be seen by staff: – emergency board meetings – complete fear – management paralysis, finger-pointing, bickering, etc. – acting in functional isolation.		

must therefore be exercised before relying on the Z-score, or indeed any predictive tool.

However, as the development of Z-scores has become more sophisticated (due to the increase of information available to develop the ratios and the processing power of computers), industry specific Z-score ratios have been developed. One of the most successful has been brought to market by a UK company called Syspass.

The reader should now be in a position to recognize some of the key symptoms of decline and therefore begin to form an opinion on whether a business may benefit from the application of turnaround techniques. Not all companies that are predicted to fail respond to turnaround techniques. Once a business is firmly in decline, it is imperative that the management leading the turnaround quickly understands the causes of decline (as opposed to the symptoms) so they can treat the real problems.

Causes of Decline

Developing a suitable system to classify the factors causing decline is not as easy as it may seem at first glance. One can, if one wants to, trace virtually all the reasons for declining performance back to 'bad management', arguing that it was either poor decisions or inaction on the part of management that was the cause of all the firm's problems. Even where the cause of decline is primarily due to environmental factors beyond management control, one can argue that management should have forecast such events and planned accordingly. David Lovett recalls being part of the 'it's all down to management' school. In the 1980s he made a number of presentations based on the idea that what separated successful businesses from failed businesses were two key features – management and luck. He observed that the management of successful businesses appeared to have had 'good luck' whereas the management of failed businesses appeared to have had 'bad luck'. Some further analysis led to the observation that good management appeared to have good luck and poor management appeared to have bad luck.

On further reflection he wondered whether management actually made its luck by the various and complex ways in which the management process was undertaken.

This rather simplistic approach was popular among the audiences of the 1980s, who liked to hear (a) that it was all down to management and (b) that it was rather straightforward. Further experience of dealing with the management of troubled companies and their stakeholders has led Lovett to conclude that this approach is not very useful. It merely locates the blame for a firm's decline without providing those charged with the recovery task with any useful analytical information. The simplistic answer may be to change management, but that is far from the whole story.

As soon as one looks deeper into the problem, however, one is confronted with a classic 'chicken and egg' situation. Which is the true causal factor and which the effect? For example, one might identify intense price competition in the marketplace as a causal factor of decline . . . but is this the cause, or is the firm's inferior cost position relative to that of its competitors the real cause? If *this* is the cause, is it due to lack of market share or to the firm's conservative financial policy of not investing in modern plant and equipment, or to both? If financial policy is to blame, what causes management to adopt such a policy? . . . and so here we are, back once again with management! In practice, a chain of interrelated causal factors and multiple causes can be identified in most situations. Which causal factors are identified, therefore, requires a considerable amount of subjective judgement, and this is reflected in the writings of various authors and researchers.

We have chosen to concentrate on what we believe to be thirteen principal causes of decline. These are shown in Figure 2.2. From time to time we come across other factors that undoubtedly play a contributory role. Unfavourable government policies with regard to exchange rates, subsidies, taxes, and so on, can make companies and whole industries uncompetitive against foreign competitors. Strikes, drought, famine, and so on, can all be causes of financial distress. In a recent study of causes of decline among entrepreneurial high-tech firms, Stuart Slatter identified manufacturing problems as a particular cause of crisis,[4] but we have omitted this factor from our list of *principal* causes.

Figure 2.2: **Causes of Corporate Decline**

Internal Causes	External Causes
1. Poor management	11. Changes in market demand
2. Inadequate financial control	12. Competition
3. Poor working capital management	13. Adverse movements in commodity prices
4. High costs	
5. Lack of marketing effort	
6. Overtrading	
7. Big projects	
8. Acquisitions	
9. Financial policy	
10. Organizational inertia and confusion	

1. Poor Management

The personal characteristics of the chief executive and the key management personnel play a major role in causing decline. Sheer incompetence and/or lack of interest in the business are common characteristics of a firm in decline. There are many books and articles on the characteristics and skills required of good managers, and we do not intend to summarize them here. What is worth emphasizing, however, are the common defects in the composition and methods of operation of a failing management team. There are six principal factors to consider:

Autocratic rule: The presence of a dominant and autocratic chief executive characterizes many failing firms. Typically, such a chief executive makes all the major decisions in the firm and will not tolerate dissent. S/he is the typical Zeus-like character described by Charles Handy in his book *Understanding Organizations.*[5] Autocratic rule, although always risky, is not necessarily bad per se. Many of the most successful firms have been built up largely on the efforts of an autocratic chief executive. As long as such companies remain financially successful, everyone points to the vision and leadership of the chief executive as a key factor for success; however, as soon as trouble occurs, that same individual is blamed for the trouble. This is just as it should be, since the causes of early success are often the causes of later failure; but it nevertheless highlights the fine line separating the positive and negative effects of autocratic rule. The main difference between the successful and the unsuccessful autocrat appears to lie in their differing attitudes towards change and new ideas. The successful autocrat is usually willing to adapt to changing business conditions and to be receptive to new ideas from subordinates and outsiders, while the unsuccessful autocrat is not.

Combined chairman and chief executive: In those firms where the positions of both chairman and chief executive are held by the same individual, there is no effective watchdog over the activities of the chief executive. The separation of these positions, while providing some safeguard to shareholders, will not of itself ensure that the chief executive's actions are monitored effectively, however. Much depends on the personalities of the individuals involved. This is particularly true where the chairman is non-executive and all the real power lies with the chief executive.

Ineffective boards of directors: Many readers might consider this to be a symptom rather than a cause of decline, but an ineffective board of directors means that planning, resource allocation and control decisions – key decisions affecting the 'guts' of the business – are poorly made. It is critical that businesses set a clear strategy and then align the operations of the business to implement that strategy. Where the board of directors is weak, it becomes very difficult to align the objectives across the business. When problems arise, this can be disastrous, as management become defensive in their functional areas and start blaming each other rather than focusing on fixing the problems.

An ineffective board of directors can arise for a number of reasons, the most important of which are:

- A poor chairman who treats the board as a 'rubber stamp', or fails to ensure that they discuss key business issues and perform their duties as required by both the law and corporate governance conventions.
- Non-executive directors who do not participate. One highly successful unit trust manager once told a class at the London Business School that he would not invest in any company which had as directors peers of the realm, members of parliament or retired generals, because in his experience they were ineffective as board members. (As an aside, he went further and said he would like to see photographs of directors in the annual reports – because he does not trust anybody who wears a beard!)
- Executive directors who participate only when the topic of discussion directly affects their area of responsibility of expertise.
- An unbalanced board in which board members are all engineers, all accountants, or whatever. Failing firms – particularly smaller firms – are often characterized by unbalanced skills at board level. In the UK the issue of having a balanced board and a balanced top management team is often one and the same issue, since most boards are heavily oriented towards executive directors. When this is not the case, both the board and the management team need to be balanced.
- Lack of communication among board members, with consequent lack of consensus agreement on the direction in which the company is going. UK research has shown that those companies in which there is a high degree of consensus among board members concerning company objectives outperform those companies where consensus does not exist.

Ineffective management: Many so-called managers are not managers at all but administrators. Maintaining the status quo is not what management is about, and many companies get into trouble because managers are simply not managing. Management is about change. Constant change is necessary for survival in today's business environment; and managers unwilling or unable to accept this proposition will inevitably be a cause of corporate decline. In some cases it is an attitude problem, in others managers lack the intellectual capability to deal with the problems they face or the ability to make and implement decisions.

Management neglect of core business: When firms reach a certain stage of development, they typically start to diversify. Diversification means further growth, something most managers find exciting and challenging. But herein lies the danger. The development of new business takes more and more of top management's most scarce resource, time, with the result that their core businesses are neglected. The consequences of this can be quite disastrous, since the core businesses are likely to be mature businesses that are generating a substantial portion of the cash flow needed to fund the acquisition and new venture programmes.

Lack of management depth: Our research has shown that lack of adequate management skills at the level below that of chief executive is a contributory factor causing decline. It is, however, nowhere near as important a factor as the quality of the chief executive. Turnarounds can often be accomplished successfully without changing any management other than the chief executive. Lack of management depth tends to be found most often in those firms where decline has been relatively slow, because in these situations the better managers have usually left long before the ultimate crisis occurs. Where the crisis is caused by one or more relatively sudden events (as was the case with Barings, for example), the quality of management is generally acceptable, although one or two heads may still have to roll.

2. Inadequate Financial Control

Lack of adequate financial control is a common characteristic of declining firms. It is a major problem because weak control usually means that management is unable to pinpoint the products and customers on which it is losing money; and sometimes more important in a crisis situation, which products or businesses are using cash and which are generating cash. As information technology and business controls have improved over the past twenty years, so the importance of this causal factor has begun to reduce. However, it is still a key factor. Often systems which have the capability of enforcing strong controls are not used correctly by management and so their effectiveness is diminished.

Lack of financial control may mean any or all of the following are absent or inadequate:

- cash-flow forecasts
- costing systems
- budgetary control
- monitoring of key performance indicators (KPIs).

There are still many firms – mainly smaller firms – in which all four are totally absent. The only financial information that exists is financial accounting information: statutory accounts prepared by outside auditors at year-end. In this situation, management may not realize until some months after the financial year-end that they lost money in the previous year. Financial accounting does not provide adequate control information – it is aggregate data and is received too late to be of use. At best it is a lagging rather than a leading indicator. From the point of view of control, what is important is management accounting information on a frequent basis. In hospitals, the patient's pulse and temperature are measured every few hours as an indicator of more fundamental problems. With firms, similar constant vigilance is required so that swift corrective action can be taken if unforeseen problems develop.

In larger firms, the problem is more typically one of inadequate systems rather than no systems at all. Budgets, costing systems and cash-flow forecasts are not new ideas for most managers these days, but the mere existence of these systems does not guarantee that they are implemented effectively. There are four common problems:

Many management accounting systems have been poorly designed: They are too complex, they produce too much poorly presented information and, more important, they produce the wrong information for general management. In fact, one could go as far as to describe many management reports as volumes of data which contain no 'information'. How many boards of directors and top management groups receive a package of monthly information which has taken many work-hours of overhead to produce, but which is totally useless? In our experience, the number is legion – and is found even among large companies. The blame for this must lie with top management. They have to ask themselves, 'What information do we need to run our business effectively, and *when* do we need it?' These are not easy questions to answer, therefore many managements delegate this non-delegatable task to accountants and systems specialists, who proceed to design systems based on what they *think* is required.

Management must produce useful, relevant, timely and accurate information on which to base decisions. They need to decide on the 'must haves' and the 'nice to haves' and then understand the cost of obtaining that information against the benefit of having it.

Management accounting information is poorly understood: Is the information provided used as a guide to management action? In large part, the answer to this question depends on whether management is numbers-oriented. There are many chief executive officers who just do not understand how to use accounting information; they do not understand the language of business. They are like businessmen trying to do business in a foreign country without being able to speak the language.

The organizational structure hinders effective control: One of the functions of a well-designed structure is to aid management control. We have noticed two aspects of this problem in our work. First, over-centralization seems to make control more difficult, because it is difficult for management to find out what is really going on. Second, the hierarchical level at which control is placed in the organization structure is often too high. In recent years many companies have found that by locating budget responsibility lower down the organization, control and productivity have been improved.

Methods of overhead allocation distort the costs: Most firms adopt a product-line costing system in which overheads are allocated to individual product lines on the basis of labour content, machine hours or total variable costs. Such a system assumes that the cost of serving one customer is the same as that of serving the next customer. This is not the case, however, unless the firm is competing in a single homogeneous market segment, which is rare. Most firms market their products or services to a range of customers in different market segments, with the result that the actual overheads associated with one transaction may be quite different from those associated with another transaction for the same product.

3. Poor Working Capital Management

Poor working capital management is a feature common to turnaround situations and is really a consequence of poor financial control. However, we have seen many situations where none of the problems identified in the previous section are present, but still the company finds itself in a cash crisis due to management's failure to focus on working capital management.

Working capital management concerns the management of debtors, stocks, creditors and cash balances. For some businesses, especially those in a start-up phase, working capital management is critical to their survival. Successful business is about generating sustainable cash flows. Increasing stocks and debtors, and decreasing creditors, all consume cash and can lead a company into crisis. For businesses such as building contractors, who may be on long-term contracts with large milestone payments, the management of their work-in-progress and invoicing is critical. Cash outlays on wages and materials, funded through an overdraft, can be very expensive, and any delays to receiving payment from the customer may take a company outside its bank covenants. Companies in seasonal industries also face difficult working capital issues as they have to stock up for the key period of sales. If they do not have sufficient funds to purchase the required stock levels, the business may fold. Furthermore, if they have inadequate planning systems, they can end up with an over- or under-stocked position, both of which lead to lost margin, and working capital difficulties.

4. High Costs

A firm that has a substantially higher cost structure than that of its major competitors is likely to be at a competitive disadvantage at all times. Even those companies focusing on relatively price-insensitive product-market segments will probably have lower profit margins than their direct competitors, with the result that they will generate less profit and less additional borrowing power. With less funds available than competitors, they will not be able to invest as much on new product development and marketing, and will, therefore, be less capable of building and defending their market position. However, the more common problem encountered in turnaround situations is the inability of firms to compete on price.

There are six major sources of cost disadvantage which can lead to a firm having to charge higher prices than its competitors:

- relative cost disadvantages due to the firm's inability to take advantage of economies of scale and its lack of experience compared with competitors
- absolute cost disadvantages which result from competitors controlling strategic variables not available to the firm itself
- cost disadvantages due to diversification
- cost disadvantages due to management style and organization structure
- operating inefficiencies due to lack of investment and poor management
- unfavourable government policies.

Each type of cost disadvantage will be explained briefly.

Relative Cost Disadvantages

There are two types of relative cost disadvantage: those due to scale effects and those due to learning-curve and experience-curve effects. Scale effects refer to the way in which the unit costs of a product decline as the absolute volume per period increases, whereas learning- and experience-curve effects depend on cumulative volume.

Scale economies: The presence of economies of scale, in whatever function of a business, give a cost advantage to the larger firm. Economies of scale arise from specialization of labour; the indivisibility of technology; spreading fixed costs over a larger volume; and the application of the concept of mass reserves. They can be present in nearly all functions of the business, and are often more important in purchasing, marketing and distribution than in manufacturing. It is very important for management to analyse each element of the firm's cost structure separately to determine the particular relationships between unit costs and scale. Where significant scale economies exist, it is the smaller firm which is usually at a cost disadvantage, unless the larger firm has moved past its optimum size and is faced with diseconomies of scale.

Learning- and experience-curve effects: These effects are independent of scale; thus it is possible for a smaller firm that has been in an industry a long time to have lower costs than a new entrant who lacks experience and is likely to incur heavy start-up costs. In practice, however, scale economies and experience-curve effects are often found side by side, since it is usually difficult for a small firm to keep its experience proprietary. Learning-curve effects apply only to labour costs, while experience-curve effects may apply to nearly all cost components.

Absolute Cost Disadvantages

Absolute cost disadvantages are independent of size or cumulative output. There are a number of sources of such disadvantages:

Ownership or control of raw material supply by competitors: Where this occurs, the disadvantaged firm is forced to buy its raw materials from a competitor who is more vertically integrated.

Access to cheaper labour: The location of manufacturing facilities can lead to significant cost disadvantages due to differences in wage rates, and differences in productivity which are independent of capital investment and training efforts. Cheaper labour is obviously an important strategic factor in industries where the manufacturing process is labour intensive, but it is a mistake to think it is important only in such industries. Access to cheaper labour is important in all industries where price competition occurs and the profit margin is low.

Proprietary production know-how: A firm relying on widely available production technology may find itself at a competitive disadvantage against a firm that has developed proprietary production processes. Many Japanese companies – Hitachi, for example – place considerable weight on this aspect of their competitive advantage.

Favourable site location: A new competitor in a market may find itself at a cost disadvantage compared with established competitors who managed to obtain property at lower prices.

Cost Disadvantage Due to Diversification Strategy

Diversified firms may find themselves at a cost disadvantage in a particular product-market area because of high allocated corporate overheads. The mix of businesses that a diversified firm chooses to be in directly affects its overhead structure. Let us assume firm X competes in three different business areas, A, B and C; its main competitor, Y, in business area A is another diversified company operating in business areas A, D and E. Firm X may find itself at a cost disadvantage if its businesses B and C have a higher overhead cost structure than businesses D and E. This situation is a direct result of the diversification strategies adopted by the two companies. A similar situation will occur if firm Y regards its business area A as a 'loss leader' business which is subsidized by profits from its other business areas, or if it regards business A as merely a vehicle for disposing of by-products from business D or E.

Cost Disadvantage Due to Management Style and Organization Structure

The issue of management style is important because it directly affects the overhead structure. The chief executive who relies heavily on staff personnel will incur heavier overheads, and thus be at some cost disadvantage, compared with the chief executive who decentralizes responsibility down to the line managers. Organization structures with large head-office 'bureaucracies' are increasingly being recognized as inefficient and cost-ineffective. This is a common problem with large, complex organizations, and inevitably leads to higher costs. Managerial style and organizational structure also have an indirect effect on labour productivity. A hierarchical organization with poor communications typically leads to lower productivity at the plant-operating level.

Operating Inefficiencies

Operating inefficiencies are due largely to poor management; they may be found in all functions of the firm. With the high proportion of bad management in turnaround situations, it is not surprising that operating inefficiency is a major cause of corporate decline. Operating inefficiencies affect all elements of the cost structure. Some of the areas in which inefficiencies may, directly or indirectly, cause higher costs are:

- low labour productivity
- poor production planning
- lack of adequate maintenance
- plant layout
- allocation of salesforce time
- allocation of advertising and promotional expenditure
- distribution and after-sales service
- terms of trade that 'encourage' a large volume of small orders
- office procedures.

Unfavourable Government Policies

Government policies in the form of taxation, foreign exchange policies and regulatory requirements can place companies located within their jurisdiction at a major cost disadvantage against their overseas competitors. We often hear captains of industry talking about the need for a 'level playing field' to compete internationally. What this means in practice is that overseas competitors have lower costs than they do due to differences in government policies. The much lower taxes on oil in the USA, for example, have given US manufacturers a significant cost advantage against the UK carpet industry.

5. Lack of Marketing Effort

The vast majority of firms that are in a period of profit-decline are characterized by management and employee complacency at all levels in the organization. This complacency is often most clearly visible to outsiders in the firm's approach to marketing. Lack of marketing effort may take many forms but, typically, one finds:

- lack of responsiveness to customers' enquiries
- a poorly motivated salesforce with a non-aggressive sales manager
- ineffective and wasted advertising
- efforts not targeted on key customers and key products
- poor after-sales service
- lack of market research/knowledge of the customers' buying habits
- outdated promotional material or a lack of promotional material
- weak or non-existent new-product development.

In those firms where lack of marketing effort has been identified as a major factor causing decline, the basic problem is usually management. The marketing director and/or the sales manager are incompetent, and are unable to provide the direction and leadership required to compete effectively in the marketplace. Lack of marketing effort alone may cause sales and profit to erode, but lack of marketing effort is often found in conjunction with more fundamental marketing problems of a strategic nature, such as severe price and product competition. Management (and their professional advisers) often fail to distinguish between marketing problems of an operational nature and those of a more serious strategic nature.

6. Overtrading

Overtrading is the process by which a firm's sales grow at a faster rate than the firm is able to finance from internally generated cash flow and bank borrowings. Overtrading can occur solely as a result of poor financial control, in which case the lack of adequate control is more accurately the cause of decline. Very often, however, there is another factor at work: the firm is going after sales growth, regardless of whether or not it is profitable. Margins are reduced and customers are added just to increase sales volume. Overtrading is a characteristic of growth firms, but most distressed firms we see tend to focus on sales volume and not profit or cash.

7. Big Projects

The 'big project' that goes wrong because costs are underestimated and/or revenues are overestimated is a well-known cause of failure. The definition of a big project is, of course, arbitrary, but we have chosen to include under this heading all 'one-off' capital and revenue projects which commonly cause decline, with the exception of acquisitions. Acquiring poor firms and poor post-acquisition management are sufficiently important causes of decline to warrant separate attention later. (Diversification as a cause of decline is not synonymous with acquisition because diversification may be implemented internally as well as by acquisition. Diversification will, therefore, be treated under both the 'big project' heading and acquisition.)

Perhaps the best rule of thumb relating to big projects is that no firm should enter into a contract which, if it goes wrong, would by itself cause the firm to become insolvent. This is more easily said than done, because many businesses by their very nature depend on a few big projects.

There are five ways in which the 'big project' typically goes wrong.

Underestimating Capital Requirements

This may arise because of:

- poor cost estimates at the project planning stage
- poor project control during the implementation of the capital expenditure
- late design changes
- external factors.

There are a variety of factors that can delay a project and increase capital costs, but over which a firm may have little control – for example, strikes by contractors; bad weather; technical difficulties with new machinery during installation; late delivery of equipment and materials. The various causes of delay feed on one another, leading to what has been described as a 'cycle of mutual demoralization'. Materials are delivered late, which leaves workers with nothing to do; they blame the management and vent their feelings by walking out. Process plant equipment manufacturers are told of the delays and decide it does not matter if they complete their orders late; and then the client company reckons the project is now running so far behind that it might just as well make a few late design changes . . .

Start-up Difficulties

Even after completion, capital projects may experience a variety of start-up difficulties which elevate operating expenses above the forecast level. Technical difficulties with plant and equipment, particularly new state-of-the-art equipment, can lead to high wastage, significant down time, and even loss of customer confidence if order backlogs develop. Sometimes the problem is organizational rather than technical, and is symptomatic of poor project planning. Perhaps the most common organizational problem leading to higher operating costs than expected is the lack of adequately trained employees. Many firms are surprised, when they open up a new plant, to see how long it takes for the new plant to operate at a similar level of productivity to their existing plants. The same applies to an even greater degree for service operations. Successful firms in service industries tend to grow only as fast as they can recruit and train personnel because they know that, if they expand too fast, poor service levels can cause the whole business to start to decline. It is not uncommon to hear the consumer say: 'They were all right until they grew too big.'

Capacity Expansion

Capacity tends to be increased either to meet growing demand or as a prelude to increasing market share, or both. The errors that companies make in this area relate to timing, and the feasibility of filling the extra capacity. The timing issue is related to the question of forecasting and cycles of demand. In a cyclical industry, a firm may be burdened with the additional overheads associated with new capacity just at the same time as demand turns down. More often than not, the error lies in believing the feasibility of filling the extra capacity at a profit. The root cause in such situations is poor strategic judgement. Very often the strategic error and timing error go together.

The decision to expand capacity is often based on whether the expansion project exceeds a certain 'hurdle' rate of return. We have seen many cases where the desire for growth has led companies to use low hurdle rates, leading to an expansion which ultimately fails to provide at least sector-average returns.

Market-entry Costs

Market entry refers to the introduction of new products into new and existing markets, or even the introduction of a firm's existing products into new markets. There are different risks associated with each type of market entry. When new products are being introduced, development costs may be higher than anticipated; when new markets are being entered, market development costs may be higher. When the firm is diversifying (i.e., introducing totally new products into totally new markets), it faces both technological and marketing risks.

Nearly all firms experience marketing failures from time to time, even firms normally regarded as highly successful – and it can be argued that, without taking the risks associated with new products and new markets, few firms would be successful.

There are many examples of growth firms in high-growth industries falling into a crisis situation as the result of marketing and/or product development costs that are higher than anticipated. E M I's brain scanner is a classic example of a good product which required much greater resources than management had originally anticipated. The large amount of cash required to market the scanner was the key causal factor in the demise of EMI. High market-entry costs are a principal cause of failure of high-tech companies.

Major Contracts

Poor cost-estimating and pricing decisions on major contracts are a common cause of decline and even failure, particularly in the construction and capital goods industries. This is most prevalent where orders are won through a process of competitive tendering. Research has shown that errors are more likely to be found in the cost-estimating process than in the pricing decision.

8. Acquisitions

Acquisitions have played an increasingly important role in the corporate strategy of large and medium-sized firms during the past thirty years. As the popularity of acquiring other companies has increased, so has the incidence of acquisitions being a direct cause of corporate decline. Acquisitions are used primarily by firms either to implement growth strategies in industries in which they already compete, or to implement diversification strategies into both related and unrelated industrial sectors. They have also been used as an opportunistic method of growth by financial conglomerates. Empirical evidence suggests that the incidence of failure varies according to the type of acquisition, but our own research reveals that there are three aspects of acquisitions that may cause firms to enter a crisis situation:

- the acquisition of 'losers' – firms with weak competitive positions in their own markets
- paying an unjustifiably high purchase price for the acquired firm
- poor post-acquisition management.

The Acquisition of Losers

We use the term 'losers' to refer to firms with weak competitive positions in their own markets. They need not necessarily be losing money at the time of acquisition, but often do so soon afterwards. Losers are typically firms that lack the key factors for success in their marketplace: they have no competitive advantage that can become the basis of a defensible business strategy. They often have obsolete products or suffer from severe competitive pressures due to their inferior cost positions. To the extent that market share is an indicator of competitive advantage, acquisitions are more successful when the acquired firm has a high market share. 'Losers' themselves typically exhibit many of the factors causing decline that are discussed in this chapter.

Conventional wisdom, coupled with empirical research on types of acquisition, has led many corporate managers to believe that related diversification is safer than unrelated diversification. This is not *always* so, and Figure 2.3 indicates why. The matrix relates the type of diversification to the existence of competitive advantage in the acquired firm. Firms which we refer to as priority candidates are those that are in related businesses and that have competitive advantage. These are the best acquisition candidates, provided the purchase price is not too high (see next section) – but they are very often the firms least likely to be for sale. Under conventional wisdom, firms falling into the top right-hand corner of the matrix would seem to be the next most attractive acquisition candidates, since they are in related businesses. However, for such acquisitions to be successful requires the successful transfer of resources and skills from the parent company to the acquired company. In practice, this transfer is very difficult to achieve, and often proves elusive even for firms in the same industry.

The worst of all possible worlds is the acquisition of unrelated firms with no competitive advantage in their marketplace. Such acquisitions are to be avoided at all costs but, unfortunately, they are very common. Typically, when a firm with a weak competitive position is acquired, the new subsidiary becomes a cash drain on the parent company. The acquisition is unlikely to be generating a large cash flow from operations even if profitable, and may require large cash in-flows to keep pace with

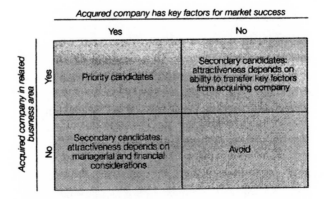

Figure 2.3: **Diversification Type and Competitive Advantage**

increased working capital requirements, and to replace old and inefficient machinery. Having just purchased the company, management throws good money after bad in the hope of justifying their acquisition decision. The sunk cost argument escapes them.

Many underperforming or troubled businesses offer great opportunity to the acquirer to rebuild value through correcting the causes that led to the current situation. There are however firms that are 'losers', and that cannot be turned around because tackling the causes of decline is beyond the scope of management. It is these acquisitions that are doomed to failure.

Paying Too Much for the Acquisition

Academic research shows that the financial benefits of acquisitions typically accrue to the seller and not to the purchaser. Many acquirers pay a considerable amount of goodwill (the amount paid in excess of net asset value) for firms they acquire. If the acquisition is of a public company, large premiums in excess of the market capitalization at the time of the bid are often paid. Firms can only justify paying large premiums if they have some unique ability to operate the acquired firm; if the acquisition will mesh with their existing businesses; or if they can see that the industry they are entering is in disequilibrium and there is therefore an opportunity to make above-average returns in the future. No wonder the more successful acquisition-oriented firms rarely pay much goodwill for the firms they acquire. Paying too much for an acquisition may destroy shareholder value but rarely leads to a crisis by itself; but if the acquisition is a 'loser', or post-acquisition management is poor, paying a high price can be disastrous.

Poor Post-acquisition Management

Poor post-acquisition management has been identified as the single most common cause of failure when making acquisitions. What happens after the acquisition depends primarily on the acquisition objective. Was the firm bought as an independent operating unit, or with the intention of integrating it into an existing operation? Acquisitions tend to be most successful when they are integrated. When they continue as an independent operating unit, what often happens is that either the new owner leaves the acquired firm alone and fails to exercise adequate managerial and financial control over its activities; or s/he becomes involved in managing the business, but in so doing meets significant organizational resistance to change. Resistance is to be expected in the post-acquisition phase, since the organizational culture of the acquiring firm is likely to be quite different from that of the acquired firm. Typically, an aggressive, power- or task-oriented organization moves into a static organization; or a task-oriented organization acquires a power-oriented (often family) firm. The result is a clash of organizational cultures which, if not well managed, can lead to inefficiency and eventual loss. The management of the new subsidiary spends its time fighting its new owners, rather than running its business.

9. Financial Policy

There are at least three types of financial policy that are direct causes of failure:

- a high debt:equity ratio (high gearing)
- a very conservative financial policy
- the use of inappropriate financing sources.

High Debt:Equity Ratio

The use of a moderate amount of debt financing (both short-term and long-term) is generally regarded as sound business practice, providing the firm can earn a rate of return on the incremental investment (made possible by the borrowing) greater than the interest payable on the debt. For many firms, a high debt:equity ratio is the result rather than the cause of corporate decline. In these situations, bank borrowings escalate as losses mount due to price competition, inefficient manufacturing, etc. Where gearing is a causal factor of decline, the aggressive use of debt financing is usually a conscious, voluntary management action. Many property companies and management buy-outs or buy-ins are characterized by the heavy use of debt.

Appropriate gearing ratios depend to a large extent on the characteristics of the industry or industries in which the firm competes. In cyclical industries with a high fixed-cost structure, high gearing ratios are likely to be riskier than in industries with only one or neither of these characteristics. What is appropriate will also depend on the debt structure (short-term versus long-term) and on the timing of the principal repayments. For example, a firm with bunched maturity dates will be able to support considerably less debt than a firm in which maturity dates are spread out.

Conservative Financial Policies

Where a firm's financial policy is characterized by lack of reinvestment in plant and equipment, a high dividend payout ratio, high liquidity and low gearing, the financial policy is usually regarded as 'conservative'. Whereas a highly aggressive financial policy can lead to the development of a rapid crisis situation, a too-conservative financial policy has the dubious merit of prolonging the decline phase of the firm.

Inappropriate Financing Sources

The failure to match borrowings and lendings was a major cause of the famous secondary banking crisis in the mid 1970s. Banks borrowed short-term money and invested in long-term projects which were illiquid in the short term. Companies are still doing this. When Laura Ashley first hit the buffers in 1990 one of the causal factors was the use of short-term debt to finance fixed-asset growth.

10. Organizational Inertia and Confusion

Distressed companies are characterized by organizational inertia. They are unable to make decisions and/or implement them, usually due to a combination of poor leadership, inappropriate organizational structures, poorly motivated staff, lack of clearly defined accountabilities and responsibilities, and inappropriate or non-existent management processes. (Sometimes staff may lack basic competencies or skills, but this is not usually a principal problem.) The organizational culture is like treacle: very slow to move!

Large companies in distress usually also suffer from organizational confusion, due to some of the same factors: unclear organizational structures, and lack of clearly defined accountabilities and responsibilities. The end result is similar: no decisions get made and nothing happens.

The typical response of senior managers when asked why an obvious decision has not been made is, 'The organization won't let us do it.' As consultants, our response is always, 'Who is the organization?' Sometimes they get the point! Once again we are back to poor management. In today's fast-moving business environment, failure to take decisions and to make things happen is an obvious recipe for disaster.

11. Changes in Market Demand

A reduction in the demand for a product or service, or a change in the pattern of demand to which the firm does not respond can be important causes of decline. A drop in demand for a product is either a long-term trend or a cyclical decline (in this case demand is tied to the familiar business cycle and will eventually recover). A third type of decline, seasonal decline, is not a significant cause of company decline except when a company is in a weak financial condition, and then it may be the trigger for change or receivership.

Long-term Decline in Demand

Just as the products of an individual firm may become obsolete because new, improved products are introduced, so the demand for whole industries, or product classes within industries, may decline over time. Trends can sometimes be reversed as new uses are found for old products, but this is rare. Long-term decline is brought about by the same environmental factors – technological change, economic conditions, changing social and cultural norms, political events – that prompt demand for new products.

Cyclical Market Decline

The world economy and the economies of all individual countries have experienced regular economic cycles of boom and recession for more than a hundred years, and maybe considerably longer. Each industry is affected in a somewhat different way by the business cycle. Some industries lead the cycle and others lag behind. Demand fluctuations in some industries are much smaller than that of the economy as a whole, while in others they are much greater. Some, like the food and tobacco industries, are affected much less than industries manufacturing capital goods and deferrable items of consumer expenditure, such as furniture.

The effect of these cyclical swings in demand can be very serious for companies that already exhibit a number of the other causal factors of decline at the start of a recessionary period. Recession alone rarely, if ever, puts a company into a turnaround situation; but recession coupled with factors such as lack of financial control, a weak competitive position, and a financial policy of high gearing (or just a weak balance sheet for historical reasons) can spell disaster. Recession tends to expose a company's competitive weaknesses, although the source of these weaknesses is often the result of management decisions or acts of omission during the previous boom phase. Management is usually too busy just meeting demand in a boom period to worry about whether it is losing market share (and hence eroding its relative cost position vis-à-vis competitors); decisions to build extra capacity are usually taken at this time with insufficient attention given to what the state of market demand is likely to be when the new capacity comes on-stream.

Sometimes the effect of severe recession is a two-stage process. The first recession weakens the company financially, but it survives. In the intervening boom the company's position improves, but it does not fully recover before the next recession comes along. In the furniture industry, for example, historically managers have operated on the basis of breaking even during recessionary periods and making good profits with which to repay their bank borrowings in boom times. Often recession takes its toll, but most businesses survive with the help of extensive bank borrowings. However, if the subsequent boom is not strong enough for companies to repay their loans and to finance working capital requirements, they enter the next recession in a relatively weak financial position. The next sudden drop in demand is then likely to send them into immediate receivership or liquidation.

Changing Pattern of Demand

Demand for a particular product may not decline, but the way in which it is distributed and purchased may change. If this is the case – and management does not or cannot respond – it will soon find itself in difficulty. Huge changes continue to take place in the channels of distribution used by many industries, and new channels such as the Internet are growing fast. The growth of out-of-town shopping centres in the UK and the declining number of visits to shopping malls in the

USA are causing financial difficulties for many traditional retailers, and distress to manufacturers who fail to adapt to the changing patterns of demand.

Competition

Both price competition and product competition are common causes of corporate decline. In practice they often occur together, although we will discuss them separately.

Product Competition

The product life-cycle concept has long been recognized as a useful tool for business analysis, although its universal validity has rightly been questioned. The idea of the life cycle is that after an initial start-up period, successful products go through a growth phase, a maturity phase, and eventually decline as new and improved products are brought on to the market. The length of the life cycle varies enormously from one industry and product to another – from a few months in high fashion clothing, for example, to many years in English reproduction furniture. The basic idea, however, is that products eventually become obsolete as new technology is developed or improved, or substitute products are introduced and consumer preferences change. The reasons why firms do not develop new products to replace obsolete products include:

- lack of success with new product introductions (the failure rate of new products is very high)
- belief that the old product is still the best on the market
- inadequate financial resources and technical know-how to develop new products
- lack of ideas for new products.

A firm that fails to respond to changing market needs, or that responds too late to changing needs, is likely to find itself heading towards extinction. Responding to market needs does not necessarily imply following market trends. The firm may not have the resources to develop any competitive advantage as technology or consumer needs change; however, if it wants to survive as an organization, it must respond by diversifying, entering joint ventures, or following some other strategy.

Price Competition

Severe price competition has probably been the most common cause of decline in manufacturing industry in Britain and other Western countries over the past twenty years.

Motor cycles, cars, cutlery, ball bearings, machine tools, textiles, paper, carpets, radio, television and household appliances are all examples of whole sectors of the economy where individual companies have declined due to price competition from lower-cost foreign competitors.

The existence of price competition in a market is largely a function of the nature of the product and the structural characteristics of the industry. The matrix in Figure 2.4, which shows the degree of product differentiation and the primary nature of buyers' behaviour, can be helpful in visualizing the extent to which a product is likely to be the subject of price competition. Products which fall in the top right-hand corner – those with a low degree of product differentiation, bought primarily on economic criteria – are true commodity products and are exceptionally price sensitive. Those products falling in the bottom left-hand corner are likely to be relatively price-insensitive products.

Few products are *truly* price insensitive, because as soon as a product is copied or a substitute product is developed, the original product, even if differentiated by brand name or design features, starts to behave like a commodity product. Although the nature of the product is important in determining whether price competition is likely, price competition will not occur automatically or uniformly in a given market. There are likely to be some market or customer segments which will be more price sensitive than others.

The severity of price competition in a market will depend on the structural characteristics of the market. Michael Porter has identified

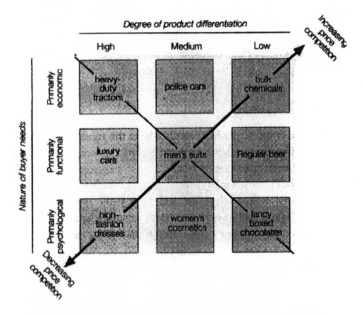

Figure 2.4: **The Effect of Product Characteristics on Price Competition**

Source. Adapted from C. W. Hofer, 'Conceptual Constructs for Formulating Corporate and Business Strategies' (Intercollegiate Case Clearing House, Boston, No 9−378−754, 1977), p 20 Reprinted by permission.

five major structural determinants of the intensity of competition in an industry: the threat of new entrants; the threat of substitute products or services; the bargaining power of suppliers; the bargaining power of customers; and the nature of the rivalry among current competitors. These are illustrated graphically in Figure 2.5. The reader is referred to Porter's book *Competitive Strategy* (Free Press, New York, 1980) for a discussion on how these five groups of factors affect price competition and hence an individual firm's ability to make profits in its industry. Some industries are clearly more profitable than others – those with a high degree of price competition are generally less profitable, since above-average levels of profitability are harder to generate.

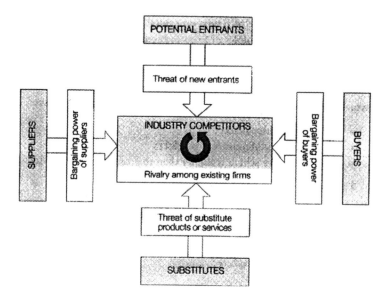

Figure 2.5: **Forces Driving Industry Competition**

Source Michael Porter, *Competitive Strategy* (Free Press, New York, 1980), p 4.
Reprinted by permission

Of greater interest when studying the causes of decline is the way in
which the degree of price competition changes over time. Typically,
price competition increases as an industry matures, with the result that
the key factors for success change. When the industry growth rate starts
to slow down, price competition begins to become more important,
and margins decline. The result is an industry shake-out in which those
competitors with higher cost structures may find themselves unable to
compete.

While an industry as a whole may be subject to increased price
competition, not all firms within that industry will necessarily suffer
the same fate. A firm's success, as measured by its profitability, is a
function not only of the industry (and other external) variables over
which the firm has no control, but also of the firm's strategy and the
quality of its strategy implementation. Work by Richard Rumelt has
indicated that a firm's character strongly outweighs industry membership

as a predictor of the rate of return on capital. Thus it is not surprising that there are many examples of firms in highly competitive, declining industries that are successful in making high rates of return. Their success is due to a combination of three elements: product-market focus, product differentiation and low costs. Conversely, those firms which get into a serious profit decline are usually characterized by:

- a lack of product-market focus
- a relatively undifferentiated product
- a cost structure which is higher than that of major competitors.

The issue is explained by Porter in the following way:

This firm lacks the market share, capital investment and resolve to play the low-cost game, the industry-wide differentiation necessary to obviate the need for a low-cost position, or the focus to create differentiation or a low-cost position in a more limited sphere.[6]

Adverse Movements in 'Commodity' Prices

By 'commodity', we refer not only to the price of commodity products such as raw materials but also to interest rates, foreign currency prices and property prices – items over which management has virtually no control and which can fluctuate widely, often over a relatively short period of time. We have seen many companies become involved in property development only to find that interest rates subsequently rise and property prices drop, causing financial insolvency. Is this just a regular business hazard which can be blamed on 'bad luck', or has management taken too big a risk? In most cases it is the latter.

Analysis of Causal Factors

Lists of causes are useful, but managers need more than just a checklist. They would like to know how often these causes occur and under

Figure 2.6: **Studies of Causes of Decline**

	Schendel et al. 1976[7]	Bibeault 1982[8]	Slatter 1984[9]	Thain and Goldthorpe 1989[10]	Grinyer et al 1990[10]	Gopal 1991[10]	Gething 1997[11]
Internal							
Poor management	✓	✓	73%	✓	✓	✓	84%
Inadequate financial control		✓	75%	✓	✓	✓	60%
High cost structure	✓		35%	✓	✓		56%
Poor marketing	✓		22%	✓	✓		20%
Big projects	✓		17%	✓	✓		20%
Acquisitions			15%				72%
Financial policy			20%	✓		✓	84%
External							
Changes in market demand	✓	✓	33%	✓	✓	✓	68%
Competition	✓	✓	40%	✓	✓	✓	44%
Adverse commodity price movements	✓	✓	30%	✓		✓	20%
Government policy	✓	✓				✓	
Strikes	✓						
Bad luck		✓				✓	

what circumstances. Are the causes of decline the same in service businesses as in manufacturing businesses? Are they the same in large companies as in small? Are they different for businesses with low market share and high market share? Do they differ by industry? By the stage of evolution of the industry? We do not have answers to all these questions, but Figure 2.6 summarizes the findings of seven studies (made between 1976 and 1997) on the frequency of these causal factors.

Care should be used in interpreting the data since some of these studies are based on very small sample sizes, and there are noticeable differences in the frequency of causal factors in the firms that eventually recovered and in those that became insolvent despite recovery efforts. Lack of financial control and inadequate top management at the level of the chief executive are the major causes of decline, but there are some interesting trends which reflect the business climate when the studies were undertaken. The latest study, by Gething in 1997, shows a dramatic increase in the frequency of acquisitions and financial policy as causes of decline. This reflects the fact that many of the turnarounds in the first half of the 1990s were caused by the effects of the late-1980s boom, which was characterized by a high level of acquisition activity funded by complex debt instruments. Many of the acquired companies were poor acquisitions which management paid too much for and then failed to manage in the post-acquisition period. Some of the same characteristics are occurring again in the mid 1990s, particularly in the MBO/MBI (management buy-out and buy-in) markets where high prices are being paid for marginal business being divested by larger companies. The growth of the private equity market in the UK is leading to a major new influence in the structure of corporate ownership which may well affect the shape of the next cyclical downturn in the economy.

Two other factors stand out from Gething's study: the increase in frequency of high cost structures; and changes in market demand. Neither of these are surprising given what is happening in business today: competitors are continually looking for radical ways to lower their costs, and the rate of change in technology and market needs is faster than ever before. Firms that fail to respond quickly are increasingly finding themselves in trouble.

Little empirical research has been carried out on how causal factors vary by industry. Our experience suggests that distressed manufacturing businesses tend to be characterized by relatively high manufacturing costs and price competition, whereas service businesses tend to get into trouble by failing to cut overheads early enough in a business downturn. Generalizations at this level can be dangerous, however, and more specific studies similar to Stuart Slatter's on entrepreneurial high-tech firms are needed.[12] In that study the special characteristics of the sector led to product competition, manufacturing problems, and the pressure for growth being important causal factors of decline.

From the analysis, it appears that a crisis situation is likely to occur most frequently when a firm already weakened by poor management, lack of control and inefficiency is subjected to adverse movements in market demand or commodity prices, price competition, and 'one-off' problems resulting from the so-called big project or acquisition. The number of factors causing decline in crisis and non-crisis situations lends further evidence to support this view. Our research showed that there are twice as many causal factors of decline in crisis situations than in non-crisis situations. The typical crisis situation is usually characterized by six or seven of the thirteen causal factors.

Notes

1. E. Altman, *Corporate Bankruptcy in America* (Heath, Lexington, Massachusetts, 1971).

2. J. Argenti, *Corporate Collapse: The Causes and Symptoms* (McGraw-Hill, New York, 1976).

3. R. J. Taffler and H. J. Tisshaw, 'Going, Going, Gone: Four Factors which Predict', *Accountancy*, Vol. 88, No. 1003 (March 1977), pp. 50–52, 54.

4. Stuart Slatter, *Gambling on Growth* (Wiley, Chichester, 1992).

5. C. Handy, *Understanding Organizations* (Penguin Books, London, 1976).

6. M. Porter, *Competitive Strategy* (Free Press, New York, 1980).

7. D. Schendel, G. R. Patton and J. Riggs, 'Corporate Turnaround Strategies', *Journal of General Management* Vol. 3, No. 3 (1976).

8. D. Bibeault, *Corporate Turnaround* (McGraw-Hill, New York, 1981).

9. Stuart Slatter, *Corporate Recovery* (Penguin Books, London, 1984).

10. Naresh Paudit, 'A Meta-analysis of Corporate Turnaround Literature' (Manchester Business School working paper number 328).

11. J. Gething, 'Turnarounds: Success v. Failure (unpublished MSc thesis, London Business School, June 1997).

12. Stuart Slatter, op. cit., Chapter 8.

3 Characteristics of Crisis Situations

If no attempt is made to reverse the causes of decline identified in the previous chapter, a crisis situation will develop. The word 'crisis' has been defined in management literature as a situation that 'threatens the high-priority goals of the organization [i.e., its survival], restricts the amount of time available for response, and surprises decision-makers by its occurrence, thereby engendering high levels of stress'.[1] Crises originate as threatening events in a firm's environment and as defects within the organization. The purpose of this chapter is to explore further the defects within the organization that give rise to crisis, but also and more importantly, to discuss the ways in which crises affect the behaviour of the firm and the individuals in it. Only once we understand the characteristics of crisis situations can we begin to understand the strategies and tactics necessary to stabilize the crisis and effect a successful turnaround.

The forces causing decline are present, to some degree, in all firms. Why is it, therefore, that some firms are able to cope successfully with the problems they face while others end up in a turnaround situation? There are a variety of factors that affect the ability of organizations to adapt to changing circumstances and cope with crisis. By studying these factors we can gain an appreciation of the firm's susceptibility to crisis, and a better understanding of what happens in a crisis situation.

Crisis, once recognized by management, induces stress. The crisis may well have existed for some time before it is recognized, but admitting the problem is often stressful to those who have to deal with it. This has a negative impact on managerial behaviour, and this in turn has a deteriorating effect on the whole organization. Crisis tends to accentuate the internal factors causing decline, reinforcing and accelerating the downward trend. A key task for crisis managers is to engage the corporate team in fighting the crisis. Clearly this cannot commence until the crisis is acknowledged. If no action is taken to effect a turnaround, the end result is insolvency and failure.

Susceptibility to Crisis

The causal factors of decline that were identified and discussed in the last chapter interact with one another to create a crisis. An interesting model of corporate crisis proposed by C. F. Smart, W. A. Thompson and I. Vertinsky identifies those corporate characteristics which increase or decrease the vulnerability and susceptibility of organizations to crisis.[2] Theirs is a theoretical model rather than one based on empirical observation, but it is interesting because it attempts to relate three groups of causal variables to market performance and susceptibility to crisis. These groups are:

- competitive and environmental variables (product-market decisions, business cycles, etc.)
- managerial characteristics, such as individual capabilities and management styles
- organizational attributes, such as resources and structures.

For those who like diagrams, the model is illustrated in Figure 3.1. The causal variables affect crisis susceptibility in the following ways:

The external environment is an important determinant of susceptibility to crisis. A firm competing in a business where there are sharp and unpredictable fluctuations in the environment will have difficulty in maintaining market alignment and will therefore be more susceptible to crisis than a firm in a stable market environment.

Managerial characteristics, such as individual capabilities, personal biases and management styles (together with the organizational attributes discussed below), determine the quality of decision-making in a firm,

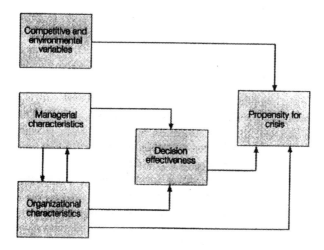

Figure 3.1: **A Simple Model of Crisis Susceptibility**
Source Adapted from a model developed by C. F. Smart, W A. Thompson and
I. Vertinsky, *Journal of Business Administration*, Vol. 9, No. 2 (Spring 1978)
p 59 Reprinted by permission.

which in turn affects its susceptibility to crisis. Where decision-making
quality is low, the firm is more susceptible to crises: it is less able to
cope with a crisis induced by the outside environment and is more
likely to generate a crisis internally as the result of operating inefficiencies,
conservative financial policies, etc.

Organizational characteristics affect the quality of decision-making, but in
addition they have a more direct effect on crisis susceptibility. The
existence of organizational slack – a concept which describes built-in
inefficiencies or reserves – can increase a firm's resistance to crisis
by spreading risk. Organizational characteristics are also important
determinants of the firm's ability to implement its decisions: for example,
effective implementation requires an organization that is neither overly
rigid nor too unpredictable. The size and complexity of an organization
also increases the chance of implementation failures.

The many interrelationships that exist between the three groups of variables have been developed into a simulation model by Smart and his colleagues, to determine the more appropriate corporate profile for five different market environments: stable, declining, expanding, cyclical and discontinuous (expanding, but with a sudden and dramatic slump). In each environment they found that the most effective corporate profile combined a democratic management style, high-quality decision-making ability, and an aggressive strategic posture. This same profile also had the least propensity to crisis, except in expanding market environments. In that environment, the researchers found that a defensive rather than an aggressive strategic posture lowered the threat of crisis, although the appropriate profile is clearly a risk trade-off: a lower propensity for crisis versus a higher product-market growth rate.

The only time an autocratic management style appeared to be halfway effective as a management style was when it was combined with effective decision-making and an aggressive posture, but even this combination was found to be definitely unsuited to *declining* market situations. This suggests that an autocratic organization is usually too rigid to adapt to a declining environment. Of the five environments, an autocratic management style appeared to be best suited to a stable market environment – the very environment where crisis situations are probably least likely to develop.

Each of the corporate profiles discussed above reflects a different organization culture. The term 'organization culture' describes the ideology of the firm: its beliefs, goals, values, ideas, morale, enthusiasm, etc. The concept of an organization culture is important to the study of turnarounds since some cultures are more susceptible to crisis than others, although no single cultural pattern leads to crisis. Firms exhibiting power cultures (the one-man-bands of the previous chapter) and bureaucratic-type role cultures (firms governed by rules and procedures) appear to be most susceptible to crisis. In the power culture, susceptibility to crisis depends on the quality of the key decision-maker(s), whereas in a role culture, the firm is 'slow to perceive the need for change and slow to change, even if the need is seen'.[3]

The reader should be careful, however, not to fall into the trap of believing that a firm's susceptibility to crisis is easy to diagnose. The processes that produce crisis are substantially the same as those that produce success.[4] There is a fine line between success and failure, and success itself can easily lead to crisis. When firms are successful, they tend to crystallize their successful activities as standard programmes; but this makes them less sensitive to their environment because they respond to their environment in a standardized way and do not perceive many of the small differences among environmental events. Successful firms are usually able to buffer themselves from their environments (by building up inventories and through vertical integration, for example) and are able to build up slack resources, both of which allow them to become less sensitive to their environments. By loosening the connections with its environment, the firm is in greater control of its destiny (which is important if it is to be successful), but at the same time is increasing the risk of developing erroneous perceptions about its environment.[5]

The Impact of Crisis on Managerial Behaviour

How do managers, both individually and as a group, respond to crises once they have started to develop? As one would expect, response to crisis situations varies with the people concerned and the type of crisis. For some individuals, crises may actually improve the quality of their decision-making, but these people are more likely to be turnaround experts who thrive on crisis situations, rather than the existing management of a firm headed towards insolvency. Where poor management is a major causal factor of decline, case studies clearly show that the capacity of managers to cope with a growing crisis is severely impaired.

We have already defined a crisis situation as one characterized by surprise, short decision time and a high threat to important values. The effect of these three characteristics is to increase the stress on both the organization and the individuals in it. It is generally recognized by students of organizational behaviour that some degree of stress is a necessary prerequisite for problem-solving, for without it is no motivation to act. However, beyond a certain point stress becomes anxiety-producing rather than motivational and may even lead some

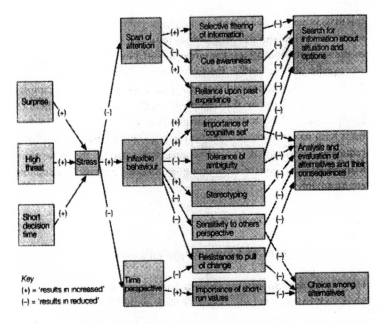

Key
(+) = 'results in increased'
(–) = 'results in reduced'

Figure 3.2: **Managerial Behaviour in Crisis**
Source: Adapted from Ole R. Holsti, 'Limitations of Cognitive Abilities in the Face of Crisis', *Journal of Business Administration*, Vol. 9, No. 2 (Spring 1978). Reprinted by permission.

individuals to believe that 'the worst would be better than this'.[6] Experimental findings tend to indicate the existence of an inverse relationship between stress and the performance of individuals and groups.[7]

A useful way of showing how crisis situations affect managerial behaviour and decision-making performance is shown in Figure 3.2, based on Ole Holsti's work. While really only a series of hypotheses (since not all the cause-and-effect relationships have been proven), it appears to be a reasonable representation of the principal effects of a crisis situation. The basic idea is that crisis causes stress, which in turn affects managerial behaviour (cognitive performance), which in its turn affects the quality of decision-making. Holsti has identified the major effects of crisis-induced stress as being a reduction in management's span of attention, an increase in their inflexibility and a reduction in their time perspective.[8] We will examine each of these three effects.

Reduction in Management's Span of Attention

The beginning of a crisis usually results in a faster pace of activity as individuals begin to realize something has to be done about the threatening situation. In many firms, particularly larger ones, the effect of the faster pace is to increase the volume of communications, resulting in information overload. The typical managerial response to this phenomenon may take any or all of the following forms:

- the search for information within the communication system becomes less thorough, and management becomes more selective in what it hears and believes
- danger signals are ignored because unpleasant information and information which does not support existing beliefs tend to be rejected
- management responds to information in terms of their own personal predispositions and past experiences
- decision-making becomes increasingly less integrated, which means that less strategic (integrated) decisions are made; instead, decisions are made on a more simplistic, one-off basis.

An Increase in Managerial Inflexibility

Intense and protracted stress tends to make individuals extremely inflexible, and to reduce their ability to cope with complex problems. The typical behaviour patterns that have been recognized are:

- tolerance for ambiguity is reduced
- the decision-maker develops a single or dominant view of the world through which s/he interprets information. The view is likely to be a learned response transferred from a previous situation
- the dominant view is maintained in the face of information which clearly calls for a reappraisal
- the decision-maker's view of the world may be characterized by stereotypes rather than an appreciation of the subtleties of the situation
- the personality characteristics of the decision-maker become emphasized – for example, the anxious become more anxious, the repressors become more repressive
- there is a trend towards increased autocratic behaviour unless democratic values are unusually well established.

The effect of this behaviour is to reduce the likelihood of identifying possible alternative actions and to limit evaluation of whatever alternatives are identified, consequently reducing the quality of decision-making.

A Reduction in Management's Time Perspective

Severe stress usually focuses attention on the present and the immediate future rather than on longer-range considerations, something which makes sense in a severe financial crisis. However, perceived time pressure may adversely affect decision-making. A moderate level of time pressure can enhance an individual's level of creativity and performance, but beyond a certain level it can be particularly harmful. Complex tasks for which there are no established decision rules or standard operating procedures tend to suffer most from time pressure. Managers tend in these situations to adopt a single approach that they have used before and to continue applying it, irrespective of whether it is appropriate. Furthermore, when decision time is short, managers' ability to estimate the consequences of a particular decision is likely to be impaired.

The Impact of Crisis on the Organization

The development of a severe crisis situation does not occur overnight. The typical firm goes through stages of crisis development, although in some firms, particularly those which we describe (later in this chapter) as fragile firms, some of the stages may be very short. There are four stages of crisis development. Figure 3.3 depicts each of these stages and their dominant organizational characteristics.

At the initial stage – the hidden crisis stage – the management group and the organization are unaware of the existence of a crisis. Often, this is due to lack of adequate control systems – not just financial control systems, but more informal systems that monitor and interpret unexpected environmental events. Typically, the firm will be complacent and may even be arrogant about its capabilities and market position. Once the signs of crisis become visible within the firm (second

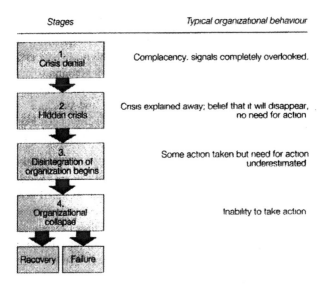

Stages	Typical organizational behaviour
1. Crisis denial	Complacency. signals completely overlooked.
2. Hidden crisis	Crisis explained away; belief that it will disappear, no need for action
3. Disintegration of organization begins	Some action taken but need for action underestimated
4. Organizational collapse	Inability to take action
Recovery Failure	

Figure 3.3: **Four Stages of Crisis Development**

stage), management begins to look for reasons to explain the crisis away. Two arguments are often put forward. First, the signs of crisis are attributed to the firm's efforts to change (new products, new capital investment, etc.) and it is claimed to be only a matter of time before performance will improve. The second argument is that the poor performance results from short-term environmental pressures beyond the control of the firm (exchange-rate fluctuations, economic recession, etc.).

Both these arguments support the view that no management action is necessary to avert the impending crisis; in effect, there is denial that a crisis exists at all, or at least a denial that any change is required. Optimism about the future is still the prevailing management rhetoric. At this stage, managers often believe sincerely that they are still on the correct path, that their overall strategy is correct, and that any problems are transient in nature. However, denial may be due to management's desire for self-preservation. Not only do managers believe that they will be blamed and perhaps lose their jobs if their previous actions are found to have been wrong but, more importantly, change – and in particular strategic change – usually involves changes in the power structure within the management group, so those people who currently hold power tend to resist change. In anticipation of these problems, management may begin to be creative with their accounts to make the financial symptoms of crisis look better than they really are.

As the crisis deepens, the firm's structure and processes start to disintegrate. Organizations that encounter crisis have been likened to palaces perched on mountain-tops that are crumbling from erosion:

Like palaces, organizations are rigid, cohesive structures that integrate elegant components. Although their flawless harmonies make organizational palaces look completely rational to observers who are inside them, observers standing outside can see that the beauty and harmony rest upon eroding grounds. The inhabitants' first reactions to crises are to maintain their palaces intact; they shore up shaky foundations, strengthen points of stress and patch up cracks – and their palaces remain sitting beautifully on eroding mountain-tops.[9]

This is the third stage of crisis development: management now recognizes that a crisis exists and takes some actions, but the need for action is underestimated. Inflexibility and many of the other behavioural characteristics discussed in the previous section begin to affect management. Decision-making groups tend to become smaller at this time as autocracy increases and the perceived need for secrecy and improved coordination grows. With less consultation and increasing time pressure, there is a greater tendency to rely more heavily on those who support the prevailing wisdom in the firm. The director or manager with an alternative point of view is increasingly ostracized from the decision-making group.

The actions taken in the third stage do little more, however, than temporarily slow down the process of decay. The palace starts falling apart. But in spite of this, management still continues to send out optimistic press reports stating that 'everything will be OK tomorrow'. The classic hockey-stick forecast (a short period of continuing decline followed by a sudden and prolonged upturn in performance) is the order of the day.

The organizational cracks eventually cause collapse (the fourth stage). It becomes evident to everyone that top management have been making faulty predictions, and severe doubts arise as to whether management are capable of coping with the crisis. If management were any good, surely they would have taken appropriate action in the first or second stage? The processes of disintegration at work in the final stage include the following:

- there is a decrease in decision-making behaviour and more general discussion of the need to make decisions
- commitment to organizational goals declines and individual managers become more self-oriented
- the budget cuts and reorganization of the third stage cause power struggles that undermine cooperation and cause top management to centralize control even further
- expectation of failure grows, thus making failure more likely
- the most able people leave, so the average level of competence falls.[10]

These processes reinforce one another. Top management becomes incapacitated and morale declines to an all-time low, causing an even further decline in efficiency. The organization has collapsed. The result is almost certain to be insolvency unless the seven essential ingredients outlined in the next chapter can be put into place.

The Reality Gap

We have observed that there is often a difference between what is really happening in an organization and what is being reported. Where businesses are doing well, better perhaps than expected, there is a natural tendency to be very conservative in reporting by maintaining healthy provisions and prudent income recognition policies. During this phase a growing company is often undervalued, but these reporting practices allow management the freedom to experiment and invest without their failures being seen by external stakeholders.

Most businesses operate in a cycle, with good times being followed by bad, and those businesses that have conserved resources during the good times are often more able to survive the downside by releasing these reserves. There is nothing startling in this observation, and so long as the area shaded 'A' (reserves accumulated) in Figure 3.4 is greater than 'B' (reserves released), then business continues reasonably uninterrupted by the interest of external stakeholders. We should not therefore be surprised that one of the unerring characteristics of turn-around situations is that the crisis is usually worse than management have reported and external advisors believe it to be. The characteristics of the hidden crisis and crisis denial stages described in the previous section mean that management usually convince themselves that the situation is not that bad. It is only when reserves released (B) exceed reserves accumulated (A) that the crisis may become obvious – at Point X–Y. The difference between the net assets reported (X) and actual (Y) is the reality gap. Even when declining financial performance is obvious and organizational disintegration is well advanced, the true situation is usually much worse. Provision accounting is often a mystery understood only by a few at the centre.

The two scenarios shown in Figure 3.5 illustrate what we mean.

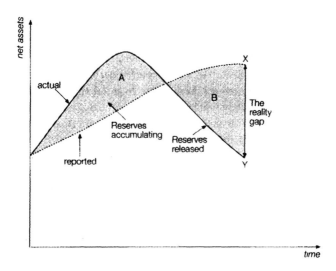

Figure 3.4: **The Reality Gap**

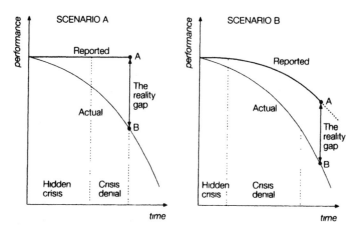

Figure 3.5: **Reality Gap Scenarios**

Both scenarios show the firm starting off in a relatively healthy position, with actual performance at least equal to reported performance. At this stage reported earnings may still be showing an increase but actual performance has levelled off or even started to decline. The cushion of provisions that management have made in good times starts to be released, but management is still confident and investing in new projects. This is the hidden crisis stage when management are unaware of the underlying trends affecting the business.

When it is clear to management that actual performance starts to drop below reported performance, the crisis denial stage begins. It is now that we begin to see creative accounting, or management's disbelief in the information presented to it. Reported results may continue to look healthy while actual performance drops off very fast (scenario A). It is only when a crisis is triggered by a sudden default on a loan repayment or a major breach of a banking covenant that investigating accountants are called in. They report that the company's actual performance is at point B and not at point A. The difference between A and B is what we call the downside reality gap. In this scenario the organization moves suddenly from crisis denial into disintegration and possibly collapse as soon as the reality gap is exposed.

In scenario B, crisis denial continues until the situation starts to deteriorate to such an extent that reported results also start to decline quite sharply. Despite management's best efforts to deal with the deteriorating financial position, reality eventually catches up when the cash-flow position becomes so out of line with reported operating performance that questions start being asked by the company's bankers and creditors. The longer this process takes, the more likely it is that organizational disintegration and even collapse will have set in. Again, it is usually the introduction of investigating accountants or a turnaround manager that will identify the reality gap. When this happens, the external stakeholders usually jump to the conclusion that existing management must be changed, or that the stakeholder must take control – either way, the game is up for the incumbent management team.

We discuss later in the book the need for the management team to face up to reality, whether or not a third party is introduced. In most cases, new management are introduced and it is absolutely essential that the new team or manager identifies the reality of the current financial position as a priority because only then can appropriate plans be put in place to remedy the situation. If the turnaround manager does not grasp the full extent of the situation – i.e., find *all* the skeletons in the cupboards – s/he can quickly become tarred with the decline when, despite considerable efforts, the properly reported results show a worsening position following his/her appointment. There is not much tolerance in a crisis, and s/he can pay the price before having the opportunity to inspect the goods!

The crisis is magnified by the reality gap. Internal and external stakeholders suddenly realize the true nature of the situation. This is a dangerous time for the company, because although the actual situation has not changed, what has changed is the perception of the stakeholders. At this time it is often difficult to separate perception from reality, and many stakeholders base their decisions on perception rather than an understanding of reality. It is vital that key stakeholders have a thorough understanding of all the key issues and an awareness of the consequences of failure. The challenge facing the management team is to resolve the real causes of decline while maintaining stakeholder support. This is a classic dilemma for the turnaround manager and we will deal with this critical issue later in the book (Chapter 8).

Fragility and the Spiral of Decline

Most firms that find themselves in a crisis situation are characterized by several of the causes of decline occurring simultaneously. As additional problems arise or existing problems become more severe, the crisis deepens. A variant of this pattern is where a company exhibits a number of causes of failure but, even when combined, the problems are offset by strong market demand for the company's product(s). However, it only needs some other problem to emerge – called here a 'trigger' problem – for the whole company to be in an immediate crisis. For companies already weakened by a number of independent causes of decline, a relatively small downturn in the business cycle, a delay in receiving a contract from a customer, or a problem with a subcontractor can act as a trigger problem.

However, the pattern of problem escalation in distressed companies has changed in recent years. What was often a slow process of decay over a number of years is often a much more rapid process and the result of a single cause of decline. Many businesses nowadays, particularly high-tech firms, fashion and some people-intensive service businesses (such as advertising and financial services) are extremely fragile. The increasing rate of technological change leading to shorter product life cycles, increased market volatility and uncertainty, increased competition in a global marketplace, and employees who change jobs more frequently than twenty years ago, mean that a firm that is apparently doing well and outperforming its competitors can be in a crisis in a matter of months. Business risk has increased and with it the speed at which firms can spiral into decline.

We see simple causes of decline – such as a competitor's new product or the loss of a key creative team – setting off a chain reaction of sequential causes and symptoms of decline. There is interdependence between a variety of causes and symptoms of decline. One problem leads to another, and a causal relationship can be identified. For example, product development difficulties lead to process engineering problems, which in turn result in lower quality products. A subsequent high level of returns then increases work in progress, with the result that manufacturing efficiencies decline further. Poor deliveries mean that customer confidence declines, sales volume drops, finished goods inventories increase, and a cash crisis develops. The sequence is shown in Figure 3.6.

Taken individually, the problems might be readily manageable, but because they are interdependent there is often a complex web of problems difficult to disentangle. The big difference between the two patterns of decline is in the position of the trigger cause. Where the causes are largely independent, the trigger comes at the end of the process, after the company has already been weakened by a series of problems. Where they are sequential and interdependent, the trigger cause comes first. Common trigger causes include:

- severe product competition due to failure to generate a new generation of products on time

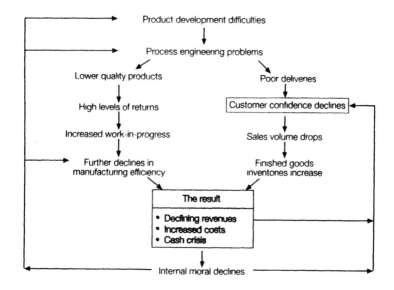

Figure 3.6: **Sequential Causes of Decline – An Example**

- new entrants competing on the basis of price
- a sudden and dramatic drop in market demand
- cancellation or delay of a major contract.

Among fragile companies we see that once the health of the company starts to deteriorate rapidly, there are two critical areas which act like cogs in accelerating the process of decline. Firstly, customers lose confidence. For example, no customer wants to buy a high-tech product from a company it thinks might become insolvent. And, secondly, the internal morale of management and staff spirals downward at a rapid rate as they hear one piece of bad news after another. Poor internal morale means some key individuals start to look for employment elsewhere – before the axe falls – and efforts to solve the company's problems become more difficult. Fragile firms can go through the typical stages of crisis development (from crisis denial to organizational collapse) in just a few weeks.

Crisis and Change

Once a crisis has become severe and both management as individuals and the organization as a whole have begun to exhibit some of the negative behavioural characteristics discussed in this chapter, dramatic action is necessary if recovery is to be achieved. If the onset of crisis is caught early enough, a serious crisis can be averted and less dramatic action *may* be enough for recovery to proceed. However, the same order of strategic change, in terms of product-market reorientation, financial policy, control systems, etc., may be necessary at that early stage, since the causes of failure will be the same. What will be different at the early stage will be the amount of organizational change necessary.

The earlier the developing crisis is tackled, the less organizational change will be necessary and the more chance there is of saving the firm and instituting a successful turnaround. Ideally, a firm will embark on a turnaround strategy before a real crisis develops (i.e., at the 'hidden crisis' stage). However, a crisis is frequently necessary before change can be achieved, since it is only then that the necessary organizational unlearning can take place.

Sometimes the disintegration that precedes the start of a turnaround can actually facilitate a turnaround. This comes about because organizations have to unlearn what they know before they can start to be 're-programmed'. For example, they have to:

- lose confidence in their old leaders before they will listen to new leaders
- abandon their old objectives before they will adopt new ones
- reject their perceptual filters before they will notice events they had previously overlooked
- see that their old methods do not work before they will invest in and adopt new methods.[11]

The problem of organizational unlearning is important because it relates to managerial judgement, and judgement is a key ingredient in the decision-making process. In making a judgemental decision, a manager draws on his/her own personal pattern of beliefs and personal biases that s/he has developed from experience over the years. Some of these beliefs are extremely personal and may be Freudian in nature; others result from the fact that the manager has operated in a given business system, such as an industry where there are well-established industry practices. Grinyer and Spender call an industry's pattern of managerial beliefs a 'recipe', although they recognize that within one industry a number of different recipes may coexist. In their study of recipes in the Newton Chambers Group, Grinyer and Spender found that the firm's commitment to a particular recipe had been reinforced by its past success, and that management adhered to the old recipe even after it had become obsolete. As financial performance declined, Newton Chambers' management adopted tighter financial controls and a policy of more aggressive implementation, which produced a temporary recovery as slack was absorbed but failed to stop the decline. Only the adoption of a revised recipe brought in by new senior executives led to an eventual turnaround after a long period of severe crisis.[12]

Most – but not all – firms that meet a serious crisis situation are already suffering from poor management, and hence poor decision-making. With the onset of a crisis, decision-making deteriorates even further because the managerial characteristics that increase a firm's susceptibility to crisis are intensified once the crisis begins. Management therefore is rarely able to serve as an effective change agent to initiate a turnaround. We shall see in the case histories later in the book that existing management is rarely capable of taking the drastic action needed to effect a turnaround. They may attempt one, but they use too few turnaround strategies, and those that they do use they do not implement in sufficient depth (they may cut costs, but not drastically enough; they may dispose of assets, but not enough of them). It is unlikely that the existing management of a firm can implement a turnaround successfully after the crisis denial stage has been in existence for any period of time.

The appointment of a new chief executive to begin the turnaround is, in some senses, a symbolic act which marks the end of the disintegration and the beginning of the recovery. It is an important step in initiating the turnaround process, although the arrival of new management is not of itself a good indicator that recovery is actually under way. The firm may continue to decline, since the new management's attempt at turnaround may fail. A turnaround can only really be said to begin at that point in time when management's actions (either new management or old) start to improve the financial performance of the firm.

For a firm whose organization has already started to disintegrate, a change in culture is a necessary prerequisite for a successful recovery, due to the need to change the negative behavioural characteristics that have developed. We have already referred to the term 'organization culture' to describe the ideology of the organization – its beliefs, goals, values, ideas, morale, enthusiasm – although we have confined our discussion to one aspect of culture: the effect of crisis on individual and group behaviour. There are, however, many factors besides the behaviour of the people within the firm that influence culture. History and ownership of the firm, its size, technology, objectives and environment may all influence the culture of a firm in crisis.[13] Just as there is no single cultural pattern that leads to crisis, there is no single cultural prescription to use in a turnaround. Many cultural patterns may work. Handy's suggestion that a power culture is more appropriate for crisis situations, however, stands up well in practice, as we shall see when discussing leadership. This may seem to contradict what has been said before about power cultures being most susceptible to crisis, but in fact it does not. The success of a power culture depends totally on the quality of the individuals within the organization and the extent to which they like to operate within that culture. The ideal culture is a power culture within a core team sharing goals and aspirations.

Intervention from the Outside

The trigger for change during a severe crisis is more likely to be an intervention from an outside source, most commonly banks or lending institutions, than from management itself. To initiate change, banks often have to precipitate a crisis or make the existing crisis more severe by refusing to extend overdraft facilities. If possible, banks prefer not to have to appoint a receiver, since there is a certain stigma attached to them doing so, and for most bankers there is a trade-off between their public image and the risk of loss.

As a firm's financial crisis becomes more severe, but before receivership, the bank may find it possible to initiate management changes at board level. Sometimes they may be able to make an extension of borrowing facilities contingent on a new chief executive being appointed; at other times, the most they can achieve is the appointment of a new finance director. It is not unknown for banks to lend a firm in distress an accountant on a temporary basis or to insist that a firm receives 'intensive care' from turnaround consultants or an independent firm of accountants. Management find that during these difficult times they lose the initiative and become subject to a third party's agenda. A key challenge for the turnaround manager during this time is to maintain the initiative while meeting the requirements of the external stakeholders. Many businesses have collapsed unnecessarily due to this balance of power being mishandled.

Another group of outsiders who are increasingly taking a role in instituting management changes are the institutional investors. Traditionally, institutions such as insurance companies and pension funds have avoided taking an active management role, as have the banks; but in recent years they have started to take a bigger behind-the-scenes role (often in conjunction with the merchant banks) in obtaining management changes. The group that is potentially most influential in obtaining change is the non-executive directors, if they exist. In theory they should have the best information, but very often they are powerless. Typically, they are appointed because they are friendly with existing management, not because they are independent outsiders who will challenge management. Non-executive directors can resign in protest against management's actions or inactions, but they rarely do. Change of ownership, usually by acquisition, is clearly the easiest way to initiate change. The old management can be replaced immediately; and the new parent company can, if it wishes, transfer resources in the form of cash and management skills to the ailing firm. These acts will not of themselves put an end to the crisis, but they do put an end to the threat of insolvency and give the necessary impetus for change.

Notes

1. Charles F. Hermann, 'Some Consequences of Crisis which Limit the Viability of Organizations', *Administrative Science Quarterly*, No. 8 (1963), pp. 61–82

2. C. F. Smart, W. A. Thompson and I. Vertinsky, 'Diagnosing Corporate Effectiveness and Susceptibility to Crises', *Journal of Business Administration*, Vol 9, No. 2 (Spring 1978).

3. Charles Handy, *Understanding Organizations* (Penguin Books, London, 1976), Chapter 7.

4. Bo L. T. Hedberg, Paul C. Nystrom and William H. Starbuck, 'Camping on Seesaws: Prescriptions for a Self-designing Organization', *Administrative Science Quarterly*, No. 21 (1976), pp. 41–65.

5. William H. Starbuck, Arent Greve and Bo L. T. Hedberg, 'Responding to Crisis', *Journal of Business Administration*, Vol. 9, No. 2 (Spring 1978).

6. See, for example, Kurt Back, 'Decisions under Uncertainty: Rational, Irrational and Non-rational', *American Behavioral Scientist*, No. 4 (February 1961), pp. 14–19.

7. See, for example, Robert E. Murphy, 'Effects of Threat of Shock, Distraction and Task Design on Performance', *Journal of Experimental Psychology*, No. 58 (1959), pp. 134–41.

8. Ole R. Holsti, 'Limitations of Cognitive Abilities in the Face of Crisis', *Journal of Business Administration*, Vol. 9, No. 2 (Spring 1978).

9. William H. Starbuck, op. cit.

10. Albert S. King, 'Expectation Effects in Organizational Change', *Administrative Science Quarterly*, 1974, No. 19, pp. 221–30.

11. Richard M. Cyert and James G. March, *A Behavioral Theory of the Firm* (Prentice Hall, New York, 1963).

12. Peter Grinyer and J. C. Spender, *Turnaround: Managerial Recipes for Strategic Success* (Associated Business Publications, London, 1979).

13. Charles Handy, op. cit.

4 Framework for Achieving a Successful Turnaround

A successful turnaround depends upon developing an appropriate turnaround prescription, and an effective implementation. The first point addresses what needs to be done and the second point how to do it. We have developed an approach for achieving a successful turnaround that consists of seven essential ingredients and an implementation framework consisting of seven key workstreams. This chapter outlines our approach, and subsequent chapters develop the ideas in further detail.

Seven Essential Ingredients

Recovery of a sick company depends upon the implementation of an appropriate rescue plan or turnaround prescription. Characteristics of the appropriate remedy are that it must:

- address the *fundamental* problems
- tackle the underlying causes (rather than the symptoms)
- be broad and deep enough in scope to resolve all of the key issues.

One of the challenges for any turnaround leader is to ensure that the rescue is built on a robust plan. Plans that try to tackle every single problem of a troubled company, no matter how big or small, will fail as limited resources are wasted on tackling 'non mission-critical' issues. The key is to focus on tackling the life-threatening problems. A recovery strategy that is based on the symptoms rather than the underlying causes may make the patient feel better temporarily, but any long-term recovery strategy has to be based on sorting out the underlying causes of distress. Turnaround plans must be sufficiently broad and deep to ensure that all of the mission-critical issues are addressed. Turnaround management involves radical rather than incremental change. Very sick companies have serious problems which can only be tackled through fundamental, holistic recovery plans. We have almost never encountered a turnaround plan which was too drastic. The chief danger to avoid is doing too little too late.

The essential ingredients of a successful turnaround plan are:

1. Crisis stabilization.
2. Leadership.
3. Stakeholder support.
4. Strategic focus.
5. Organizational change.
6. Critical process improvements.
7. Financial restructuring.

Successful turnaround situations are characterized by significant actions in each of these seven areas. Failure to address any one of them may endanger the successful outcome of the turnaround.

We put crisis stabilization at the top of our list because it plays a critical role in any successful recovery situation. By securing a short-term future for the business, the turnaround leader creates a window of opportunity within which s/he can develop and implement medium- and long-term survival plans. That breathing space is an essential prerequisite for a successful turnaround, as is our second ingredient, strong leadership.

The third ingredient addresses the critical role of stakeholders in the recovery process and the importance of reconciling their often conflicting needs and rebuilding their confidence. The next three elements recognize the integrative nature of a business. Successful organizations are based on developing a viable strategy, and then aligning and integrating it with an appropriate organizational structure and effective business processes. Our final ingredient addresses the prerequisite of establishing a sound financial base and appropriate funding for the recovery. A financial restructuring which involves the injection of new funds is unlikely to succeed unless the other six key ingredients are tackled cohesively and successfully.

Figure 4.1: **Generic Turnaround Strategies**

Seven Key Ingredients	Generic Turnaround Strategies
1. Crisis Stabilization	<ul><li>taking control</li><li>cash management</li><li>asset reduction</li><li>short-term financing</li><li>first-step cost reduction</li></ul>
2. Leadership	<ul><li>change of CEO</li><li>change of other senior management</li></ul>
3. Stakeholder Support	<ul><li>communications</li></ul>
4. Strategic Focus	<ul><li>redefine core businesses</li><li>divestment and asset reduction</li><li>product-market refocusing</li><li>downsizing</li><li>outsourcing</li><li>investment</li></ul>
5. Organizational Change	<ul><li>structural changes</li><li>key people changes</li><li>improved communications</li><li>building commitment and capabilities</li><li>new terms and conditions of employment</li></ul>
6. Critical Process Improvements	<ul><li>improved sales and marketing</li><li>cost reduction</li><li>quality improvements</li><li>improved responsiveness</li><li>improved information and control systems</li></ul>
7. Financial Restructuring	<ul><li>refinancing</li><li>asset reduction</li></ul>

Each of these core areas of the turnaround plan is supported by a range of generic strategies which address the problems most usually encountered in that area. Our list of generic strategies is set out in Figure 4.1. Clearly it is not an exhaustive list, since each situation has its own specific characteristics that require a tailored solution. Nevertheless, there are a number of actions that are sufficiently common to most situations that we consider them to be generic turnaround strategies. These are discussed in detail in the chapters that follow, but first we must give the reader an overview of each of the seven ingredients.

1. Crisis Stabilization

In most turnaround situations, crisis management will have to commence immediately. Substantially underperforming companies typically suffer from a rapidly worsening cash position and a lack of management control. In many situations companies are in free fall; senior management are paralysed in the face of an apparently hopeless situation and the business faces the very real prospect of running out of cash in the very short term. The turnaround manager or whoever has effective management control at the time must move very rapidly to take control of the situation and commence aggressive cash management.

The objectives of crisis stabilization are:

- to conserve cash in the short term and thereby provide a window of opportunity within which to develop a turnaround plan and agree a financial restructuring
- to rebuild stakeholder confidence by demonstrating that senior management have taken control of the situation
- to begin to reintroduce predictability in the operation.

The approach requires very strong top-down control. The turnaround manager moves quickly to impose a very tight set of controls for the entire organization. Devolved authority to spend money, incur credit or commit the business in any way is removed. Short-term cash generation becomes the top priority.

A critical element is to rebuild predictability into the business, and the generation of rolling short-term cash-flow forecasts becomes a key management tool. The process of forecasting the short-term cash position, communicating the information to the stakeholders on a regular basis, and then *achieving* the forecasts is crucial in rebuilding their confidence.

Crisis management requires robust leadership; in most cases the turn-around manager is forcing a radical mindset change on the organization.

The other key element is launching a series of cash generation strategies. Working capital is reduced by liquidating surplus stock, improving debt collection and stretching creditor payments. All capital expenditure, except the most essential, is put on hold. Sometimes there is an opportunity to increase short-term revenues by price increases or provisional events – but this is the exception rather than the rule.

2. Leadership

New Chief Executive

Inadequate senior management is frequently cited as the single most important cause of corporate decline, and therefore many, but not all, turnaround situations require a new chief executive officer (CEO). Many investors and turnaround practitioners argue that in almost every case a change of CEO is required for two reasons. The first point is that since the CEO was the principal architect of the failure, it is very unlikely that s/he can form part of the solution. The second argument is that a change of CEO has enormous symbolic importance: it sends a strong message to all stakeholders that something positive is being done to improve the firm's performance.

An alternative view is that the immediate removal of a CEO may not be in the best interests of the company. It is a decision that may make stakeholders feel positive in the short term, but which they may come to regret at their leisure. It is important to remember that many CEOs of troubled companies have a strong track record of prior success; today's villain was yesterday's hero. Furthermore, the CEO is often the person with the most knowledge and experience of the company and the industry – skills that may be vital to the recovery. An existing CEO who is not in crisis denial, who understands the reality gap, is acutely aware of the causes of decline, and is determined to restore the company's fortunes is often a less risky choice than a new CEO.

A second important consideration is the type of CEO to appoint to a turnaround situation. The basic choice is between a candidate with substantial industry expertise but no prior turnaround experience, or the converse: an experienced turnaround manager or company doctor. The appropriate choice will inevitably depend on the specific circumstances. On balance, however, we would tend to favour a candidate with previous turnaround experience rather than industry knowledge for most situations. A good company doctor is usually a highly effective general manager, and experience suggests that such people can usually work across most industries, except for the most specialized. A non-specialist is also more likely to challenge established industry norms.

A further consideration is whether one person can lead an organization through the complete recovery process from crisis stabilization to restructuring and on to corporate renewal. The manager who is good at taking control, generating cash, downsizing and cutting costs is often no good at developing and implementing viable market-driven strategies for the longer term.

The immediate task of the turnaround leader is to rebuild stakeholder confidence by re-establishing a sense of direction and purpose. The leader must move quickly to initiate the development of a rescue plan and communicate it to stakeholders. Finally, the leadership must be seen to be taking action quickly; it is essential to achieve some early wins.

Other Senior Management Changes

Apart from the change of CEO, many turnaround situations are characterized by other senior management changes. Again, views vary enormously among experienced company doctors. There are those who argue for wholesale change, irrespective of the competence and willingness to change of the incumbent management. Proponents argue that such action eliminates resistance to change, sends a strong message throughout the organization, and is a necessary part of the shock therapy that troubled companies require. The opposing view is that, as far as possible, the new CEO should work with existing management, with the proviso that the individuals are sufficiently competent and show a willingness to change. Irrespective of which approach is taken, most turnaround managers will introduce a new finance director because of the critical importance of strong financial management in a turnaround environment.

Turnaround managers rarely have the luxury of working with a world-class management team and workforce. However, large-scale management change is rarely an option in the early days because it is not easy to attract good managers to highly unstable situations. Consequently, one of the major leadership challenges for the turnaround manager is to deliver superior performance from a relatively weak team. But the organization does need to have sufficient human resources for the challenge ahead. Embarking on a turnaround with a team that lacks the basic expertise and experience required is a foolhardly exercise. The turnaround leader needs to conduct a rapid management skills audit at an early stage. The objective is to establish where the gaping holes exist and to consider ways of filling these skill gaps. At the very least, most organizations require effective financial, operations, sales and marketing management.

Improved Communications

Most companies could have better internal communications, but in a turnaround situation a quantum leap is usually necessary. As the company has gone into decline, less and less information has been communicated, cynicism has increased and morale has declined. The turnaround manager and his/her top team have to develop external credibility very quickly if they are to harness the organization's resources. They therefore have to decide what to communicate, how to communicate it, to whom and where. In doing this it is crucial that they all communicate the same message.

Building Commitment

The turnaround leader needs to motivate the whole workforce at an early stage. The priority here is to prevent good people leaving and to start to mobilize the organization for the challenge ahead. Particularly during the early stage of the recovery, the organization will move through very turbulent times, and having a committed workforce is a key factor for success.

3. Stakeholder Support

Troubled companies typically suffer from poor relations with their key stakeholders. These, comprising debt and equity providers, suppliers, customers, management and staff, and government regulators, can normally be split between 'mission critical' and less important. The power, influence and importance of stakeholders will vary according to each situation. In most cases some or all of the stakeholders will be aware of the distressed nature of the organization and will be concerned primarily about their own risk exposure to a failure of the business. A history of poor trading, inadequate communications, unfulfilled promises from management and unpleasant surprises, coupled with the risk of failure, will have eroded their confidence in the business. The other key issue is that the stakeholders will have different objectives and priorities. If the company is going to be rescued, these differing agendas have to be reconciled and stakeholder confidence rebuilt.

The guiding principle is that the turnaround manager must start to rebuild stakeholder confidence through a process of open communications and the provision of reliable information. Predictability must be restored and unpleasant surprises avoided at all costs. The role requires both impartiality as regards facts and at the same time a robust advocacy of the company's position. Success depends upon getting the stakeholders to recognize and accept the reality of the company's position and work cooperatively towards a solution to the business's actual problems.

Gaining stakeholder support requires careful stakeholder management. The first stage involves the clear, unbiased communication of the company's true financial position to relevant stakeholders. Based on that, the turnaround manager can commence a preliminary assessment of stakeholder positions, and identify at an early stage the level of support for a turnaround plan (compared with other options such as sale or insolvency). It may be necessary to reach a standstill agreement and negotiate ongoing support from the company's bankers during this period. During the early stages of the turnaround, there should be regular communication of the short-term cash and trading position. The turnaround manager should seek the involvement of stakeholders in the development of turnaround plans. Finally, the stakeholders' formal approval and agreement to the company's detailed rescue plan should be obtained. Ongoing communication of trading performance and progress of the recovery should occur during the implementation process.

4. Strategic Focus

Substantially under-performing companies generally face one or more serious strategic problems. Strategic issues are invariably 'mission critical' because they have an impact on the *raison d'être* of the business. Few organizations have a natural right to exist. Continued existence depends upon establishing a business that delivers a service or product in such a way that it generates a return on capital that exceeds the cost of its capital. This requires a robust and viable strategy that incorporates a clear sense of purpose and direction, realistic long-term goals that are based on genuine commercial opportunity, viable plans for achieving those long-term goals, and an ability to outperform competitors based on genuine competitive advantage. Our experience with troubled companies is that they very rarely have a robust and viable strategy. Typically, a formal strategy has not been clearly articulated and written down, resulting in confusion across the organization. Any strategy that exists is usually based on long-term goals that are either unrealistic or lack commercial common sense. Alternatively, the business may not be well-equipped to achieve its long-term goals; it may lack the basic resources and capabilities required to develop any competitive advantage. The key business objective for a turnaround manager is to develop a recovery plan that tackles these generic problems.

All the basic principles of strategic planning apply in turnaround situations. The strategic problems faced by most troubled companies, although very serious, are rarely complex. The solutions tend to be simple in concept but more complex in their execution. The desired end-state or vision for the business must be clearly understood across the organization. That destination must be intrinsically attractive, i.e., profitable, and based on an underlying demand for that service or product. The business must be capable of delivering a range of services or products, taking into consideration the resources it has at its disposal (infrastructure, people, know-how, technology, etc.), and it must be able to do so more effectively and efficiently than its competitors. The strategy must be written down and widely communicated throughout the organization. It should incorporate a simple definition of the goals and objectives of the business. It should encompass the 'what' and the 'how': what products/services are we going to deliver and to whom; and how are we going to do it?

The choice of strategy must take into account the existing resources and capabilities of the organization. To the extent that the recovery strategy depends upon skills and capabilities that the organization lacks, this gap must be manageable. A focus on the key success factors for the strategy must be at the heart of the recovery plan, since they provide the parameters within which the entire plan must be developed. The product-market mix provides the target or focus for the organization; it defines what products/services will be sold to whom. The importance of clarity on this issue cannot be overstated. Establishing a viable product-market strategy must be based on identifying a genuine customer need.

In many cases the strategic analysis will have to be quick and dirty. In our experience it is better to be 80 per cent right and act than 100 per cent right and have missed the opportunity. At the same time, the approach must be bold and broad. The danger for any turnaround leader is to use the excuse of insufficient time and analysis to postpone major strategic change. However, a sense of balance is also required.

Below we set out a brief summary of the most common generic strategies used in recovery situations.

Redefine the Business

This is the most fundamental form of strategic change. The long-term goals and objectives of the organization are changed; the management mindset changes; and the nature of the business is redefined. For example, a diversified multi-industry conglomerate becomes an industry-specific focused business; a vertically integrated company splits; a multi-process organization restructures around a single core process.

Divestment

A divestment strategy is often an integral part of product-market refocusing. As the firm cuts out product lines, customers, or whole areas of business, assets are liquidated or divested. The focus here is the disposal of significant parts of the business (division or operating subsidiaries), rather than the liquidation of current assets or disposal of surplus plant and machinery, which we consider to be part of crisis management.

Growth via Acquisition

This is a somewhat surprising but quite common recovery strategy. It does not necessarily mean diversification into new product-market areas unrelated to the firm's existing business. It may mean the acquisition of firms in the same or related industries. Acquisitions are most commonly used to turn around stagnant firms: firms not in a financial crisis but whose financial performance is poor. Growing by acquisition rather than organically means turnaround can be achieved faster. It is a strategy available to few firms in a crisis situation, however, because they lack the necessary financial resources – though, once their survival is assured, acquisition may be part of the strategy to achieve sustainable recovery.

Product-market Refocusing

Less radical than a complete redefinition of the business, but still involving fundamental strategic change, is refocusing the product-market mix. This occurs at the operating-company or business-unit level and involves the firm deciding what mix of products or services it should be selling to what customer segments. As we saw in Chapter 2, the distressed firm has usually lost focus by adding products and customers while continuing to compete in all its historical product or market segments. Pareto (80:20) analysis quickly shows that there is usually an excessively broad product range and broad customer base, much of which consists of loss-making or low-margin business. In the early stage of turnaround the appropriate product-market strategy usually involves dropping unprofitable products and customers and refocusing on those that are relatively more profitable.

Outsource Processes

Outsourcing addresses the position of an organization in the value chain of the enterprise system within which it operates. The rationale behind outsourcing is to focus on profitable processes where the company has a relative advantage and to outsource the remainder to third parties who can perform them more effectively. Outsourcing one or more businesses or functions is a core element of enterprise transformation. Traditionally outsourcing has been applied to non-core support processes with a heavy emphasis on finance and information systems. Increasingly, however, it is being applied to core functions and processes as multi-process organizations restructure to focus on only one or two core processes. Outsourcing is equally relevant to turnaround situations and is one of the generic strategies available as part of a strategic change plan. The emphasis within a turnaround environment is usually on the urgent need to replace or enhance a substantially ineffective process.

5. Organizational Change

People problems are usually among the most visible signs of a troubled company. Typical symptoms include a confused organization structure, a paralysed middle management, resistance to change, and demoralized staff. Staff turnover is probably high, the most able people have left, and the remaining workforce lack key skills and capabilities. Dysfunctional behaviour, where employees fail to cooperate to achieve the corporate objectives, may be encouraged by isolationist thinking and a rewards system not aligned with the strategy. Significant organizational change is therefore required.

New Organizational Structure

Changing the organizational structure can be a powerful way of rapidly changing the operations of an ailing business. A revised structure that facilitates clear accountability and responsibility will make the implementation process more straightforward. The turnaround leader will be able to see clearly who in the organization is working to the plan and who is not. Any revised organizational structure should emphasize an external, market-facing perspective, empower middle management, and seek to break down isolationist thinking. As we shall see in Chapter 10, however, structural change should be kept to a minimum in the early days of a turnaround.

The People

People are more important than structures. Capable and motivated staff are critical to an effective turnaround, since it is they who have to implement whatever recovery plan is agreed. Thus a top priority is assessing the people in the organization – particularly the management – and deciding who, if anybody, should be changed and when. In undertaking this assessment it is as important to assess skills and capabilities as it is to assess attitude to change. One without the other is no good.

Building Capabilities

The generic strategies required for process improvements all involve the organization doing things differently. Activities and sub-processes are reconfigured, organizational structures change, and new measures of success are introduced, with the consequence that employees will have to be trained to work in the new ways. Adequate training to support the change programme is therefore a vital element of successful recovery.

Terms and Conditions of Employment

We believe that an effective reward system can play a major role in tackling the people problems of a business. The entire organization should be given strong incentives to implement the recovery plan. It seems to us quite obvious that people who feel they have a stake in the business, and who are financially motivated to implement a recovery plan successfully, are more likely to give their best efforts than those who are not.

In recent years changing contracts of employment and union

agreements have also been used as effective mechanisms for organizational change.

6. Critical Process Improvements

Substantially underperforming companies typically have serious problems with both their core and support processes. These are often characterized by high cost, poor quality and lack of flexibility/responsiveness. The underlying causes of these problems vary. Many processes are poorly managed due to a lack of focus on cost, quality and time. Problems with the physical infrastructure, such as machines in need of repair, outdated IT systems, or an organizational structure that breaks natural links in processes, can exacerbate problems.

The tools and techniques of mainstream business-process re-engineering (BPR) substantially apply. However, it is important that the turnaround plan does not become a BPR project. Turnaround plans are broader and deeper than conventional BPR. The emphasis in turnaround situations is on 'quick win' process re-engineering. Stand-alone BPR projects are characterized by a strong link with technology and management information systems (MIS) improvements. These projects tend to be large-scale and long-term, with the emphasis on process improvements through improved computer technology. In a turnaround environment the reverse tends to be true. The approach is 'quick and dirty', with the object of focusing attention on the core processes. Typically this will cover procurement, conversion, logistics, sales and marketing. The emphasis is on achieving a rapid quantum-leap improvement in time, cost or quality without the need for major MIS improvements.

Business process improvements generally fall within the following dimensions:

Time improvements: typically the focus is to make the organization more responsive and more flexible by reducing the time taken to bring a product to market, or reducing manufacturing lead-times.

Cost improvements: the approach is to simplify processes to reduce both the fixed and variable costs.

Quality improvements: this is self-explanatory and is about reducing the level of rework by systematically analysing the reasons for non-conformance, and putting in place corrective actions to improve processes.

Generic strategies deployed across the various business processes can be summarized as improvements to demand-generation, demand-fulfilment and demand-support processes.

Demand Generation

Assuming that product-market refocusing decisions have been taken, improving the selling process and the effectiveness of the salesforce is a key area for process quick-wins. Marketing mix improvements include brand management/repositioning, promotions and, particularly, pricing. New product development and improved customer responsiveness may also provide important improvement opportunities. Although this area tends to be more important in enterprise transformation rather than turnaround situations, increasing innovation rate and improving product engineering are important longer term initiatives.

Demand Fulfilment

Typically this is the core area for process improvements and will involve substantial cost reduction and improved effectiveness in procurement, manufacturing/conversion, logistics and after-sales service. Simple procurement initiatives can reduce cost, working capital and inventory risk, and improve quality and service. Gaining control of the shop floor and improving efficiency typically involves layout changes and the introduction of cellular manufacturing, just-in-time (JIT) and Kanban principles.

Support Systems

The introduction of a production planning function to balance the supply-and-demand side of a business is an important generic response to a very common business problem. Other improvements will be targeted at head-office functions and will include the introduction of new performance measures, improvements to the management of the physical infrastructure, and the restructuring of the finance department to deliver timely, relevant and accurate information.

7. Financial Restructuring

Companies in need of a turnaround typically suffer from one or more of the following:

- cash-flow problems, i.e., insufficient future funding or an inability to pay debts as and when they fall due
- excessive gearing (too much debt/too little equity)
- inappropriate debt structure, e.g., excessive short-term/on-demand borrowing and insufficient long-term debt
- balance-sheet insolvency.

Irrespective of the health of the underlying business, if the operating cash flow cannot finance the debt and equity obligations, the company will remain fatally wounded. In these circumstances the only solution is a financial restructuring.

The objectives of any financial restructuring are to restore the business to solvency on both cash-flow and balance-sheet bases, to align the capital structure with the level of projected operating cash flow, and to ensure that sufficient financing in the form of existing and new money is available to finance the implementation of the turnaround plan.

A financial restructuring usually involves changing the existing capital structure and/or raising additional finance. Capital restructuring usually involves an agreement between the ailing firm and its creditors (usually the banks) to reschedule and sometimes convert interest and principal payments into other negotiable financial instruments. The raising of new funding may involve additional debt, typically from the existing lenders, who may be persuaded that the best prospect of recovering their existing lending is via the provision of further lending. The provision of new equity from existing shareholders via a rights issue or from outside investors (vulture funds, etc.) frequently accompanies new bank lending. Existing funders may accept a financial restructuring even if progress in the other six key ingredients is not good because they believe restructuring represents the best option for recovery of their investment. However, to attract new money from new investors there must be a convincing plan and the prospect of appropriate returns in the restructured company must be real.

The Implementation Framework

The starting point for the implementation of the turnaround process is always a diagnostic review to establish the true position of the troubled company and to determine whether a turnaround – as opposed to insolvency, immediate sale or liquidation – is a viable option.

Once the decision to proceed with a turnaround has been taken by the principal stakeholders, seven separate implementation processes – or as we prefer to call them, 'workstreams' – have to be undertaken to ensure the seven key ingredients are in place:

Crisis management: taking control of the distressed business and implementing aggressive cash management.

Selection of the turnaround team: appointment of a chief executive to lead the turnaround and selection of his/her team.

Stakeholder management: rebuilding stakeholder confidence and reconciling their different interests within an overall recovery plan.

Develop the business plan: the development of a detailed recovery plan for the business covering strategic, operational and organizational issues.

Implement the business plan: the implementation of the detailed turnaround initiatives contained within the recovery plan.

Prepare and negotiate financial plan: restructuring the capital base and raising the money to fund the turnaround.

Project management: the integration and coordination of the above six workstreams, i.e., overall management of the turnaround process.

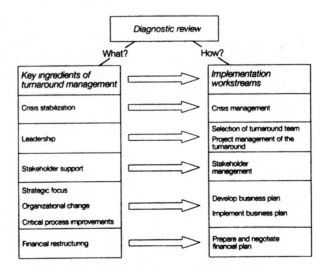

Figure 4.2: **Key Ingredients and Workstreams**

Figure 4.2 illustrates how these seven workstreams are linked to the seven key ingredients.

Our experience is that in most turnaround situations the turnaround leader will have to undertake all seven workstreams, although financial restructuring may not be required where the troubled company is a subsidiary of a healthy parent.

These workstreams are the essential implementation tasks of the turnaround process. Together they address the priority issues of managing the immediate crisis, fixing the operations, managing the various interests of those with a stake in the company, and ensuring that the company has sufficient cash to survive in both the short and long term.

Clearly a diagnostic analysis must be done first because the company doctor cannot cure the patient unless s/he knows what is wrong. However, in many situations it will be crucial to begin other workstreams in parallel with the diagnosis, particularly dealing with the stakeholders and managing the immediate crisis. One of the first things the newly appointed turnaround leader must do is advise the stakeholders of his/

her appointment and explain how s/he intends to tackle the situation. On day one the discussion may be limited to an explanation of the process s/he intends to follow. Such early initiatives start to rebuild confidence, demonstrate management control, and can help prevent the stakeholders taking any adverse action prematurely. The other immediate priority is crisis management. The turnaround leader needs to rapidly assess whether the company has sufficient cash to survive in the short term whilst s/he carries out a diagnostic review and starts to formulate the recovery plan.

The analysis phase typically lasts between one week and three months, depending on the size and complexity of the problem. During the later stages of the analysis, the turnaround team will have already started developing the detailed business plan. Our approach to business planning is intensive; the plan is the 'bible' for the rescue. It sets out in detail the specific actions needed to restore the business to profitability, together with associated trading projections. The process involves several iterations as each stakeholder adds their input to the plan. How long this takes will depend on the size and complexity of the company, but we would normally expect the plan to be fully developed within three to four months, and much sooner in some cases. Even before the plan is finalized, implementation can commence. Many of the initiatives are 'no-brainers' and can be implemented before the plan has been fully and finally approved. The implementation phase typically lasts between six months and two years, and comprises an emergency phase, a strategic change phase and possibly a growth phase. The financial restructuring is probably the last workstream to get under way. The key input for it is the operating cash-flow forecast and funding projections for the business, contained within the business plan. As soon as these projections have been finalized, work can commence on restructuring the debt and equity and raising new money.

Diagnostic Review

Variously described as a strategic review, diagnostic review or business assessment, this critical phase must be the first step in the turnaround process and has the following objectives:

- to establish the true position of the company from a strategic, operational and financial perspective
- to assess the options available to the company and to determine whether it can be turned around
- to determine whether the business can survive in the short term
- to establish the stakeholders' position and their level of support for the various options
- to make a preliminary assessment of the management team.

In many situations the troubled company may be rapidly running out of cash and the priority is therefore to move as quickly as possible through this phase. The approach is likely to be 'quick and dirty'; analysis is high-level, broad in scope, and in-depth only with respect to the key issues. The value of such a review depends upon who does it, and clearly the more experienced the practitioner the better. This is one reason why we generally prefer an experienced turnaround practitioner to undertake the review, rather than an industry expert.

The diagnostic review needs to combine the elements of a conventional strategic and operational review with those of a corporate recovery/insolvency analysis. The team carrying out the review will therefore use traditional consultants' methodology: the strategic and operational review will cover both the internal and external environment with a view to establishing the causes of decline and possible recovery strategies. The financial review will focus on establishing the current financial position and future trading prospects.

The review will need to consider the various options available to the company – typically the sale of part/all of the business, turnaround, insolvency, or closure/liquidation – and evaluate the financial outcome for the stakeholders under each scenario. The techniques for the review phase follow conventional consulting methodology: analysis of financial and operational data; interviews with management and staff; tour of facilities; discussions with suppliers, customers and industry experts; analysis of the industry and competitors. At the end of the diagnosis the turnaround leader must have concluded whether turnaround is a viable option; the outline shape of the turnaround plan (and the approximate level of funding to support it); preliminary management changes; and the extent of stakeholder support.

At the beginning of this phase the prospective turnaround manager may not have taken a formal management position with the troubled company. At this early stage, it may not be apparent whether turnaround is a realistic option or not. However, within a relatively short period of time (a few days to a few weeks) the proposed CEO must decide whether to take on the turnaround assignment or not. Having made this initial decision, the turnaround assignment can begin in earnest, and the turnaround manager can move quickly to begin the crisis management and stakeholder management workstreams.

Crisis Management

As soon as the turnaround option has been chosen for the distressed company, crisis management should commence forthwith, if necessary even before a turnaround manager has been appointed. Where this is the case, interim management or consultants can be brought in to deal with the crisis. The most likely cause of failure in the short term is that the business runs out of cash thereby preventing wages, rent, etc. from being paid. The priority is therefore to establish what critical payments have to be made in the short term to keep the company alive, and to determine whether the existing bank facilities together with short-term cash receipts (such as debtor collections) will be sufficient to cover the critical payments. If the analysis indicates a funding shortfall, the turnaround manager must move rapidly to bridge the funding gap by arranging additional funding, pursuing aggressive cash realization strategies, and restructuring critical payments wherever possible.

Simultaneously, the turnaround leader must move rapidly to take control of the organization. The priority in the short term is to try and limit the scale of the continuing decline by focusing attention on the most serious and urgent problems. The key issue is to determine what factors, if any, threaten the survival of the business in the short term.

Selection of the Turnaround Team

Ideally an appropriate person will be appointed to lead the turnaround – usually a chief executive – as soon as the process is triggered by one or more of the stakeholders. This may or may not be before a diagnostic review has been undertaken. If the diagnostic review has been carried out by consultants or investigating accountants, their report is usually the trigger to appoint a turnaround manager and/or begin crisis management. Changing the top team may however take time: incumbents have to be assessed, and where a replacement is necessary the recruitment process can take several months. Getting the right top team in place is usually a time-consuming task for the turnaround leader.

Stakeholder Management

We have previously described the key elements necessary to obtain stakeholder support. As stated above, we strongly believe that stakeholder management should commence forthwith. The duration of the process varies considerably but our strong preference is for a longer rather than a shorter duration. Experience suggests that debt and equity providers like to remain closely involved at least until the 'patient' is almost fully recovered. In practice this is likely to be towards the end of the implementation phase, i.e., a duration of up to about two years, although in some cases it can be much longer (the case of Brent Walker lasted for about six years). One certainty is that the recovery path will not be smooth and uneventful. The company is likely to experience continuing uncertainty and turbulence during much of the early recovery period. It is much easier to retain the confidence of the stakeholders if they are kept fully informed of both positive and negative developments.

Develop the Business Plan

We believe that successful leaders of turnaround situations move very quickly to commence the development of a business plan which sets out their rescue strategy, following the conventional consulting model. Problems are initially identified during the diagnostic review. Further analysis will identify the underlying cause(s) of each problem so that one or more remedies can be developed. Clearly there is a natural link between the diagnostic review and the plan development workstream. In our experience the two have a 'paralinear' relationship – they are partly sequential and partly parallel processes. Clearly recovery strategies cannot be developed until the problem has been satisfactorily diagnosed. However, turnaround initiatives for problems that have been rapidly diagnosed can be developed while analysis continues on other more complex problems.

We strongly believe in the development of a comprehensive business plan. The plan should clearly state the long-term goals (vision/mission) for the business together with the chosen strategy for achieving those goals. The plan should clearly define the products or services offered by the company and what its chosen markets are. The core business processes for delivering those products/services must be explicitly defined. The plans should contain a detailed programme of turnaround initiatives that together form the rescue plan. Each turnaround initiative should be described in terms of responsibility, proposed action, implementation timetable, required resources and proposed impact.

The number of initiatives varies according to the size and complexity of the organization. The size and scope of each initiative may also vary from a major restructuring improvement ('rationalize ten factories to four') to a more modest action ('hire a new design director'). Clearly the larger initiatives may involve a major project and thus require a number of sub-tasks. In our experience turnaround plans rarely comprise less than fifty recovery initiatives.

Finally, the plan should contain detailed financial projections for Year 1 and higher-level projections over a three- to five-year period. The plan forms the 'bible' for the implementation process over the next six to eighteen months. By the time the plan is endorsed, each and every executive who is to play a part in its implementation must understand it and his/her role. Managing the implementation of the plan becomes the key focus for the senior management.

Implement the Business Plan

The focus during this phase is the implementation of the turnaround initiatives incorporated in the business plan. The implementation of the business plan becomes the principal role of senior management. Although this may appear simplistic, it is generally the case that if an issue has not been addressed in the business plan, it should not be an issue for management during the implementation phase.

We believe that rigorous project management is the key success factor for implementation. The plan sets out a programme of prioritized actions with timing, responsibility and planned impact. The implementation process employs conventional project management tools (Gantt charts, progress reports, etc.) to drive accountability; the priority is to get people/teams to deliver their initiatives on time and on budget. Progress must be monitored against the plan on a weekly basis; key issues must be dealt with when they arise; and next steps must be continuously identified. Action becomes the defining watchword for the implementation phase.

Management of the implementation process is driven by regular progress meetings supported by continuously updated rolling implementation reports. Ordinarily the coordination or steering group will meet on a weekly basis during the early stages; as the turnaround progresses the frequency of these meetings may become fortnightly or monthly. The focus for the meetings is the review of progress against each initiative.

Prepare and Negotiate the Financial Plan

The business plan is the basis of the financial restructuring plan – if that is necessary. The financial projections accompanying the business plan will be based on the cash-flow forecasts which are the key input into assessing the future funding requirements of the business.

Project Management

We have already mentioned the need for detailed project management of the implementation initiatives. However, the whole turnaround process needs project managing by the turnaround manager. S/he needs to fit the various parts of the turnaround jigsaw together at different stages of the turnaround process.

The turnaround manager does not therefore have the luxury, enjoyed by many other participants in the turnaround, of being able to concentrate solely on one phase of the turnaround at a time. This is a difficult challenge, as the objectives of each phase can be quite different. For example, the mindset and style required for crisis management is quite different from that required in business planning, yet these phases of the turnaround are managed side by side. The role of the turnaround manager is to achieve balance between the workstreams and build momentum into the implementation processes so that the overall objectives are afforded the best prospect of success.

Timing

The turnaround process is characterized by considerable overlap of the planning and implementation phases. We identify four distinct but overlapping phases in the implementation process:

- analysis
- emergency
- strategic change
- growth and renewal (beyond turnaround).

Figure 4.3 illustrates how the workstreams discussed in the previous sectors are phased throughout the turnaround process.

The Analysis Phase

This phase encompasses more than just the diagnostic review. We have already stated that stakeholder interface management and crisis management often need to begin in parallel with the diagnostic review, and that the diagnostic review itself is the starting point for the development of the business plan. Thus some generic strategies – such as cash

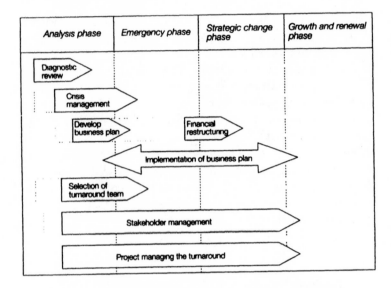

Figure 4.3: **Phasing of Workstreams Throughout the Turnaround Process**

management, change of chief executive or tighter financial control – may start to be implemented in the analysis phase.

The Emergency Phase

The emergency phase consists of those actions necessary to ensure survival and therefore tends to focus on those generic strategies that can most easily be implemented in the short term. The distinction between implementation of the business plan and crisis management can become blurred. Cash generation, cost reduction, increased prices and increased selling effort are the principal generic strategies used in this phase of recovery. Organizational change to facilitate control and management may also happen now.

The emergency phase is often characterized by surgery: divesting subsidiaries, closing plants, making employees redundant, firing incompetent managers, reducing surplus inventories, selling obsolete inventories, cutting out unprofitable product lines, etc. – all actions designed primarily to improve the cash flow and stop the losses.

It is during the emergency phase also that the firm may seek additional financing to implement its recovery strategy, and so there is overlap with the financial restructuring workstream. The emergency phase usually lasts from six to twelve months, or longer if appropriate recovery strategies are not adopted or are not well implemented.

The Strategic Change Phase

Whereas the emergency phase tends to emphasize operational factors, the strategic change phase emphasizes product-market reorientation. By good implementation of an appropriate recovery strategy in the emergency phase, the firm has assured short-term survival and can begin in the emergency phase to focus strategy on those product-market segments where the firm has most competitive advantage (usually, but not always, those segments where it is profitable). However, product-market change usually takes time to implement and may require some investment, which may not be possible in the early phase of recovery. It is at this strategic change phase that management and/or shareholders may realize that the long-term viability of the firm looks doubtful, or that the investment of money and time required to achieve sustainable recovery is not worth the risks involved. They may, therefore, decide to look for a suitable purchaser for the business.

Assuming product-market reorientation appears viable, the strategic change phase is also characterized by:

- An increased emphasis on profits in addition to the early emphasis on cash flow. Return on capital employed is still unlikely to be satisfactory during this phase, although losses have been eliminated.
- Continued improvements in operational efficiency.
- Organization-building – which may be important, bearing in mind that the organization may have been traumatized in the emergency phase.

This phase is sometimes referred to as the stabilization phase, because the organization needs time to settle down and prepare for a phase of renewed growth. New management will probably have brought with it a new organizational culture which will take time to become institutionalized. Stabilization is important, yes; but alone it is insufficient to give the firm a sound base for the future. That can only be accomplished by refocusing the firm's product-market position or sharpening its existing competitive advantages.

The Growth Phase

Before this can begin, the firm's balance sheet must have improved. Once it has, the firm can start to grow, either organically through new product and market development, or via acquisition, or both. This is the final phase of the turnaround process and the beginning of what is sometimes called corporate renewal. However in some industry sectors, such as high technology, a rapid return to growth maybe a prerequisite for a successful turnaround.

Characteristics of Successful Recovery Situations

There are substantial differences between the recovery strategies adopted by successful turnaround leaders and unsuccessful ones. Successful recovery situations are:

Comprehensive: They incorporate the seven essential ingredients. A very common source of failure is to initiate too narrow a turnaround. The turnaround leader has to not only manage the immediate crisis and tackle the strategic and operational problems of the business, but also rebuild stakeholder confidence and ensure the company has adequate funding for the future.

Non-linear: They address the key issues simultaneously rather than in a linear sequence. In the early days, the turnaround leader should start the process of rebuilding stakeholder support in parallel with the early stages of managing the crisis and developing the business plan.

Wide-ranging: They are broad in scope, i.e., they tackle cost reduction and revenue growth, deal with hard and soft issues, incorporate strategic and operational initiatives, and address both short- and long-term priorities.

A study comparing successful and unsuccessful turnaround efforts undertaken by one of the authors in both the UK and USA showed that successful turnarounds are characterized by:

- management changes, particularly the appointment of a new chief executive and a new financial director
- the use of multiple cash-generating strategies
- improved financial control systems, used by management to install a performance-oriented culture
- an understanding that cost-reduction strategies, although important, are usually insufficient to effect a successful turnaround
- fundamental product-market reorientation alongside improved operational marketing
- significant organizational change in terms of structure processes and improved communications

Two key messages stand out in examining successful turnarounds. Firstly, successful firms use twice as many generic turnaround strategies as unsuccessful firms: they undertake a lot of generic strategies in parallel. And secondly, they implement more vigorously. There is nearly always a need for more rather than fewer actions. We see this in practice when the initial turnaround manager is replaced because s/he is failing to make a real financial impact within the first twelve months. The replacement turnaround manager will always use more strategies and implement those of his/her predecessor more vigorously.

5 Diagnostic Review

Objectives

The diagnostic review is essential to ensure that the business is capable of being turned around and that it can survive whilst a detailed business plan is developed and implemented. The review is typically undertaken by investigating accountants or by a company doctor acting in a consulting capacity. Most experienced company doctors insist on undertaking their own diagnostic review before committing themselves to becoming the turnaround manager. The key objectives of the review are:

- To assess whether the business can survive in the short term (a minimum of three months) or the extent to which external funding is required to underwrite short-term survival.
- To determine whether the company may be viable in the medium to long term.
- To assess the options available to the company and identify which offers the best value to the various stakeholders. These options could include turnaround, immediate disposal, workout or formal insolvency.
- To diagnose at a high level the key problems, whether these are primarily strategic, operational or both, and what mix of strategies and actions are needed for short-term survival and beyond.
- To assess the positions of the key stakeholders (lenders, shareholders, management, employees), their willingness to support and if necessary help fund a turnaround, their relative bargaining power and ability to influence the outcome.

- A preliminary assessment of management. Who is part of the problem? Who is part of the solution? Can we work with them? Should anyone be asked to leave immediately?

The desired outcome of the review is an agreed course of action plus provisional stakeholder support for the business. The conclusion should be supported by a financial analysis that demonstrates the financial value and risk profile of the alternative courses of action that have been considered.

The Approach

The approach is 'quick and dirty'. The analysis must be sufficiently accurate to ensure that the right option is selected, but time is desperately short. The analysis may take from a few days for a small company to several weeks or even months for a large firm, but typically there will be time pressure to report back to the board or stakeholders with findings, conclusions and recommendations. It is helpful to keep the following points in mind in determining the approach:

An external stakeholder, typically the lender(s), equity-holders or a new chief executive or chairman, often initiates the process. They want answers quickly and may also want feedback during the process, particularly if they are maintaining or even extending lending facilities during the review period.

Only do sufficient work to address the key objectives outlined above. Although the analysis will be broad in scope, covering the business's strategy, competitive position, core operations and current financial position, it is unlikely to include extensive analysis in any of these areas. You need to get to the key issues quickly: don't get side-tracked by non-essential areas that are not critical to the short-term survival or medium-term viability of the business.

Objectivity is key: Assumptions and opinions must be substantiated by analysis and facts and there can be no 'sacred cows'. Consultants can play an important role here, providing objective, analytical support to the turnaround leader and speeding up the diagnostic process.

In large companies it will not be possible to evaluate all business units at the same time, although it is important before any detailed strategic analysis is undertaken to categorize operating companies roughly into 'winners', 'losers', and 'satisfactory but unexciting'. An experienced turnaround manager can accomplish this through an analysis of available financial data and by a one-day meeting with the managers responsible for that unit. Diagnostic effort can then be focused on the 'losers', while detailed investigation of the remaining business units is postponed to a later date.

Analysis of Ability to Survive in the Short Term

The key issue is whether the business can survive for the period required to develop turnaround strategies, prepare a detailed business plan and negotiate a financial restructuring or refinancing. Typically this will take at least three months; for more complex businesses, you may need to consider a six-month time period. The assessment requires a rolling daily or weekly cash flow going forward three months. This must be based on up-to-date financial information and should incorporate aggressive but realistic working-capital management targets.

If the cash flow indicates a need for short-term financing, a survival plan is needed which identifies:

- what funds can be generated internally
- what funding gap this will leave and for how long
- what level of short-term funding is required from external sources
- what the business might be able and willing to offer in return (such as security) in order to get short-term funding.

If short-term funding cannot be secured, the only realistic options facing the business are immediate (distressed) sale or insolvency.

Viability Assessment

Not all crisis situations are recoverable. For a recovery strategy to be successful, it must eliminate the financial crisis, reverse the causes of decline, overcome the resistance of stakeholders, overcome the constraints of the firm's internal environment and, in many situations, overcome an unattractive set of industry characteristics. Therefore not all turnaround situations are viable independent businesses.

The chances of recovery vary according to the combined effect of six major factors:

- causes of decline
- severity of the crisis
- attitude of stakeholders
- firm's historical strategy and internal environment
- external environment and industry characteristics
- firm's cost/price structure.

These are each discussed in greater detail below.

Causes of Decline

Turnaround situations are usually characterized by several different causes of failure, each one of which usually requires several generic strategies to correct (see Figure 5.1). However, it is not so much the number of strategies required that influences turnaround viability but the nature of the underlying causes of decline. Companies suffering from operational weaknesses and poor management, or those suffering from an ill-conceived debt burden taken on during an earlier financing, are much easier to turn around than those where the problem is the result of competitive weakness, severe price competition from competitors with a much lower cost base, or a completely outdated product line.

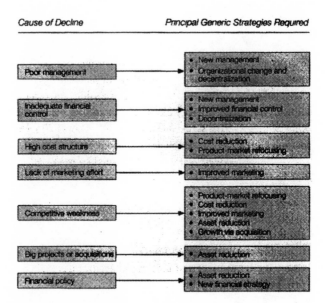

Cause of Decline	Principal Generic Strategies Required

Poor management	• New management • Organizational change and decentralization
Inadequate financial control	• New management • Improved financial control • Decentralization
High cost structure	• Cost reduction • Product-market refocusing
Lack of marketing effort	• Improved marketing
Competitive weakness	• Product-market refocusing • Cost reduction • Improved marketing • Asset reduction • Growth via acquisition
Big projects or acquisitions	• Asset reduction
Financial policy	• Asset reduction • New financial strategy

Figure 5.1: **Influence of Causes of Decline on Generic Strategies**

Severity of the Crisis

The severity of the crisis facing the turnaround firm is a function of the causes of failure and what stage the crisis has reached (i.e., the degree to which the firm has progressed towards insolvency). The fact that a firm has been losing money for years means that it is clearly a potential candidate for turnaround treatment, but does not necessarily mean that there is a crisis. Whether a cash crisis develops is a function of the firm's balance sheet. The balance sheet will usually deteriorate when a firm is losing money, but the situation can continue for a number of years if management has adopted conservative gearing policies in the past, has maintained reasonable financial control, and the losses are not becoming progressively worse.

In a severe cash crisis, crisis management and financial restructuring must take priority over all other strategies, and long-term viability cannot be reasonably assessed until short-term survival has been secured.

Strategies such as process re-engineering and product-market refocusing may help generate cash flow, but the additional cash they are likely to contribute in the short term is likely to be small compared with that from crisis management and financial restructuring. In situations where no further capital is available, the firm's cash-flow limitations will usually mean that most investment and growth strategies cannot be implemented until after survival has been assured and the balance sheet has recovered.

Similarly, the severity of the firm's profit crisis (measured by the extent to which the firm is operating at below breakeven) determines the extent to which the revenue-generating strategies (product-market reorientation and re-engineering of demand-generating processes) will be necessary in addition to a cost-reduction strategy. Even the most dramatic cost-reduction strategy may be inadequate to bring a firm back to breakeven, as is illustrated in Figure 5.2.

Attitude of Stakeholders

In a turnaround situation, the relative power of the various stakeholders may be important in determining whether the business is viable in the medium to long term. If the shareholders act through their representatives on the board of directors to change management before the firm reaches a crisis, recovery may be initiated relatively simply. In the absence of a crisis, new management usually has fewer constraints determining the recovery strategy, although it is to be hoped that management action will take place under the watchful eye of the board and the principal shareholders. Few turnaround managers have this freedom unless the ailing firm has just been acquired – in which case the objectives of the acquirer determine the recovery strategy.

Once a crisis occurs, it is more likely to be the firm's creditors, usually the banks, that initiate the turnaround process. Bank influence varies enormously from one situation to the next, but in some instances the bank can be virtually running the firm and, in the process, be deciding

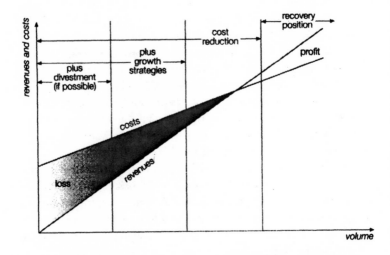

Figure 5.2: **Influence of Firm's Breakeven on Recovery Strategy**

which generic strategies should receive most management attention. Typically, an asset-reduction strategy designed to repay or reduce the bank's outstanding loans takes precedence (as it does, for example, when a receiver is appointed). If the bank or banks require a workout of this nature, this may rule out medium- or long-term survival of the business in its current form. As banks become global in nature, their attitude in a particular country is increasingly affected by pressures elsewhere. If the turnaround manager is to maintain bank suport s/he needs to establish the banks' real agenda before deciding what approach to take to the turnaround. Powerful trade unions may also act as a constraint on both cost-reduction and asset-reduction strategies if there is the likelihood of loss of jobs and changes in job practice.

Thus, stakeholders act in two ways to influence the recovery strategy: in a direct way when they stipulate what strategy should be followed or given priority, and in an indirect way when they act as constraints on strategy implementation.

Firm's Historical Strategy

The firm's historical strategy directly influences future viability, even if the historical strategy was not a cause of decline. Both the firm's product-market scope and the deployment of its assets influence which generic strategies are feasible. A diversified firm, for example, can generate cash by selling business units, an option not available to a more focused business.

Organizations embarking on a programme of strategic change do not have the luxury of starting with a clean sheet of paper. Any revision to strategy has to take into consideration the constraints imposed by the status quo position. Enterprises have a heritage that they carry with them: their existing products, customers, assets, human and financial resources, know-how, etc. These represent parameters or constraints on what is possible in the future, particularly in the short term.

Industry Characteristics

The characteristics of an industry in which the firm competes always influences the strategy formulation, whether the firm is in a turnaround situation or not. However, some key industry characteristics are favourable to turnarounds while others are not.

The prospects for the industry in which the company operates, including the size and growth rate of the industry. The importance of industry growth rate is based on the premise that cash usage is proportional to market growth rate, that the feasibility of increasing market share varies according to the stage of growth, and that management should focus on different functional strategies at various states of growth.[1] The lack of financial resources, poor management and lack of financial control which usually characterize turnaround situations may change substantially the traditional pattern of strategic responses expected at different stages of the life cycle. This is particularly true in the growth phase of the market, when sales growth and investment strategies would normally be appropriate. Instead, asset-reduction, cost reduction and product-market refocusing strategies may be necessary to ensure survival.

The nature of the product, which influences the ability to implement certain turnaround strategies. For example, product-market focusing and increasing price, which are often necessary in a turnaround, become increasingly difficult as the product becomes less differentiated and more price sensitive. Revenue-generating strategies are extremely difficult for capital goods where long lead times exist between order and delivery.

The degree of market segmentation: A market that is highly segmented due to varying customer preferences is more likely to allow the turnaround firm the opportunity to develop a focused and defensible product-market strategy.

The rate of technological change: A slower rate of technological change favours the turnaround firm because it makes it more feasible to implement viable product-market and investment strategies. The greater the rate of change, the more financial resources are required to bring the firm back to a competitive position.

The relative strength and size of competitors and the intensity of competition.

The bargaining power of customers and suppliers. This will affect the ability of the turnaround firm to raise prices, and its chances of achieving substantial reductions in supply costs.

Many of the industry characteristics that influence the formulation of recovery strategies are the same as those identified by Porter as factors influencing industry profitability.[2] This should not be surprising, since a firm's profit potential, and hence its recovery potential, are partly functions of the industry it is in. The chance of sustainable turnaround in an industry with low profit potential must be lower than in an industry with higher profit potential, because in the latter case it is easier to attract additional finance for investment and to follow an asset-reduction strategy of divestment since there are likely to be new firms willing to enter the industry.

Firm's cost/price structure

The strategies required to obtain short-term profit improvement are dependent to a large degree on the firm's cost/price structure at the time of crisis. This in turn is determined in part by industry characteristics and in part by the causes of decline. The cost/price structure is extremely important in determining whether management should focus short-term attention on a cost-reduction strategy, a marketing improvement strategy, or both, to achieve a rapid improvement in profit margins. If the cost/price structure does not allow certain strategies to be implemented, it may indicate that turnaround is not a viable option.

The firm's cost-price structure is derived by analysing the inter-relationship of the revenue and cost components of the profit-and-loss statement and then doing a sensitivity analysis. Management controls the three components of the profit-and-loss statement – price, volume and costs – through its ability to implement marketing improvement and cost-reduction strategies. For small changes – say 5–10 per cent – in the value of these three components, the relative importance of pricing, volume-generating and cost-reduction strategies can be ascertained.

Sensitivity analysis of this type determines which are the most profit-sensitive components in the cost/price structure but takes no account of which components it is most feasible to change. The actions to influence components vary enormously in the ease with which they can be implemented and the time horizons over which they can be changed, and thus managerial judgement and common sense are required to determine the relative importance of the strategic alternatives. As desirable as further price increases might be, the price elasticity of demand for the firm's product may effectively close this option. Similarly, once costs have been reduced to a certain point, additional cost reductions may not be easily obtainable, in which case management must turn to increases in sales volume to obtain additional profit – which is usually very difficult in a turnaround situation (see Chapter 10).

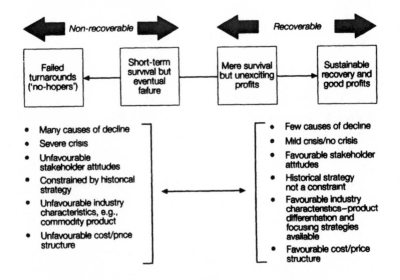

Figure 5.3: **Factors Determining the Feasibility of Recovery**

Types of Recovery Situation

The chances of recovery vary according to the combined effect of the six groups of factors outlined in the previous section. There is a range of likely outcomes, from complete and sustainable recovery, through mere survival, to short-term survival and, at the opposite end, failed recovery. The range of outcomes is shown in Figure 5.3 and provides a useful classification of recovery types. Figure 5.4 shows a graphic representation of typical profit trajectories for the four types of recovery situation.

It is important to identify quickly a situation that is not recoverable. This will maximize the time available for implementing an alternative course of action, such as sale, workout or formal insolvency, and thereby maximize the returns available to the various stakeholders. If the business is a basket case, it is not realistic to aim to restore the company to the state in which it was originally created.

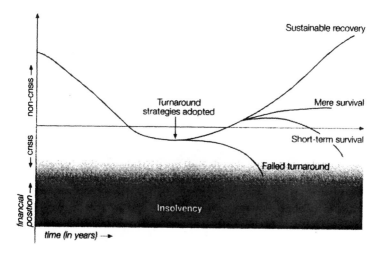

Figure 5.4: **Types of Recovery Situation**

The possible outcomes for an organization in a turnaround situation are:

No-hopers: These are firms that cannot exist as viable, independent entities even in the short term. They will inevitably fail, and from an economic point of view are not worth turning round. They are characterized by some or all of the following factors:

- decline in their core business area as the result of severe price competition from lower-cost producers who possess significant cost advantages due to scale and experience-curve effects
- indivisible assets – they are single-plant, and often single-product, firms that cannot divest assets to generate cash flow
- high fixed cost as a percentage of value added
- very fast decline in market demand (30 per cent or more in a single year)
- loss of regulatory licence with little chance of immediate restoration
- total loss of confidence by customers.

Short-term survivors: These are firms that, if analysed over a three- to five-year horizon, look as if they have recovered. They may well have succeeded in improving profits for several years, yet eventually they go into insolvency because they are unable to overcome significant competitive disadvantage. This does not mean to say that such firms are not good turnaround candidates, providing the investors sell the business as soon as they have added value by adopting short-term turnaround strategies.

Mere survival: Even if survival is possible, sustainable recovery may not be. There is a big difference in both the strategies and the management time and effort required to bring a firm to a survival situation and those required to achieve sustainable recovery. Sustainable recovery usually requires a shift in product-market emphasis and growth-oriented strategies such as new product development and/or growth via acquisition. In many situations, sustainable recovery will be impossible to achieve, due to industry characteristics and the limited resources of the firm compared with competitors. Where survival has been achieved, stakeholders need to reappraise their investment and decide whether they will sell the firm while the going is good or stay with it for the long term, with the aim of achieving sustainable recovery and a better return on their investment. The danger of sticking with a firm that achieves the mere survival stage and no more is that it is more susceptible to crisis than a firm in a sustainable recovery mode, even if it is adequately managed. A 'mere survival' firm may become a sustainable recovery firm under new ownership, where the benefit of the merger may move the firm to a higher level of performance.

Sustainable recovery: Achieving sustainable recovery means successfully implementing a recovery strategy that permits the firm to make above-average profits in the long term. It is the ideal situation to aim for, but the dice are often loaded against this happening. Where the causes of the firm's decline are due to poor management, lack of control, general operating inefficiency or product-market weaknesses in a subsidiary, sustainable recovery is usually feasible; but if the causes of decline are related to the firm having a weak product-market position in its core business area, sustainable recovery may be impossible. A firm may have more chance of recovery as a subsidiary of a larger firm if the acquirer is prepared to invest large sums of money and time into turning the firm around. But even then recovery is not assured, as many acquisition-minded firms have subsequently found out. Sustainable recovery is usually easiest to achieve in a non-crisis recovery situation since, by implementing a recovery strategy before the onset of a crisis, the firm has greater financial resources available to it and a stronger competitive market position on which to build for the future.

Problems of classification do arise, particularly between what is sustainable recovery and what is mere survival or even short-term recovery. While the classification of recovery types is presented here as a useful conceptual framework, few firms stay in a static position for very long, due to the changing nature of both internal resources and the external environment. All firms are susceptible to crisis, with the result that there is a natural tendency for firms to slip back towards less recoverable positions. Considerable managerial effort – and perhaps some luck – is required to keep a firm in the sustainable recovery box for a long period of time, due to rapid technological change and the increased competition which comes from slower growth in the world economy.

Options Assessment

The next step is to analyse the financial implications and the risks inherent in pursuing each available option. This should indicate the net present value of each alternative, so that a decision can be made based on hard financial data as well as other considerations that may prevail, such as stakeholder concerns over publicity, the risks associated with each option, and the timescale within which each option can be executed. The options to be considered might include:

- immediate disposal
- 'quick fix' turnaround and disposal
- turnaround leading to long-term sustainable performance

- workout leading to liquidation, solvent or insolvent
- solvent liquidation (members' voluntary liquidation – not usually a viable option if the business has severe financial problems, as it is likely to have net liabilities)
- insolvent liquidation (administration, receivership, creditors' voluntary liquidation).

It is useful to consider a range of possible financial outcomes for each option, based on clearly documented assumptions regarding asset valuations, the timing of realizations, the cost of meeting actual or contingent liabilities, etc.

Stakeholder Assessment

The attitude of stakeholders is critical in determining whether a turn-around is feasible or an alternative course of action should be pursued. Therefore, it is vital to meet each stakeholder group as soon as possible. The aim of the initial meetings should be to assess:

Understanding: The stakeholder's level of understanding of the business and of the severity of the crisis. Frequently, there is a 'reality gap' (see Chapter 3) that means the stakeholders are unaware of the extent of the firm's operational or financial difficulties, or they are still in a state of denial. This is frequently true of stakeholder groups who are remote from the day-to-day operations of the business and whose perceptions are based on out-of-date or misleading financial information. Denial is normally associated with management but it often applies to stakeholders as well, and all concerned need to acknowledge the reality of the situation in order to give the turnaround process a chance. It is important to remember that the position of the people representing the stakeholders in their own organizations will have a big affect on their understanding and response. Different levels of management and different organizational units may have very different attitudes to the investment risk.

Confidence: The stakeholder's level of confidence in the business and the extent to which this is founded on an accurate and up-to-date understanding of its situation.

Objectives: The agenda or objectives of each stakeholder group. These can vary considerably: for example, a bank may be concerned primarily with reducing or eliminating its exposure in order to 'clean up' its lending portfolio, or may be keen to support the business because of its relationship with associated businesses or concern over adverse publicity if the business were to fail. Its attitude will also be strongly influenced by the level of any security held, the perceived value of that security, and any provisions which currently exist in its books against the outstanding debt. With the growth of the secondary debt market, it is important to appreciate that lenders may have acquired their interests at different price levels. Similarly, an equity investor's objectives will reflect the value at which the investment is carried in their portfolio, their ability to invest further monies (particularly true of private equity providers whose funds may cap the level of investment permitted in one company), and the relative importance of this investment in the portfolio as a whole. Employee groups or union stakeholders are likely to be concerned primarily with the preservation of jobs, whilst management stakeholders may be concerned with preserving their individual jobs and maintaining their status or powerbase.

Power: The relative power of each stakeholder group. If the business's short-term survival depends heavily on the support of a particular stakeholder group – to maintain current lending facilities or to pass on a dividend payment, for example – then it is vital that this stakeholder is brought 'on side' and involved in the assessment process from the outset.

Preliminary Management Assessment

One of the main causes of corporate distress is the incumbent top management team. The resolution to this problem varies from case to case, but no turnaround can be successful unless the management team has the capabilities, motivation and initiative to bring about positive change. It is critical to get the right management team in place early on in the turnaround; it is not a question of good or bad management but of the *appropriate* management, with the right skill sets and approach, to achieve the desired turnaround. The team which has successfully managed a start-up or a fast-growing business may no longer be appropriate in a crisis. The options to consider in these circumstances include:

- bringing in a new management team
- refocusing the existing management and possibly providing new leadership through a change of chairman or CEO
- retaining existing management but with extensive support from external advisors or consultants.

Hiring a new management team can have symbolic importance as concrete evidence of change to the company's stakeholders, particularly if the existing team are (or are perceived to be) a major cause of the company's problems. Replacing the existing team, however, should not be considered to be automatic for they, with some guidance and external support, may be capable of delivering the turnaround. It is worthwhile attempting to harness the knowledge of the existing team and galvanize them into making changes before considering any replacements. Continuity in management retains their knowledge of the business and this can be a great advantage when speed of change is all-important. However, if current management is unwilling or unable to embrace and implement change, then it is imperative to bring in new management. Before these decisions can be made, however, there first needs to be an assessment of the senior management team as individuals, their effectiveness as a team, and the effectiveness of the current organization structure.

Evaluating management is an integral part of a turnaround situation and is often demanded by outside stakeholders, such as shareholders and banks, before they will agree to any further financial support. The objectives of this section are to provide a framework to assess and comment on the ability of the existing management to support the continued viability of the business and to determine whether the organizational structure will support its long-term objectives. The diagnostic review covers an assessment of:

- the capability of the existing team to effect change
- the effectiveness of the board as a team
- the effectiveness of the organization structure
- the effectiveness of individual board members – their commerciality, personal qualities and functional competence (especially in finance, marketing and production).

A complete assessment of the management and organization will not be completed at the diagnostic review stage, but it is vital to carry out a preliminary assessment that considers:

- who is part of the problem
- who is part of the solution
- who, if anyone, needs to leave immediately due to their obstructive attitude or resistance to change
- who holds real power or influence within the organization (which may not be consistent with the official hierarchy or organization chart); these individuals must become champions of change.

The Capability of the Existing Top Management Team to Effect Change

In assessing the management, it is necessary to determine whether or not the current team or its members have the capability to implement the required strategies. Poor financial performance is usually caused by poor management. Poor management may exacerbate problems that arise from external factors. Management's performance is largely based upon their ability to manage the risks resulting from external factors. In developing an opinion on the management it is more important to look for certain characteristics, particularly those pertaining more to the style and approach required in a turnaround situation, than specific business or industry experience. Questions to consider include:

- is there autocratic leadership, a policy of 'divide and rule', or an environment of secrecy? (implementing change or achieving budget is often difficult in a troubled company with these characteristics)
- does the management team have the ability to operate the company effectively? (no turnaround is feasible without a management team that is willing and capable of changing)
- is there a common objective?
- how is the CEO perceived by the rest of the board?
- what are the board politics like – who supports whom?
- how successful have they been at implementing change programmes in the past?
- does the structure reflect the needs of the business?
- does the team appear to be competent and well balanced?
- how long has it operated as a team?
- how many of the team have experienced a turnaround before?
- do they have the ability to work effectively in a turnaround, i.e., can they meet the challenges they are likely to face in the immediate future?
- do they have flair and vision?
- do they have the capability to implement the required strategies?
- do they have the ability to manage the risks resulting from the external factors?
- is there an atmosphere of trust and communication within the management team?
- are there any perceived conflicts in the management team?
- is there any evidence of disruptive competition between corporate functions, or lack of cooperation?
- is information shared (both good and bad) to enable managers to assess the impact on their own department?
- do they have the capabilities, integrity, skills and desire to undertake and successfully implement a turnaround?
- what is the role of non-executive directors?

Assessing the Organization Structure

The organization structure and communication channels can have a significant effect on the corporate culture. Typical structures include:

- pyramid – traditional hierarchy and reporting structure
- matrix – multiple reporting lines
- flat – very few middle-management layers

There is no 'right' organization structure, but it is important to understand whether the structure supports or hinders the company's strategy. The points to consider in this assessment include:

- what are the formal and informal structures?
- does the structure reflect the needs of the business?
- are there weaknesses in the structure that could have an impact on the desired results?
- how often does the structure change? when did it last change and why?
- does the structure encourage open, two-way communication?
- is decision-making carried out by people with access to the right level and quality of information?
- how many of the management team report directly to the CEO? is that too many?

Effectiveness of Individual Directors or Senior Managers

A useful technique is to draw up a questionnaire using open-ended questions. Each individual on the management team should then be asked the same core questions, plus additional ones relating to the particular function s/he performs.

The questions to ask the management team will depend on the nature of the crisis that the company faces and the culture of the company. The questions should be aimed at assessing 'commerciality', personal qualities and objectives, and the functional competencies of each senior manager.

Commerciality

The manager:

- recognizes the problems at the company and their seriousness
- is able to explain why the company has not been able to deal with its problems to date
- has demonstrated sound decision-making in the past
- is an innovator not a follower
- possesses a personal plan to improve the company's performance
- demonstrates understanding of the company's strengths and weaknesses
- understands what business the company is in and has a good comprehension of:
  - the industries in which they compete
  - the industries' size and growth
  - the competition
  - how their products are viewed by customers
  - the company's position in the market
  - the company's strengths and weaknesses
  - opportunities and threats faced by the company.

Personal Qualities

Generally speaking, an astute observer with limited access to the senior management team can draw some very quick conclusions about an individual's ability to effect turnaround by focusing on some personal characteristics. Inherent traits such as integrity, judgement, decisiveness, motivation, leadership and commitment to change are often key in determining whether the management in place is able to rectify past mistakes and move the company forward. In addition one might consider:

- desire to be part of the team to solve the problems
- creativity and enthusiasm
- ability to balance conflicts of interest between corporate and personal goals

- commitment to getting the job done
- ability to implement change and willingness to do so
- tendency not to blame others for the failures of the organization
- possession of the skills, energy, expertise and commitment to implement the tactics for recovery
- positive and cooperative attitude.

Functional Competence

Assessing the functional competence of management in each of the core process and support functions requires looking at management outputs (plans, systems, achievements, etc.) as well as holding in-depth discussions. Input from specialists is often necessary to provide an accurate assessment of functional competence.

Output

The output of the diagnostic review should include:

An accurate analysis of the business's current financial position.

An assessment of short-term funding needs, including a cash-flow forecast that covers at least the next three months.

A funding plan that meets any shortfalls in funding identified by the short-term cash flow.

A high-level assessment of the key strategic and operational issues facing the business.

A conclusion as to the viability of the business – is it a no-hoper, a short-term survivor, or is it capable of sustainable recovery? This should include an initial assessment as to which strategies are required to achieve a turnaround, whether it is feasible to implement them, and the likely timescale for implementation. It is important to strike a balance between hopeless optimism and undue pessimism in reaching a conclusion. Bear in mind that the calibre of the business is more important than the state of the industry in which it operates – do not underestimate the potential of a fundamentally good business in a poorly performing sector or overestimate the chances of recovery for a lousy business in a highly regarded industry.[3]

An options assessment that compares the different courses of action available and the financial and non-financial implications of each alternative. This should consider both the cost/benefit (and net present value) of each alternative, the risks inherent in pursuing each option, and the likely timescales implied.

A recommendation as to which course of action should be pursued.

Stakeholder agreement as to the selected course of action and provisional support for the recommendation or plan. This will be easier to achieve if regular communications have been maintained with the stakeholders throughout the analysis phase, and the objectives, concerns or agendas of the key stakeholders have been considered in reaching the recommendation.

An assessment of the management team and a proposed management and organization structure that is appropriate and able to execute the recommended course of action. If this includes the removal of senior management from key positions, the recommendations must include a plan to plug the gaps using resources already identified – interim managers or consultants, as appropriate.

The value of the diagnostic review is in its conclusion, and whereas it is beneficial if this can be supported by logical analysis, the reviewer should not let this analysis lead him/her to a conclusion that is at variance with instinct or gut feeling. The review needs to be conducted by experienced practitioners, and the conclusion will often be difficult to support by clear analysis alone.

Outside consultants who are not experienced turnaround managers often over-analyse the situation, whereas an experienced practitioner will form a view fairly swiftly. Clearly, the less analysis there is, the more important the track record of the reviewer, and this trade-off needs to be clearly understood by the stakeholders, whose support will be critical to the process.

Notes

1. Standard books on strategic marketing and competitive strategy give a more detailed explanation of these concepts. See, for example, G. Day, *Market Driven Strategy* (Free Press, New York, 1990).

2. M. Porter, *Competitive Strategy* (Free Press, New York, 1980).

3. C. Baden Fuller and J. M. Stopford, *Rejuvenating the Mature Business* (Routledge, London, 1992).

6 Crisis Stabilization

This is day one of the turnaround, and should begin just as soon as the key stakeholders decide to follow the turnaround route as opposed to insolvency or immediate sale 'as is'. Ideally a turnaround manager will be in place on day one, but it is not unusual for an accounting firm or turnaround specialists to be brought in as interim management to begin crisis stabilization.

The key components of crisis stabilization are:

- short-term cash management
- new management and financial controls
- first-stage cost reductions
- compliance with legal and regulatory matters.

In this chapter we aim to provide practical guidance on how to take initial control of a business in crisis and to explain the techniques that can be used to generate cash for the business quickly.

The Guiding Principles of Crisis Stabilization

To achieve stabilization requires focused, strong leadership coupled with resilience and resourcefulness. Our experience is that one should not be too prescriptive about the steps to be taken but instead keep an open mind with a clear focus on the goal. There are, however, certain overriding principles which are recurring themes in the decisions and actions needed during the crisis stabilization phase:

Cash is king: Many businesses take cash for granted and yet once crisis strikes, cash becomes the priority. This requires a different mindset, and management need to accept that the preservation and generation of cash often need to take precedence over the delivery of profit in the short term. There will be plenty of time to focus on profit as long as the crisis is successfully averted. There are few businesses in our experience where there is a historic accountability for cash delivery. This mindset exists not only in stand-alone businesses but, more importantly perhaps, in subsidiaries of major companies where the parent has acted as a banker. The management of the subsidiary knows that at the end of the day the parent company will provide the funding.

Predictability: As we mentioned earlier, a key feature of crises is that they come as a surprise, and consequently they shake external stakeholders' confidence in the ability of management within the company. It is vital that stakeholder confidence is rebuilt, and that can be done through the crisis stabilization phase by ensuring that all promises made are adhered to, even where this involves making full disclosure of difficulties which previous management would have withheld (in the expectation of being able to resolve the matter and report on the solution). Even at times of crisis it is common for management to produce optimistic forecasts, because they fear negative reaction to a cautious forecast. However, what is needed now is stability and nothing helps stability more than a period of management delivering what they promise. Clearly, viability and performance improvements need to be addressed, but too often we see management confuse the need for viability and the need for predictability.

Accountability: Effective crisis stabilization needs to be very closely managed. Actions need to be prioritized and individuals within the organization made responsible for delivery. This can often involve the turnaround manager in wide reallocation of responsibilities within the company to ensure that there is accountability for the lifeblood of the organization – its cash.

Communications: Effective crisis stabilization requires constant communication and reassurance. Internally, all those who are affected by, or can influence, the management of cash need to understand the new priorities – what is expected of them and what new procedures are being adopted. The external stakeholders, whose continued support is vital during this stage, need to see that their interests are being preserved.

Autocratic leadership: The change process required to implement effective cash management and new controls has to be somewhat autocratic. The turnaround manager has to *take* control, which involves imposing discipline and demanding that staff go along with the new systems and controls. There is no time for the softer approach of education and persuasion in a severe crisis situation.

Short-term Cash Management

The turnaround manager's first task is usually to generate enough cash to survive the short term. In some situations this may mean generating cash to pay wages which are due at the end of the week (or in some cases, overdue), whereas in other cases it means managing the working capital to ensure the firm's principal creditors (usually the banks) do not start formal insolvency proceedings.

In a severe crisis, cash management usually takes precedence over everything else, since without cash the company cannot survive long enough to effect a turnaround. However, in almost all turnaround situations there is considerable scope for releasing cash by more effective working-capital management – with no adverse effect on the trading operations. Introducing cash management is often a culture shock for existing managers since the procedure usually involves difficult decisions and significant change. They will usually complain that any change will adversely affect the ability of the business to achieve sales. This is rarely true, unless the implementation is overenthusiastic. Just introducing the short-term cash forecasting process described in this chapter can usually improve cash flow without any new cash-generating initiatives being introduced.

There are four tasks the turnaround manager needs to undertake:

- assess the immediate cash requirements of the business
- develop an action plan of cash-generating initiatives
- establish and implement emergency cash-management controls
- introduce cash rationing.

Assess Immediate Cash Requirements

Assessing the immediate cash needs of the company requires the preparation of detailed short-term cash forecasts. These should be prepared for a minimum of six weeks, and we generally like to see them for twelve weeks, with the first four weeks being done on a daily basis and the next eight on a weekly basis. A system should be introduced whereby key forecasts are revised each month so as to give a rolling twelve-week forecast, with the first four weeks on a daily or half-weekly basis. The forecasts need to be driven from an opening balance sheet that has been critically reviewed as part of the process of establishing the real financial position of the company. For the purpose of cash management, the critical items are the working capital items in the balance sheet. The turnaround manager can usually expect to meet resistance from management who are not used to managing cash in such a controlled way, but there are in fact few businesses that cannot product cash flows on this basis.

The cash flows should be prepared on a strict receipts-and-payments basis because these documents will form the heart of the control mechanisms. This is very detailed work and a turnaround manager may find it useful to enlist the assistance of the company's existing auditors or other experienced consultants to help produce this information. Where the company is funded under a multi-bank arrangement, it is essential that the short-term cash forecast clearly identifies the funding through each of the banks so that a sensible position as to the headroom or shortfall against existing facilities can be identified. Normally there is a positive lead time between cashbook figures and bank-statement figures, and we recommend that companies produce such short-term forecasts on a cashbook basis. Cash flows should be prepared initially on the basis of normal trading with suppliers. This will enable the turnaround manager to see to what extent cash management initiatives are required to live within existing facilities.

Even though the short-term cash-flow forecast is prepared over a period of three months, it is likely to require some short-term sales forecasting. The sales forecast should be produced on a realistic or prudent basis rather than on the basis of sales targets. In practice, it will be possible to amend any over-optimistic forecasting, since the forecasts are revised monthly; but the practitioner should be aware that the external stakeholders will not expect to see actual cash flows worse than those contained in the initial short-term forecast prepared by the turnaround manager. It is not in the company's interest or that of the stakeholders for the crisis to be understated. There is of course a balance to be struck, because should their position be stated in a worse light than turns out to be the case, external stakeholders may take precipitate action which otherwise could have been avoided.

Develop Cash-generating Initiatives

Having assessed and established the 'as is' position (the base case), the turnaround manager is able to develop potential cash-flow initiatives. This requires the preparation of a formal plan indicating the steps that can be taken to improve the cash requirements initially indicated for the business. In an ideal situation the turnaround manager will wish to keep some initiatives in reserve, but if the cash crisis requires all possible initiatives to be implemented successfully to ensure survival in the short term then there is a heightened risk that without further funding the stabilization will not be successful. Where a good relationship has been struck with the firm's bankers, shared information can lead to the banks supporting the company where initiatives are delayed or ineffective. Naturally the banks will only do this if they are part of the solution and trust the management.

Each cash-flow initiative needs to be identified, and its potential benefits and costs recorded. Clearly some cash initiatives have an adverse profit effect, and that needs to be identified at this stage. Having identified all the possible initiatives which can be applied, recorded them, and subjected them to a thorough reality check, the turnaround manager needs to prioritize the actions. Responsibilities for implementing actions need to be specifically assigned within the team responsible for crisis stabilization. The detailed short-term forecast referred to above needs to be amended to include implementation of the cash-flow initiative. Cash-flow initiatives need to be analysed separately within the cash-flow table, so that the cash effects of normal trading and the effects of the new initiatives are clear to any reader.

Where this exercise results in the existence of a shortfall, it is clear that the turnaround manager needs to enter into very early discussions with the providers of funding to establish whether or not they are in a position to provide additional cash. This is discussed in greater detail later in this chapter.

Implement Emergency Cash-management Controls

Once a sensible and prudent short-term cash-flow forecast has been produced, the turnaround manager needs to ensure that the business is managed in such a way that the actual out-turn is at least equal to, and hopefully better than, the short-term cash-flow forecast. There are three aspects to establishing an effective cash management system:

- implement strong cash controls
- dedicate resources to managing cash
- ensure ongoing reporting and forecasting systems are in place.

The appropriate system for cash control will depend on the size, nature and organization structure of the business, but whatever those features of the business are, the system must provide tight day-to-day control. Whereas small- and medium-sized businesses will generally lend themselves to a completely centralized control system with one focal point, larger multi-site or multinational businesses may need a hierarchy of controls applying some of the techniques which we discuss in the next section, on cash rationing. Where some form of decentralization is necessary for pragmatic implementation reasons, centralized cash control is still crucial. Whereas in an ongoing situation we often find that banks may run several different facilities from several different countries, or several institutions within a banking group, as soon as a crisis arises the banks move to a centralized control system and this must be reflected in the company's own system. There is the need to build a strong central team to keep overall control, regardless of the size of the company. A full schedule of those who are authorized to remit money either telegraphically or through the use of chequebooks needs to be established and reviewed to ensure that they are part of the overall control system. Almost always this review results in a reduction in the number of authorized persons and a tightening of authorization limits.

A complete review of the banking arrangements needs to be undertaken. Typically these will have developed over several years, and need to be simplified as much as possible to minimize the number of accounts which need to be controlled.

Automatic payment runs also need to be reviewed, and authorization systems reconsidered, to ensure that cash control is in accordance with the short-term cash forecast. Because much of the financial management infrastructure of the group will be realigned to meet the top priority of conserving cash, it is important for the turnaround manager to ensure that those with spending authority are involved in the system. Managers should not be allowed to override agreed initiatives, particularly as regards the settlement of liabilities and the collection of monies from customers.

The second key area in establishing effective cash management is to dedicate resources to the task and to manage the task itself. Almost always this involves increasing the number of people who are involved in this area, and it is important to ensure that the calibre of the staff is appropriate for the task in hand. Managing the process involves communicating – to whatever level is considered appropriate – the nature of the procedures which are being implemented for crisis stabilization. An infrastructure of daily and weekly meetings should be instituted for those who are directly concerned with incurring liabilities or collecting cash. The daily meetings should be attended by all those collecting cash and the weekly controls by those who feed into the short-term forecasting process. Not only does this process give sharp focus to the priority of cash management, it also begins to build peer pressure, which is important when changing behaviour in an organization. The meetings enable those who have to make the difficult decisions about cash rationing to prioritize payments from a real understanding of the different demands on limited resources.

Finally, an effective cash-management system needs an ongoing reporting and forecasting system in place, even though the twelve-week rolling forecast is updated on a monthly basis. Internally, the weekly cash report needs to be checked, actual against forecast, for any variances, and responsibilities need to be reviewed. In the early stages of introducing a tight cash-management system, many promises and undertakings are given which are not delivered. This is counter-productive and should be stopped as soon as possible. The company needs to rebuild confidence with its external stakeholders and that cannot happen while promises continue to be broken. Where the ongoing viability of the company relies on external stakeholder support, it is also important that the formatting of the cash flow and its reporting be agreed with the recipient(s) and that there be an easy communication of variances.

Implement Cash Rationing

The fourth key step is cash rationing. This is normally required in a multi-company or multi-site operation. It provides a method of central control where pragmatism has decreed that decentralization is required. Where cash controls and influence are operated at a divisional or subsidiary level, the central controller needs a mechanism to ensure that the division operates in accordance with the short-term cash-flow forecasts that they have signed up to and which have been consolidated into the critical short-term cash-flow forecast which is used by the company in obtaining support from its bankers and on which the process of rebuilding stakeholder confidence is based.

Effective cash rationing operates when the central controller only authorizes payments in accordance with the forecasts, subject to those payment authorizations being reduced by any cash shortfall in cash receipts as forecast. The system usually operates with a weekly time-lag so that any shortfall in receipts in Week 1 will result in rationing of cash by the same amount against Week 2 payments.

In such a situation we find that some divisional controllers are better than others, and consequently the central controller will be well advised to build in a central contingency. S/he should not allow over-collections to go out in additional payments but instead divert them to the centre. This allows the central controller to deal with group-wide surprises and maintain effective control.

Clearly cash management is an *after-the-event* control system, and the turnaround manager will wish to control the management actions which result in the generation or absorption of cash. We discuss this under the heading of management controls later in this chapter.

Strategies for Short-term Cash Generation

The short-term forecasting process we described above often indicates an immediate or short-term funding gap between currently available facilities and the forecast cash requirement. What are the options for bridging this gap? There are five main ones suitable for the crisis stabilization phase, all of which can lead to numerous cash-generating initiatives:

- reduction of debtors
- extension of creditors
- reduction of stocks
- stopping planned expenditure
- short-term financial support.

There are a few other cash-generating strategies available, such as divestment and fixed-asset sales. However, unless negotiations are already well advanced at the time crisis stabilization commences, divestment of part of the business or sale of surplus fixed assets are not generally regarded as strategies for short-term cash generation.

Reduction of Debtors

Tight management of the sales ledger can often generate cash faster than any other cash-generating strategy. We have seen turnaround managers do nothing else during the first few days of a turnaround but focus on where there are overdue accounts.

Our experience is that many troubled businesses fail to deal with difficult and old balances, particularly those where there have been disputes. Unfortunately one of the characteristics of a troubled business is that it has often experienced delivery problems or quality problems with its customers which have resulted in payment being delayed or withheld. Debts outstanding for more than ninety days, or debtors in dispute, can provide a substantial source of short-term cash for a company if proper focus is applied to the problem. Focusing on these accounts will also provide hard evidence of whether provisions in the accounts for bad debts are adequate.

A specific person or team needs to be established to identify an agreed list of old and disputed debts. Responsibility for recovery of the balance needs to be removed from those usually responsible so that they may concentrate on ensuring that all 'good debts' are recovered as soon as possible without being diverted to dealing with dispute resolution. Dispute resolutions often become a ping-pong game between the delivery department and the finance department. The delivery department do not wish to acknowledge the quality or delivery issue and the finance department do not want to have to settle a dispute at less than full recovery due to the unavailability of provisions.

The way to break this impasse is to establish a team who have no responsibility other than to sort out the dispute, set target dates and recover the agreed balances. Not only does this result in cash flowing into the company but it often reduces the mountain of paperwork which builds up around disputed accounts. The turnaround manager should ensure that VAT bad debt relief (often an ignored source of cash) is recovered as disputes are resolved. Once the bad part of the ledger has been identified and actions taken to clear whatever can be achieved, the turnaround manager will wish to ensure that operations in this area do not slip back into the old habits.

Should further cash be needed from the 'good' part of the ledger, this can be achieved by:

- offering early settlement discounts on good debts (but this is expensive money)
- entering into a factoring or an invoice-discounting arrangement with a finance house (also expensive)
- renegotiating trading terms towards a reduced credit period
- prioritizing production and sales to better-paying customers
- persuading customers to pay in advance of order delivery.

Extension of Creditors

The extension of creditor payments can be a major area for cash generation in the short term. This is a particularly sensitive area. Any extending of credit needs to be handled with care because many suppliers operate within credit reference rings. Information quickly builds which can result in suppliers reducing their credit terms because they fear the credit-worthiness of the company.

Best practice dictates that any extension should be done through agreement with the supplier by a proper renegotiation of payment terms. This is time-consuming and it is vitally important that any renegotiated terms are complied with to ensure that confidence is not damaged. The turnaround manager will of course be aware that buying time for the business to survive is often in the supplier's own interest, as they will probably not want one of their customers to fail. Indeed, there are many examples of major companies supporting their smaller customers through extended credit terms.

Suppliers are a key external stakeholder group and are often *the* major external stakeholder. This is particularly true in the distributive trades. In the oil industry, for example, where major oil companies supply partly through distributors, the debts due from the distributors to the major oil companies can be substantially higher than their debts to their banks. The major oil companies require the distributors to survive since they provide the distribution network for the eventual sale of their product. The turnaround manager needs to have a full understanding of the part that credit insurers play – a supplier may not be able to extend terms even where they wish to if the debt is insured. One of the positive sides to extending payment terms is that once the credit dates are extended and new terms agreed, they often remain in place, thereby giving a permanent benefit to the company.

The practical steps that need to be adopted to extend creditors are as follows:

Identify an individual or team who will be responsible for delivering the initiatives outlined in the short-term forecast.

Obtain trading terms for all major suppliers: As a practical step, apply the 80:20 rule rather than merely running alphabetically through the purchase ledger.

Understand the payment routines that are currently in place and, where automatic payment runs are in place, check the payment arrangements against the agreed terms. It is not unusual to find that even companies in crisis are paying their suppliers ahead of the agreed payment date.

Where trading terms are not clear the company can communicate its trading terms to the suppliers and negotiate advantageous trading terms with future suppliers. The whole area of procurement management is one which is discussed in more detail in Chapter 12; quick wins can be achieved here during the crisis stabilization period.

Consider the possibility of moving to consignment stock arrangements with existing suppliers; and finally, consider alternative suppliers if better credit terms can be obtained.

Arrangements with government bodies, particularly the Inland Revenue and Customs and Excise, can often provide scope for conserving cash, and some fairly straightforward VAT-planning steps are normally available to improve the cash flow within a company. As with other external stakeholders, our experience is that government bodies generally wish to be supportive, but naturally require information and continuous communication to enable them to move to a position of stability and predictability. There are many examples where the Inland Revenue in particular has helped businesses by agreeing a rescheduling of existing outstanding liabilities. The turnaround manager should have no hesitation in going through the detailed forecasts with the Inland Revenue or Customs and Excise so that they can see quite clearly what it is that is being asked of them and how they are to be treated in comparison with other suppliers. Poor management of these relationships can lead to fairly rapid default procedures being instituted which can lead to winding-up petitions against the company.

It is notoriously difficult to renegotiate rents with landlords, although some will agree to vary leases to enable payment of rents on a monthly basis rather than quarterly in advance. The turnaround manager needs to be particularly careful in negotiations with landlords, since major assets are often represented by the premiums available in leases. Where rent is withheld this can lead to foreclosure and loss of value.

Reduction of Stocks

Releasing cash through the better management of inventories is a major area of opportunity for the turnaround manager, but during the crisis stabilization period the key area for the turnaround manager to concentrate on is the realization of obsolete and slow-moving stock. A review of the whole supply-chain management process, which we discuss in Chapter 12, shows how cost containment with proper inventory control can improve company performance.

The initial focus should be on identifying and clearing old, obsolete or slow-moving stock lines of both raw materials and finished goods, even though to do so will probably result in a heavy hit to the profit-and-loss account (as a result of the under-provision against realizable value).

The turnaround manager needs to install a system to identify and monitor slow and obsolete lines on an ongoing basis. An individual or a team needs to be given the task of identifying stock for clearance. A normal procedure is to identify and then ring-fence this stock and then move to a stock-realization programme. It may be possible to incorporate or redesign surplus raw materials into current products since this provides greater recovery than the alternative of distressed disposal or scrapping. One can consider returning goods to suppliers for either credit or cash, particularly where commodity products are concerned. The original supplier is more likely to know of an alternative customer for the product. Alternatively, the raw material can be sold through third parties, either through clearance companies or at auction, but our experience is that disposals via this route are unlikely to achieve more than 10 per cent of original cost. Companies should not shy away from scrapping obsolete and slow-moving stock, because at the very least it can free up space and reduce handling and administrative costs within the company.

For finished goods, an individual or team needs to devise a viable plan. One of the difficulties facing companies when dealing with the disposal of slow-moving finished goods is the danger of diluting or damaging the existing product range or brand. It is sometimes better therefore to sell into markets where the business is not already operating. When disposing of stock, particularly when disposing to jobbing agencies, being paid is a prime concern. There is little benefit in converting obsolete stock into an uncollectable debt, but unfortunately that is quite common. Similarly, selling obsolete stock on a sale-or-return basis leaves the acquirer with all the upside and the vendor with all the downside and no improvement in cash management.

Stopping or Reducing Planned Expenditure

The turnaround manager will want to conduct an urgent review of all capital expenditure and discretionary revenue expenditure to establish the possibility of limiting cash outflows. Firstly, all capital expenditure will probably be halted during crisis stabilization pending the preparation of the business plan. The typical business planning process involves a thorough review of all existing and planned projects. Secondly, discretionary expenditure such as advertising campaigns, trade exhibitions and training will usually go on hold – in fact any spending not directly related to the operation of the business. And finally, there may even be opportunities to save cash by negotiating reductions in non-discretionary cost items, such as raw materials and wages costs.

As a general rule, cost-reduction strategies do not generate short-term cash flow – since either the benefits take time to work through the system (as in the case of better purchasing), or they cost money to implement (making staff redundant). However, there are situations where the turnaround manager may be lucky enough to negotiate an immediate price reduction from a major supplier or to persuade staff to take a temporary drop in salary.

Short-term Financial Support

If it is quite clear, after considering all the above cash-generating options inside the company, that the company cannot survive without an injection of outside funds, the turnaround manager has to approach the external stakeholders. The first call is usually to existing banks for an extension of overdraft facilities. This is sometimes referred to as support financing. While the banks are the obvious source of additional short-term financing, equity shareholders might be approached for an emergency rights issue (as was the case with Sketchley in 1991), joint venture parties may provide an equity injection (as happened at Laura Ashley in 1990), or a supplier may provide a loan or equity money. Where additional bank support is required, the turnaround manager should only ask for the minimum necessary. S/he thus balances the cash needs of the business while maintaining the support of major shareholders. In some cases, the turnaround manager must also balance cash needs with profit imperatives, particularly where facilities contain covenants relating to the operating performance of the business. The crisis stabilization stage is not the best time to renegotiate bank facilities because to do so will often result in changes being granted at a very heavy cost to the company. Quite understandably, the external stakeholders are seeking to improve their position, and until the full turnaround plan is developed, the turnaround manager will not be in a position to know what s/he should or can give away in order to secure ongoing support. If the crisis is so deep that support is required at almost any cost, we would caution the turnaround manager to revisit his/her assessment as to whether the business can be returned to viability in the medium term.

The turnaround manager needs to understand what options are available to the external stakeholders so that s/he can assess the likely response to a given request for support. Where a request is made that is likely to make matters worse in the short term for the stakeholder, without any prospect of a materially better subsequent position, it is likely that the request for support will be turned down. Communication with the external stakeholder is critical here since they will often take a decision based on the personal credibility of the turnaround manager. Generally speaking, the turnaround manager can anticipate ongoing support from external stakeholders if s/he can devise a stabilization plan under which the stakeholders' position does not worsen while the recovery plan is being developed. Where their position may worsen, the turnaround manager needs to be prepared to offer security over the assets or some of the assets of the company to mitigate the additional risk being requested. Turnaround managers are often under pressure to give security which would in fact improve the position of one stakeholder at the potential expense of others. Such approaches should be resisted, not only because of the turnaround manager's personal exposure to legal actions, but also because it may restrict his/her subsequent flexibility as the turnaround develops. The turnaround manager needs to get the best s/he can with the little s/he has, and this is rarely achieved by giving everything away to the first stakeholder who demands it.

Further discussion of short-term financing is included in Chapter 14.

New Management and Financial Controls

Whoever is leading the turnaround at the start of the crisis stabilization has to take control of the business. Taking control means putting in place a set of simple but effective management controls on day one. One of the simplest and most commonly used controls – particularly in small- to medium-sized companies – is for the turnaround manager to take the chequebooks away and sign all the cheques him/herself. This will give him/her a real insight into what is happening in the company. In most cases there is little the turnaround manager can do but sign the cheques, since the goods or services being paid for have already been consumed; but the knowledge gained about the business is enormous. As one company director said, 'The mind boggles at what one sees going through.' This is the reason why the turnaround manager needs to install 'upstream' management controls as described below, so that incumbent staff are unable to take actions or make decisions that might make the existing situation even worse.

The basic controls that should be automatically installed on day one are as follows:

Freeze on all hiring of staff: An immediate stop on issuing offers of employment to new staff – and perhaps rescinding offers already made to new staff – is common practice. The turnaround manager will want to assess for him/herself if there is a real need for an additional hiring or a replacement hiring. If the position to be filled is a senior position, the turnaround manager will want to interview the would-be recruit. Imposing a blanket ban on recruitment does not mean to say that essential replacements are impossible – but in each situation a strong case would need to be made and any hiring decisions signed off at a very senior level.

Stop any planned salary increases and promotions: An immediate stop will allow the turnaround manager to assess both the situation and the people. It is clearly far better to delay decisions which would later be regretted and/or have to be reversed.

Ban all capital expenditure: Either a total ban or a ban on all items above a nominal value is necessary pending the development of the turnaround business plan.

Purchasing controls: Any purchase orders above a certain size, or fixed purchase contracts for longer than a few weeks, should need the approval of the turnaround manager. Any price increases from suppliers should automatically be rejected. Purchasing is the largest cost item for many businesses and it is critical that the turnaround manager gets control of this area immediately. Waiting for suppliers' invoices to arrive is too late – the firm has already been contractually committed, often by a low-level employee. If the turnaround manager fails to put in immediate controls over purchasing, s/he will find several months later that the firm is contractually bound to volumes, prices and contractual terms that do not make commercial sense. In some situations, the turnaround manager may find it worthwhile to look at outstanding purchase orders (orders placed but where the goods have not yet been delivered) and either cancel or renegotiate some of the orders. It is not unknown for turnaround managers to refuse deliveries of goods on order (in spite of having a legal contract with the supplier) if they believe the goods are overpriced or likely to be surplus to requirements.

Contract and order controls: The last thing a new turnaround manager wants is for his/her subordinates to accept new orders and contracts after his/her arrival which are going to be unprofitable, place big demands on working capital, constrain future product-market flexibility or increase the firm's contractual risk. Thus any orders or contracts over a certain size and/or duration need to be approved by the turnaround manager. As with purchasing, a quick review of recent contracts or orders may give the turnaround manager an opportunity to reject some recently accepted new business before it is too late.

Pricing controls: Pricing is a crucial decision for any company, since any change in price directly translates to the bottom line. No price changes should be allowed and no discounts should be given (other than those already agreed as part of the standard pricing structure) without the approval of the turnaround manager. Any price increases or decreases planned but not yet implemented should be frozen pending review by the turnaround manager.

Stakeholder communication controls: Crisis stabilization is a delicate stage of the turnaround and so it is imperative that all key parties retain as much confidence in the business as possible. It is not usually possible, or sensible, to ban or centralize communications with customers, suppliers and employees, but all communications with the press and financial stakeholders should be referred to the turnaround manager.

Where implementing these controls involves rescinding contracts with customers or suppliers, or offers of employment to new staff, the new controls may lead to legal claims against the company. However, the new turnaround manager is often in a strong position to negotiate, since few outsiders will want to order goods from a company that might not be able to deliver them, or supply goods to a company that might not be able to pay for them.

Deciding on appropriate controls and announcing them to the organization is the easy part. The experienced turnaround manager knows, however, that the announcement of a set of controls does not mean that management and staff will automatically adhere to them. There are countless examples where clear controls have been imposed, only for managers to continue to operate in the way that they always have. The turnaround manager needs to strike a balance between making staff aware of the consequences – usually dismissal – if they disobey the controls, and creating a situation where day-to-day operations grind to a halt because staff fail to take any decisions at all. Business as usual should be encouraged, so the new management controls should be sensible and focus on critical items. In situations where management and staff blatantly ignore the new controls, a highly visible dismissal in the first few weeks is often enough to send a shock wave through the rest of the organization – a realization that the turnaround manager means business.

Besides installing an appropriate set of management controls, it is essential that the turnaround manager takes immediate steps to install basic financial controls. The diagnostic review will probably not have been in sufficient depth to check the veracity of the accounting systems; and so it is crucial for the turnaround manager to ensure that these are providing an accurate assessment of the company's financial situation. This is a different exercise from installing the cash-management systems described earlier in this chapter. What is required here is a review to:

- check that accounting procedures are accurately capturing accounting data (e.g., all supplier orders are actually being processed)
- ensure that prudent accounting policies are being used (e.g., regarding the timing at which profits are recorded on multi-stage contracts)

- ensure that ledger account definitions are clear and that items are posted to the right account
- ensure that the critical parts of the monthly financial accounts give a true picture of the company's financial situation.

Accurate financial data is a sine qua non for the turnaround manager. In the early stabilization phase, the focus is likely to be on financial reporting, but as the turnaround team starts to prepare the business plan, the focus will need to shift towards improved management accounting systems. Improved budgeting systems are obviously an integral part of a new system of financial controls.

First-stage Cost Reduction

While the primary focus during crisis stabilization is on managing cash and gaining control, some cost reduction may also be undertaken. This will be a top-down process focusing on easy wins, and requires little detailed analysis for the experienced turnaround manager. The target areas for cost reduction at this stage in the turnaround are likely to be obvious overmanning, purchasing and overheads.

Obvious Overmanning

The experienced turnaround manager will be able to tell very quickly if the company is overstaffed. Where volume, or in the case of a service business, revenues, have declined sharply it may be clear that there are just too many people employed and the company needs to downsize (or right-size). Sometimes the same situation occurs where a firm has built up staff numbers in anticipation of growth that fails to materialize. In some businesses there are rules of thumb about turnover per employee which can give a guide as to how much overmanning might exist – although the turnaround manager should not attempt to downsize to anything like best-practice levels of efficiency in the early stages of the turnaround.

All that can realistically be achieved at this stage is to take excess capacity out of the system and remove those clearly not adding value. What cannot be, and should not be, attempted during crisis stabilization is to change existing business processes and working methods. The turnaround manager and his/her team will not have the time, or possibly the knowledge, to do anything other than remove the *obvious* overmanning.

Recently one of us was involved in a cost-reduction exercise of this nature with an engineering maintenance company: a simple analysis showed that the direct labour was only working 55 per cent of the time they were at work! Reducing the workforce by 25 per cent immediately had no detrimental impact on operational performance. In another situation, in a technical consultancy business, revenues had dropped by about 25 per cent over two years, and industry rules of thumb indicated a total workforce of about 230 was appropriate, instead of 388. A decision was taken to reduce numbers by 100 immediately, and not by 150, because new management felt, quite reasonably, that existing staff would not be able to 'ramp up' their productivity overnight and that delivery promises and quality could suffer.

The problem in downsizing during the crisis stabilization period is often the cash cost of implementing this strategy. We have seen many firms in the past that have continued to be overstaffed (and make losses) but have been unable in the short term to fund the necessary redundancy payments. In this situation, cash has to be generated by asset reduction strategies and/or new funding before redundancy is possible.

Of course, the turnaround manager can always minimize redundancy payments by implementing a last-in, first-out redundancy programme. Some good new recruits could be lost by this process but it might help the company survive, which is often the only objective that matters at this stage.

Purchasing

Purchasing is often a neglected area in distressed companies, and yet in manufacturing firms it is usually the single largest item in the firm's cost structure. There may be some easy wins which can be achieved in this area. The turnaround manager is likely to take a quick look at the larger suppliers and assess if there is any scope for negotiating lower prices and/or changing suppliers. A new turnaround manager is often in a stronger position to negotiate with key suppliers than s/he may think. We have been involved with a number of turnaround situations where a 15 per cent reduction in purchase costs has been achieved on key components and raw materials.

In looking for easy wins in the purchasing area, the turnaround manager should not forget that sub-contractors and temporary staff are also 'purchased' items and may offer immediate cost-reduction opportunities.

Overhead Costs

Overheads that are clearly unnecessary or obviously do not add any value to the business are always prime targets, especially those that can be eliminated without any cash costs. Travel, conferences, trade exhibitions, subscriptions, mobile phones, consultants, entertaining, external training and advertising are all examples of costs that can be cut quickly with little or no short-term penalty. Where there is a cash cost, as would be the case with redundancies or exiting a lease arrangement early, the turnaround manager usually waits until the business plan has been developed.

Legal and Regulatory Compliance

Once a company enters a crisis and becomes a possible candidate for turnaround treatment, the directors face a new regulatory framework – one which has been designed to protect those who deal with companies that are unable to meet their liabilities. In the UK, this is set out in the Insolvency Act 1986. The main provisions relate to the offence of wrongful trading.

Directors entering this arena are well advised to seek advice from lawyers and others experienced in dealing with the legal and commercial realities of the new environment. Many company directors, and some turnaround managers, find themselves in unfamiliar waters and take on personal risk way beyond what they intended to at the time of becoming involved in the company.

The allegation of wrongful trading arises where

a) the company concerned has gone into insolvent liquidation;

b) at some time before the commencement of the winding up of the company, that person knew or ought to have concluded that there was no reasonable prospect that the company would avoid going into liquidation; and

c) that person was a director of the company at that time.

Although the court will not make a declaration of wrongful trading if it is satisfied that as soon as the condition specified in (b) arose, the relevant person took all possible steps to minimize creditors' losses, the court can order the relevant person to make a contribution to the company's assets as it thinks appropriate. Furthermore, a person who has been declared liable to make a contribution for wrongful trading may also, if the court thinks fit, have a director's disqualification order made against him/her. For the purposes of wrongful trading, a company goes into insolvent liquidation if it goes into liquidation at a time when its assets are insufficient for the payment of all its liabilities and the expenses of winding-up. The test of insolvency to be applied is based on a balance sheet, rather than a liquidity basis.

Directors should be aware that they are reviewed individually, not as a board, and the expectations of behaviour may well vary within a board on an individual basis. Furthermore, the Act does not recognize non-executive directors as having any different status or duty to executive directors.

The turnaround manager should implement the cash management system described earlier, mindful of his/her obligations to creditors. This is not usually a problem for a turnaround manager, but s/he needs to keep careful records documenting any agreements with creditors and the reasons why trading should continue as a better alternative to insolvency.

It would be foolhardy for us to do anything in this section other than alert directors, turnaround managers and those very closely involved with the company who could be regarded as 'shadow directors' to be aware of wrongful trading. It is a grey area and is rarely a problem for a new turnaround manager clearly seen to be acting competently and in good faith. Legal advice should always be sought if in doubt.

We have focused this section on wrongful trading because it is often raised as a concern by those involved in turnaround management, but the crisis stabilization stage ought to take a wider look at legal and regulatory compliance. The turnaround manager ought to find out quickly:

- if the company is in breach of any legal agreements (it may well be in breach of banking covenants)
- if the company really owns the assets on its balance sheet
- what legal liabilities might exist that are not apparent
- if the company is in breach or likely to be in breach of any regulatory authority's requirements.

The impact of these types of problem on crisis stabilization could be much more severe than wrongful trading – although we would not expect those leading a turnaround to incur unnecessary personal liability.

7 Leadership

Within the seven essential ingredients (see Chapter 4), the one which often receives greatest attention is the subject of leadership. Who should lead the turnaround is often the first question asked. Everyone has an opinion and yet there is no simple answer. We know, however, that if the company or its external stakeholders get this wrong it can have a major effect on the outcome. This often leads both external and internal stakeholders to the tantalizing view that all you need to do is get the right man or woman for the job and the rest will fall in place – stakeholder value will be restored and job security ensured. What a seductive argument this is, and one often supported by examples of how when so-and-so was appointed everything was OK, as if some magic potion had been applied. One rarely hears of the cases when so-and-so was appointed and nothing changed, or when so-and-so was appointed and after the early honeymoon days when everyone was sure the right actions had been taken, the situation reverted to crisis.

What is so engaging about the question of leadership is that it is quite clear that success or failure in a company's fortunes is normally attached to one person. We find it easier to understand, and can short-circuit all that has to go on to redirect and radically transform a business, by looking for an individual who can take the plaudits for success. Similarly when a business fails or becomes a turnaround candidate, life is so much easier when there is a villain about – someone to blame.

It is against this background that stakeholders clamour for change. We hear that 'the people who got the company in trouble are not the right people to get it out of trouble'. We hear that bad management caused the problem, and indeed most of the academic studies have shown

that successful turnarounds have featured a change of management –
but so have many unsuccessful turnarounds. It is curious that the
management who are blamed today for corporate malaise are often the
same team who were being lauded yesterday as 'a team to back'. The
whole question of leadership in a turnaround situation is a very complex
area and there is no easy formula to be applied.

Each turnaround situation is different, and we argue that the analysis
of the causes of failure and an understanding of the requirements to
fulfil the strategic intent will help design an appropriate management
to lead the company through this process. We discussed the causes and
symptoms in Chapter 2, and how to undertake the relevant diagnosis
in Chapter 5. However, that is history. It aids our understanding about
what might be viable in the future, but in the end recovery is not based
on the past but on the successful implementation of a relevant and
viable strategy. The key drivers of that process are, without doubt, the
management team and their leader. We cannot therefore duck the issue
of turnaround leadership, but we need to understand the type of
management appropriate in a turnaround situation. Once we are clear
on that we can assess the current leadership and management team; and
form a considered view as to whether they are appropriate, and more
or less likely to achieve the turnaround than a new team.

In this chapter we explore the nature of successful leadership in
turnaround situations. This, we hope, will help existing management
evaluate themselves and form a view as to whether they consider their
own capabilities and attitudes are appropriate, and where any gaps may
exist. Our aim is also to give external stakeholders a perspective against
which to judge the existing team and any future candidates. As we
indicated earlier in the book, there is little prospect of a turnaround
being successful unless the leader meets not only the requirements of
the company but also those of the stakeholder groups.

It is tempting for external stakeholders to demand change early on
in the turnaround process. Indeed, change is often demanded as soon
as the reality gap (discussed in Chapter 2) is acknowledged, and as a price
for support during crisis stabilization. This is sometimes appropriate,
but eagerness for action can result in short-term comfort and long-
term pain if the wrong person is appointed. However, if the external

stakeholders wait until after the business plan is prepared and then press for change, a new team or leader may well want to review the position and plans, leading to delay and an even worse financial situation.

The frequency with which management is changed in turnaround situations is one of the reasons why times are very tense in the immediate aftermath of recognizing the problem. It helps us understand why incumbent management often prefer to struggle on, keeping the crisis private and confidential, with the objective of returning the business to stability without anyone knowing it has gone through a crisis. It also explains why incumbent management will allow, indeed encourage, the development of the reality gap. They would argue that it gives them time to deal with the issues, after which they can return to the more prudent policies previously adopted. Management fears that they will not get a fair hearing if they share the realities with external stakeholders, whose position is often known, and rarely supportive – hardly an incentive for full disclosure. Yet we know that if there is not full disclosure, the prospect of obtaining their continuing support is greatly reduced. We discuss the question of managing stakeholders in the next chapter.

Appointing the Turnaround Manager

Choosing the right individual to lead the turnaround is of course the responsibility of the board of directors; although when a company is in a crisis, the banks, or sometimes the institutional shareholders, will put pressure on the board to make management changes. When the crisis is severe and insolvency is being considered as an option by the banks, they may impose a turnaround leader of their choice on the company as a prerequisite for their continued support.

In large public companies the initial catalyst for change may be a new non-executive director or chairman, who then recruits a new chief executive, usually from outside the organization but sometimes from within. This is what happened at NFC, the logistics and distribution group where Sir Christopher Bland was brought in as chairman, and then recruited Gerry Murphy as chief executive. Brian McGowan has also done this at House of Fraser, and Stuart Wallis at Scholl. Unfortunately the time taken to appoint a new chief executive often delays the start of the turnaround process by many months.

In severely distressed situations, the banks will often turn to a company doctor with a proven track record. While there are many experienced executives calling themselves company doctors, the reality is that there are very few who have the complete set of skills to provide all seven key components of a successful turnaround. Some have turned around subsidiaries of larger companies but lack the experience and credibility to undertake crisis stabilization, stakeholder management and financial restructuring. Others who are recognized as company doctors are in fact 'financial engineers' who are good at stabilization and restructuring but do not actually fix the business. They are more workout specialists than turnaround managers.

The turnaround manager is usually appointed as chief executive, but may not start out in this position. Most experienced turnaround managers, such as Howard Dyer (currently chairman of Ascot Holdings and Hamleys), tend to work as consultants while undertaking the diagnostic review (explained in Chapter 5), and then join the board when they have assessed the situation – usually within two to four weeks.

In owner-managed businesses, banks may introduce a turnaround manager to work alongside the owner, and insist that no cheques will be honoured unless approved by the turnaround manager. This is an unenviable situation for the turnaround manager, since it often leads to major conflict. We have even seen situations where the turnaround manager and indeed his family have been threatened with violence since the owner sees the turnaround manager as a threat to his livelihood and self-esteem. The ultimate threat is, of course, insolvency unless the owner will cooperate.

Qualities Required in the Turnaround Manager

It is unusual to find all the required qualities in one person, since the ideal turnaround manager will be both a strong leader and a good manager. The perfect person and/or team would have:

- considerable leadership skills
- flexibility, the ability to listen and modify views
- the ability and courage to make rapid decisions based on a minimum of data and analysis; be analytical and able to prioritize quickly
- the ability to balance short-term vision (doing the same things better) and longer-term vision (doing better things)
- the courage to take unpopular decisions
- high integrity
- confidence in his/her own abilities
- experience at driving through change in difficult times
- entrepreneurial instincts – uncomfortable with the status quo.

And be:

- a tight controller (particularly in the crisis stabilization stage)
- a facilitator able to release the creative potential of employees
- a good negotiator
- able to work long hours under stress
- a tough, no-nonsense manager who knows very clearly what s/he wants to do and will not allow anybody or anything to get in his/her way
- a bit of a loner but also a team player
- self-reliant and independent of mind and spirit.

Our list probably describes the excellent general manager, and here lies one of the problems, because turnaround leadership in its widest sense is everyday excellent management. However, turnaround managers have to take many more tough decisions under extreme time pressure than the typical general manager. S/he must be very action-oriented, and not surprisingly many company doctors are characterized by the archetypal bulldog spirit. In other words they are:

- focused – they can quickly identify the important issues
- hard-nosed and able to overcome the politics of the organization
- able to evaluate management and operations
- clear thinkers with common sense
- able to inspire confidence and reassure people
- able to instil standards and discipline throughout the organization.

Inner toughness and ruthlessness is only part of the picture, however, and the turnaround manager will need many other skills in his/her armoury. S/he must react flexibly to changing circumstances, often daily, and cut through the politicking within the company, showing effective leadership by motivating employees into implementing the appropriate turnaround strategies. S/he must be visible, hands-on and an excellent communicator, focusing the organization on those strategic priorities that are fundamental to the group's survival. Finally, the turnaround manager must be a juggler, keeping as many balls as possible in the air at the same time. Previous experience is a vital qualification for these situations.

A successful turnaround manager is likely to be one who leads by example. Many companies going through a turnaround need to adopt a new culture, something which is evident once one has examined the existing behaviour and values inside the company. It takes time to change the values of an organization, and to do it one must first change its behaviour.[1] The starting point for behavioural change is the turnaround manager him/herself.

The archetypal turnaround manager is often a crisis manager, the person who has the qualities to deal with short-term critical control issues. These are, of course, vital because as we have argued earlier the most important thing in a turnaround is to survive – without that you will not have the ability to reposition and relaunch the business. The appointment, as a turnaround manager, of someone who has all the short-term skills often results in crisis stabilization, but not much else. A different person is then needed to lead the renewal stage, but this requires yet another management change. An alternative approach is

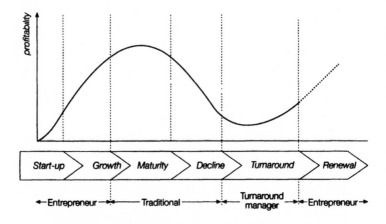

Figure 7.1: **Appropriate Management: The right people at the right time**

to build a turnaround team which has the blend of skills required for different stages of the turnaround process.

Appropriate Management

Most businesses that find themselves in a turnaround have gone through some sort of life cycle. The business goes from start-up to growth and then into maturity and decline, although decline can set in at any stage after start-up. Turnaround is then necessary, followed at a later stage by renewal. The situation is illustrated simplistically in Figure 7.1. We would argue that there are three broad types of management associated with these six stages of growth (see Figure 7.2). An enterprise will have the best prospect of success where there is a clear alignment between the type of management and the stage through which the enterprise is passing.

Many large companies operate in a number of different product-market areas, which will be at different stages of the corporate life

Figure 7.2: **Characteristics of Management Types**

Entrepreneurial Manager	Traditional Manager	Turnaround Manager
Innovator 'Scatter-gun' strategy Associate thinker Focus: new product Hires others to implement Does not recognize need for change	Shareholder value Linear thinker Focus: market share/ growth Hires similar personalities Resists change	Aim – survival and recovery Downside planner Defensive strategist Tireless seeker of cash Strong leader and communicator Drives change

cycle. The resulting diversification often enables the corporate entity to continue without experiencing crisis. A turnaround crisis arises where the declining profits of a business affect the financial viability of the whole enterprise. Part of the diagnostic phase of a turnaround is concerned with identifying the position of each of the different business units in the cycle and then assessing whether each is led by an appropriate team.

Assessing the Appropriateness of the Top Team

In all but the smallest of turnaround situations the turnaround manager needs to be supported by a turnaround team. Assessing the existing top team is therefore a priority task, and one in which the chairman is usually involved. We have spoken before about the importance of management retaining the initiative with regard to stakeholders, but unless incumbent management are honest and realistic in their self-assessment, they will quickly be found wanting when decline sets in. Then it becomes external stakeholders who assess the appropriateness of individuals and the team and, as we have shown earlier, the prejudices in the system are such that it is unlikely that the team will get a fair hearing. It may be, of course, that the team does not deserve a fair hearing because they have over-indulged themselves in the past and are incapable of realizing the true nature of the situation they are now in.

In assessing the management, it is necessary to determine whether or not the current team members have the capabilities and the right attitudes to implement the turnaround. The team should have those characteristics of the perfect turnaround manager listed above, as well as the technical competence necessary to do their jobs.

Questions that might be taken into account when considering the team's appropriateness to deal with the challenges ahead include:

- does the team and all its members recognize the difficulties that lie ahead?
- is there a congruency of purpose within the team to do what is necessary to deliver the turnaround?
- is there a leader within the team who is prepared to readjust priorities to concentrate resources on delivering a turnaround?
- how has this team weathered previous storms?
- are there any gaps in the team where outside help, either temporary or permanent, may enable the team as a whole to deliver?
- will this team, and particularly its leader, balance short-term imperatives with medium- and long-term aspirations?
- is there an atmosphere of frank and mutual support, or is there a danger of division and factional infighting?
- is the information flow accurate, relevant and timely? does the team know what they want and does the organization provide it?
- who within the team is part of the problem?

This is a time for critical self-evaluation and it is far better if the company achieves management changes voluntarily rather than having them imposed from outside. However, it is inevitable that the team and its members will go through a very challenging period during which their credibility will be questioned by external stake-holders. Any infighting during this period is likely to be very counter-productive.

Turnaround is about dynamic change in critical circumstances: it is vital that the appropriateness of the team is continuously assessed, but not to the extent that it provokes unnecessary insecurity among those who are committed to doing what it takes to deliver the turnaround.

The chairman, who may have been appointed to effect the leadership change, often plays a key role in this process.

One risk of removing incumbent management and replacing them with turnaround specialists is that there will be a massive loss of knowledge and experience. Therefore, at least in the short term, where change has been accepted there needs to be a significant knowledge transfer to the new team. Also, key industry contacts may be a prerequisite for rebuilding value, and hence must not be forsaken. As a result, it may be more appropriate to retain some of the better senior management and to harness their valuable knowledge base. They may even respond favourably to the change of leadership or increased responsibility.

Change of Management

The pressures for substantial changes in the top management team at the beginning of a turnaround are often immense, and existing teams would benefit by understanding why this is because that will enable them to understand the challenge of remaining in place and delivering a successful outcome.

In a recent survey of UK turnarounds, 100 per cent of the companies examined made some change in the senior management team. Why is a change in management considered to be so necessary? There are a number of answers to this question:

It is necessary to replace poor and weak incumbent management, and/or those resisting change.

New management skills are necessary to conduct the turnaround. The necessary skills of the turnaround manager are not always available in the business, which means that existing management has to be changed.

It helps to overcome legacy issues created by management's history of mistakes. Legacy issues frequently dictate whether or not existing management has the chance to change the direction of the business without losing face. This will particularly be the case where the decline has been caused by management's refusal to cancel a 'pet' project which is clearly not working. A change in management will immediately overcome such issues, removing the tarnished image and permitting U-turns in the business strategy, free from embarrassment.

It restores confidence and credibility with the company's stakeholders (external and internal). Generally in these circumstances, relationships with the key stakeholders are extremely poor, tarnished by their perception of weak management and poor decision-making. The introduction of new management helps to overcome these problems, gives recognition to the problems of the past, and introduces new management with the expectation that changes will be made.

The injection of new management 'brings mystery, the opportunity for a new style, and during the honeymoon period, bold initiatives can be taken'.[2] Seeing the company from a fresh, objective point of view will increase the likelihood that radical changes will be made and accepted throughout the organization.

New management typically instils a sense of energy and urgency to the situation which can prove infectious, helping to build the momentum for change and overcoming any resistance. The new leader nearly always announces, 'We need to change,' or 'We are going to change'. This is not done to create a crisis but to initiate a sense of urgency and anticipation and to raise the stakes for both leader and subordinates.

A change at the top is a signal to the whole world, both internally and externally, that 'We mean to change, we mean to succeed'.

Leading the Turnaround Process

We outlined in Chapter 4 the various workstreams that need to be managed to effect a successful turnaround. One of these was project managing the turnaround process. This is clearly the responsibility of the turnaround manager, and requires him/her to fit the various parts of the turnaround process together at the right time. This involves deciding when the priorities of the turnaround need to be changed, and managing the transition from crisis stabilization to strategic change and then to growth. It is a gradual process which requires not only judgement from the turnaround leader but also careful management. Different management styles are required at different stages of the process.

The Early Days

In the period up to completion of the business plan, typically lasting three to six months, the turnaround manager will be at his/her most stretched and will be required to juggle many balls simultaneously. In the first few days the turnaround leader will need to:

- implement crisis management measures, principally cash and working capital management, and establish a set of controls (as discussed in Chapter 6)
- commence the critical task of trying to rebuild stakeholder confidence (see Chapter 8; the importance of managing stakeholders effectively cannot be overestimated and is a sine qua non of the whole turnaround process).

In many cases the 'quick and dirty' diagnostic review of whether a turnaround is possible will have been completed prior to the turnaround leader taking on the challenge. S/he will therefore have formed views on whether s/he believes the business can survive in the short term, and whether it is likely that the business can be turned around. The turnaround leader may therefore already have some knowledge of the magnitude of the problems facing him/her. Thus, in many situations, the turnaround leader will begin the process of crisis management and stakeholder management whilst the diagnostic review is being undertaken.

In these early days, therefore, two or three distinct phases of work need to be managed at the same time. As the company is in crisis, time pressures in each of these two or three areas are immense, and it is extremely easy to become immersed in one area and neglect the others. This occurs at the turnaround leader's peril.

Good turnaround leaders have developed methods of effectively managing these critical areas in tandem. The essence of effective project management during this critical first few days is the personal and visible intervention of the turnaround leader in the key issues in each area, whilst at the same time delegating responsibility to experienced competent (turnaround) managers.

It is perhaps helpful to outline our approach here. This involves the appointment of a separate experienced turnaround manager as team leader for each of the three areas of work. This team leader and his/ her team work only in their designated area (cash and working capital management; stakeholder management; or diagnostic review). The turnaround leader gives clear instructions and sets the key objectives and deliverables for each of the teams. Supervision is close and involves progress reports – perhaps several times a day – and hands-on involvement where necessary. This close supervision and direction also helps with culture change within the organization by the imposition of deadlines, allocation of responsibilities, the requirement for deliverables, and the promotion of a can-do attitude.

The bulk of the turnaround leader's own time in the first few days is likely to be spent in meetings with the key stakeholders. The extent to which the leader manages to build confidence in the key stakeholders and achieve buy-in to his action plan will ultimately determine the success of the turnaround. The key challenge for the turnaround leader is to assess quickly who the key stakeholders are, their relative bargaining positions, and their current views on the company and its incumbent management (where appropriate). In many cases the company's relations with its stakeholders will have deteriorated to such an extent that a very adversarial relationship exists.

The turnaround leader will need to commence the crucial process of rebuilding stakeholder confidence immediately. This will require him/her to:

Set out an overall action plan clearly, identifying key deadlines and the way s/he intends to attack the turnaround.

Overcome any hostility to the company which may exist, by listening to the requirements of the stakeholders and ensuring that their valid concerns are accommodated rather than ignored.

Set clear deadlines for deliverables: The best example here is probably the short-term cash-flow forecasts which will be prepared in the first few days of the turnaround. Preparing these forecasts quickly, showing that the right actions are being taken and that the concerns of the stakeholders (primarily the company's bankers) are being met, will go a long way to restoring some confidence amongst the stakeholders.

In this critical early stage, honesty about the reality of the company's predicament, and frequent open communication as further information and issues emerge, are key. The early establishment of a 'no surprises' culture will help in the building of trust between the turnaround leader and the key stakeholders and this, of course, is much more likely to make them supportive.

By the end of the initial phase the turnaround leader must have managed his/her own activities and those of his/her team to enable him/her to answer these critical questions:

- will the company be able to survive in the short term based on the cash-flow forecasts which have been prepared?
- what additional financial support is required, if any?
- will the key stakeholders be supportive?
- is turnaround possible (based on the results of the diagnostic review)?

Answers to these questions require the turnaround leader to prioritize his/her own time and to manage the project teams (discussed above) effectively. Once the turnaround leader is able to satisfy him/herself on the above questions, then s/he will commence the business planning process. Our approach here is to assign an experienced manager as 'team leader' for the business planning process. The team leader will deal with this area only, and will often be the same person who conducted the diagnostic review.

As we will explain in Chapter 9, the business planning process is extremely intensive and focuses on all areas of the company's operations. The turnaround leader will be heavily involved in this process and in the setting of targets, objectives and deadlines. Throughout the business planning process, however, the turnaround leader needs to ensure that continuing priority is given to both crisis management (principally now cash and working capital management) and stakeholder management. The turnaround leader will need to ensure that s/he exercises close supervision of the crisis management aspects, ensuring that progress continues to be made and, importantly, communicated to the key stakeholders through a formalized reporting mechanism.

During this period, the turnaround leader will have to blend quite different styles: the short-term mindset of crisis management must work together with the longer-term mindset required to ensure the turnaround of the underlying business via the planning process. When dealing with the crisis, one of the key checks which the turnaround leader needs to make is to ensure that none of the short-term actions being pursued will unduly harm the underlying business.

During the business planning process the turnaround leader will need to:

Ensure there is a good infrastructure in place to manage the business planning process (see Chapter 13). Regular reviews will identify whether planning is on track and provide an opportunity for corrective action to be taken, involving additional resources if necessary.

Ensure an appropriate balance between short-term and longer-term objectives. This involves ensuring that the concerns of key stakeholders, which may be more short-term, are accommodated, whilst not irreversibly harming the business (e.g., by 'turning off' research and development).

Implement non-contentious quick wins identified during the business planning process. This will build confidence amongst the external stakeholders and build momentum internally.

Involve the non-executive directors in brokering solutions with the key stakeholders, if it is helpful.

Ensure the business plan is professionally presented as part of the process of confidence-building. This applies to any documents that are provided to key external stakeholders.

Post Business Plan

Once the business plan has been completed, the turnaround manager will still have three key areas to address:

Cash and working capital management systems: These will still need to be implemented with vigour. The crisis will not be over and the business not yet stable. There will still be significant further improvements to make, and the turnaround manager will want to continue to develop his/her credibility through a track record in this area, which will prove useful in securing ongoing financial support. Accordingly, the turnaround manager needs to continue to supervise this area strongly via his/her relevant team leader or cash champion, and to ensure that detailed (weekly) reports are circulated.

Ongoing funding arrangements: The turnaround manager will generally need to agree these with key stakeholders. This will almost certainly include the company's bankers and possibly also equity investors, suppliers and customers. Clearly the number of stakeholder groups, and stakeholders within each group, involved in this process will determine how complex the process is and how many different conflicting interests the turnaround manager has to balance. In almost all cases this will be a complex process, even if just banks are involved. If the business planning process has been managed effectively, as discussed above, the plan should present no surprises to the key stakeholders and should accommodate their concerns where possible. Accordingly, the business plan should be approved relatively easily. Nevertheless, complex negotiations will follow concerning detailed terms, conditions, amounts of funding, investment returns, etc. (as discussed in Chapter 14). Negotiations for funding are likely to be extremely time-consuming for the turnaround manager and other members of the management team, and can easily distract them from the key task of implementing the business plan. Perhaps the key challenge of the turnaround manager is to ensure that s/he does not take his/her eye off the ball as regards business operations as a result of the intense activity associated with the funding negotiations – there will be a natural feeling amongst the management team that they can relax once the intense period of business plan preparation is over.

Implementing the plan: The turnaround leader needs to take quick action to establish a framework and processes for the implementation of the business plan (as discussed in Chapter 13). A hiatus period between completion of the business plan and the commencement of implementation can be extremely damaging. If this does occur, the first few critical deadlines for action steps included in the business plan are likely to be missed. This will have the effect of damaging both stakeholder confidence (thus jeopardizing the negotiations towards financial restructuring), and internal confidence, causing the turnaround to lose momentum.

Once a revised funding structure has been agreed with the key stakeholders, competing demands on the time of the turnaround leader lessen and his/her clear priority becomes the implementation of the business plan.

It is important to recognize that the priorities as regards the implementation of the business plan and operations in general will change as the turnaround progresses. The turnaround manager will ensure that there is an effective framework in place to help him/her manage business-plan implementation and the business's operations. This will allow regular visibility on progress in relation to the schedule. (These processes are considered in more detail in Chapter 13.) S/he must also be flexible and encourage the emergence of new initiatives and the abandonment of inappropriate ones. Receptiveness to continuing and evolving change and the reassessment of priorities will increase the likelihood of a successful turnaround.

Moving Beyond the Turnaround

The constant assessment of progress, together with the judgement and experience of the turnaround manager, will enable him/her to consider when the time is right to move into a more advanced strategic change or growth phase. This later phase is quite likely to be accompanied by further financial restructuring and, in particular, additional fund-raising. It is important to emphasize that this shift will be a gradual process.

In determining whether the next stage of strategic change or growth is appropriate, the turnaround leader will need to consider:

The mood of the key stakeholders and whether they will be receptive to the change in priorities. The key stakeholders will retain major influence over the direction of the turnaround and need to be persuaded that a change in priorities will serve their interests as well as the company's. This of course emphasizes the continued need to communicate regularly with stakeholders throughout the turnaround.

Whether sufficient progress has been made in the turnaround to date. This is particularly relevant where additional funds need to be raised and funders will be looking for evidence of a satisfactory track record. For this reason it is likely to be some significant time before a growth phase can be contemplated – probably at least a year and possibly two years into the turnaround.

The turnaround leader must ensure that s/he anticipates the likely change in the priorities of the turnaround well in advance. To this end s/he should always have an endgame in mind. This is important so that preliminary steps and negotiations can commence early enough for the company to benefit from additional strategic change or growth.

Growth is likely to be accompanied by the need for additional funding. This may be by means of conventional debt or equity financing, or some form of merger and acquisition activity. Whichever route is chosen is likely to be extremely time-consuming for senior management, with the resultant risk that the underlying business operations may be neglected. The turnaround leader must not let this happen (in the same way that financial restructuring negotiations must not interfere with the implementation of the business plan). This is sometimes a difficult area to manage because the crisis will now have been averted and the business will be reasonably stable. There is a natural inclination at this stage in the turnaround for management to sink back into their old ways. It is critical therefore that the turnaround leader overcomes the resistance s/he is likely to face from the senior management team and continues to impose proper executive management processes for managing the business's operations. Any deterioration in operational performance at this stage is likely to destroy any prospect of raising additional finance and investing for the longer term.

Mobilizing the Organization

People are a key success-driver in any business, and particularly in the change process necessary to achieve a turnaround. Those leading a turnaround *must* be able to motivate and enthuse their people at the same time as achieving organizational stability. However much communication takes place internally, there is no guarantee that communications alone will generate commitment from senior and middle managers. This group of key managers are likely to bear the burden of implementing top management's turnaround strategy, and unless they feel ownership of and commitment to the turnaround plan implementation will at best be patchy. In many cases this ownership and commitment are difficult to achieve because top management often lack basic managerial capabilities.

Typically top management will involve the key managers in extensive one-to-one discussions, group meetings, data-gathering and analysis projects, and problem-solving sessions – which over time may build ownership. However, many of the survivors of any initial cost-reduction exercise or management changes that have already taken place are likely to resent the extra pressures put on them, and feel hard-done-by because they were not offered or did not accept redundancy. Thus the turnaround manager may need to look for other ways of bringing the key managers on board. 'Away days', management conferences, and even social events can all be useful mechanisms for involving management in the business, but may fail to provide the managers with a deep enough understanding of why the firm and they themselves need to change.

In her book *The Change Masters*, Rosabeth Moss Kanter proposed five people-related ingredients for successful change.[3] Our experience is that this is an extremely useful framework for turnaround leaders. The five ingredients are summarized briefly below:

Pressure for change: Change is usually externally induced but may be internally resisted. It is difficult to come into an organization and get people to believe in the need for change. There often needs to be some galvanizing event or crisis that requires a response, before action is triggered. There are, however, situations where change is not internally resisted. For instance, where a company has an autocratic leader whose strategies and decisions have been the subject of widespread internal dissatisfaction, the appointment of new leadership may release internal pressure which was built up over a period of time. Whatever the catalyst, the change reaction must then generate its own momentum for real progress to be made.

Frequently the pressure will be triggered by the introduction of a new CEO, providing the organization with the clear message that 'things are going to change'. In a turnaround the financial crisis is usually the trigger for change, but in the absence of a clear crisis (at, say, the crisis denial stage – see Chapter 2), pressure for change may have to be artificially induced through the creation of a crisis.

There are many sources of pressure for change, but a characteristic of companies facing a turnaround is that the pressure for change will have come about suddenly, and more often than not will have been triggered by an external stakeholder.

Leadership and vision: The need for strong leadership (as discussed in this chapter) and a clear, uniting vision for the business – supplied by the leader – will provide a motivational stimulus for change and help break down the barriers impeding progress. The vision needs to be something more than mere survival in the short term, otherwise the better people in the organization will look for challenges in other organizations where they can believe in a medium- to long-term vision. People can often understand the need for short-term hardships but need something more compelling for the longer term.

Capable people: The right team must be built to implement the turn-around. (This has been the subject of part of this chapter.) Clearly the right people doing the right things at the right time is what is needed.

Actionable first steps: The change process needs to be guided by a coherently constructed plan. This must break down tasks, assign responsibilities for delivering them, and provide deadlines by which the actions must be completed. People need to know what they are to do on Monday morning. It is rarely satisfactory for this to be what they did before, because without any enhancement or amendment, that hardly constitutes an actionable first step to effect change. (This is discussed in more detail in Chapter 13.)

Effective rewards: The final ingredient for change is to establish effective reward systems for employees, which are closely linked to the newly developed action plans. (Again, this is discussed in more detail in Chapter 8.)

The absence of any one of these five ingredients will normally frustrate efforts to implement successful change. Figure 7.3 illustrates the effect of missing ingredients. The Kanter model provides a very effective framework for the management team since it demonstrates the need for a successful turnaround to be holistic and people-inclusive.

Communication

Extensive communication down the organization by the top management team, and by the turnaround manager in particular, is a characteristic of nearly all successful turnarounds. Good communication is part of the visible leadership that is expected of the turnaround manager. It is crucial to motivating employees after a crisis.

Communication is a line-management function, so the chief executive must always be the chief communicator. In a turnaround, the chief executive usually has to have direct communication *further down* the organization than may be common in a healthy firm. The reason for this is that the management and organizational culture which the turnaround manager has inherited is usually not used to open communi-

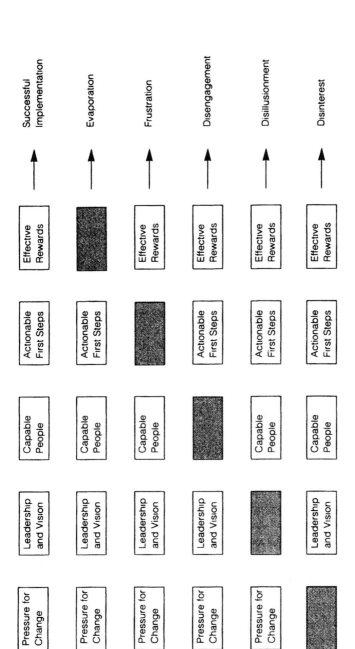

Figure 7 3 **Ingredients of Successful Change**

cation. In fact, as we said in Chapter 3, secrecy is a common characteristic in crisis situations. Thus, unless there is a large number of new managers down the organization – which is unlikely, at least in the emergency phase of recovery – the turnaround manager must take on more of this burden.

It is very easy in the heat of the emergency phase to forget about or to postpone communications, despite having good intentions. In particular, it is easy either to think your subordinates know what you want, or to think that because you have told them once, you really communicated with them. What a turnaround manager may think is communication overkill will rarely be seen as such in practice. The type of turnaround strategies adopted in a recovery situation and the speed with which they have to be implemented are often so alien to the existing management that effective communication is more important than ever.

Communication down the organization should begin on day one of the turnaround: managers and staff want to know who the turnaround manager is and what s/he is going to do. If possible the turnaround manager needs to grab the attention of the organization quickly – to make employees realize that the old days are over. This is easier said than done because old attitudes die hard, but in some situations an opportunity may exist to make a dramatic point. In a turnaround of a small up-market Swiss watch company in the early 1990s, the turnaround manager melted down finished watches to sell the gold in order to pay the wages at the end of his first week. Imagine the horror of the Swiss craftsmen – but what a way to grab their attention!

Throughout the early days of the turnaround there will be endless rumours, and misinformation and conspiracy theories will abound. Only frequent and clear communication will offset the negative forces likely to be at work within the organization. There is usually a honeymoon period when existing management are waiting to see what happens while the new team prepares its turnaround plan. Once the team starts to implement some of the classic short-term strategies – tighter financial control and cost reduction, for example – the morale of those employees resistant to change will drop very fast.

It is at this time that the turnaround team needs to have something more specific to say about where the company is going and how it is going to get there. Messages must be simple and consistent, and they must make very clear to the whole organization what the current priorities are. The communication of early wins and positive progress will be vital in maintaining enthusiasm and the momentum for change. A feature of troubled companies is a stream of bad news. There is a need for good news and this should be communicated in clear, concise terms to enable people to understand their role in the turnaround and facilitate further 'buy-in' to the turnaround process. Communication must cascade down to the lowest levels of an organization to avoid a feeling of secrecy being built up around the turnaround team. All communication should reinforce the key message the leader wants to give.

The role of communication is to reduce uncertainty. This is done by providing historical information and facts; providing perspectives and vision and confirming the psychological contract between the employees and the firm. Communication is of course a two-way exercise. The top-down direction should be complemented with bottom-up communication, providing senior management with an ear to the market and organization. It is vitally important for the turnaround manager to plug into the corporate grapevine at an early stage of the process, and not to rely on formal briefings by incumbent senior management.

As a general rule, communication is more powerful the less filtered it is, and the fewer intermediate steps there are between the sender and the receiver. This is particularly true given the nature of turnaround situations. Therefore, direct communication between the turnaround manager and the employees is the ideal situation. Short, regular meetings are the ideal format.

The leader can choose from an array of communication means, including direct conversations, electronic media and written communications (such as an in-house newspaper). Many examples have shown that direct verbal communication is the most effective way to convey credibility and urgency. The most practical method will depend on the size of the firm and the geographical spread of its operations. The following examples show how varied the ways to communicate messages concerning turnaround and fundamental change can be.

Percy Barnevik, CEO of ABB (Asett Brown Boveri), describes the challenge:

Communication. I have no illusions about how hard it is to communicate clearly and quickly to tens of thousands of people around the world . . Last year, for example, we made a big push to squeeze our accounts receivable and free up working capital. We called it the Cash Race. There are 2,000 people in accounts receivable, so we had to mobilize them to make the programme work. Three or four months after the programme had been started – and we made it very visible when we started – I visited an accounts receivable office where twenty people were working. These people had not even heard of the programme, and it should have been their top priority . . .

You don't inform, you over-inform. That means breaking taboos. There is a strong tendency among European managers to be selective about sharing information . . .

We faced a huge communications challenge right after the merger. In January 1988, just days after the birth of ABB, we had a management meeting in Cannes with the top 300 people in the company. At that meeting, we presented our policy bible, a twenty-one-page book that communicates the essential principles. It's no glossy brochure. It's got tough, direct language . . . I told this group of 300 that they had to reach 30,000 ABB people around the world within sixty days – and that didn't mean just sending out a document. It meant translating it into local languages, sitting with people for a full day and hashing it out.[4]

Here is the challenge of communication in a global organization with disparate locations – and one way to permeate the organization with a new policy. Clearly, cascading down the messages through the various hierarchies is one of the very few possibilities in an organization of this extent. The fact that the communication of the cash management initiative was a failure could have been fatal in a truly severe turnaround situation. In this case, a bottom-up mandatory feedback system and monitoring would have closed the communication loop and ensured that the initiative was widely understood and implemented.

The second example concerns a mid-size engineering company in the UK. Insufficient profitability due to its strategic positioning and the loss of a major customer necessitated the lay-off of some 600 people in several locations. Management together with outside turnaround consultants designed and implemented a communication programme. The key challenges were:

- information about the lay-offs was leaking through and the rumours were corroborated when the manufacturing orders for the major customer failed to materialize
- disparate locations and a three-shift system
- minimal disruption of the ongoing operations in terms of quality, costs and delivery
- potential publicity of the lay-offs.

First, the general situation of the company was explained to staff via a written announcement from the chairman. This announcement was meant to prepare the ground for further steps. The lay-offs themselves were announced by the managing director in person. Timing was critical, and the break between two shifts was used to gather the workforce so that a maximum number of people at the chief location could be reached. At exactly the same time, senior line management announced the redundancies at various satellite operations. A press comment as well as a 'questions and answers' sheet (covering questions most likely to be asked) were prepared. The press were informed with a standardized statement about one hour after the internal announcements had been made. Questions from the press were directed to a nominated spokesman.

The lessons from this example are twofold: first, bad messages (and the majority of major announcements in organizations are received with at least mixed feelings) should be released in a concerted and pointed effort, otherwise rumours start spreading, ultimately affecting output. Also, uncertainty among the workforce is dragging on. Wherever possible, surgery should be carried out in one big move. Secondly, the correct sequence of events is important. There is nothing worse for the employees than reading in the morning newspaper that they have been made redundant. It is management's duty to treat everybody, each individual member of the company, with respect, both those who stay and those who have to leave.

Notes

1. J. P. Kotter and J. L. Heskett, *Corporate Culture and Performance* (Free Press, New York, 1992).

2. Tony Eccles, *Succeeding with Change: Implementing Action-driven Strategies* (McGraw-Hill, New York, 1994).

3. R. M. Kanter, *The Change Masters* (Simon & Schuster, New York, 1983).

4. William Taylor, 'The Logic of Global Business – An interview with ABB's Percy Barnevik' in Christopher Bartlett and Sumantra Ghoshal, *Transnational Management*, second edition (Irwin Professional Publishers, United States, 1995).

8 Stakeholder Management

A stakeholder is any party with an interest (financial or otherwise) in a business, and hence an interest in or an ability to influence the outcome of a turnaround. Differing degrees of interest and influence will attach to different stakeholders, between whom there may well be significant tension. Stakeholder management is a critical part of the turnaround process: the relationships between stakeholders need to be managed to ensure that these natural tensions do not disrupt the process.

The most critical group of relationships are those between management and external stakeholders. In a turnaround situation the confidence and credibility of management are likely to be weakened. On the other hand, the external stakeholders are likely to be extremely anxious both about the future of the company and about management's ability to manage. Management cannot assume that it continues to attract the support of stakeholders on whom it may have been accustomed to rely. It is likely that the firm's recent history has been characterized by a lack of progress, broken promises and late delivery of information. There may even be a growing feeling within external stakeholder organizations that the subject company is seeking to withhold information. The reality may be that there is just chaos in the company because nobody with experience is dealing with the crisis. The turnaround leader will want to engage the external stakeholders in the turnaround process and to rebuild credibility and confidence. S/he will want to introduce a 'no surprises' culture and show that the performance of the business can be predicted, albeit that initial predictions are of poor performance, probably substantially worse than that which was being predicted prior to the acceptance of the crisis.

In spite of their anxiety, stakeholders need the company to succeed, and so it falls to the turnaround manager to bring confidence and clarity to the situation. Management often has to be persuaded to give thoughtful and structured attention to those who in good times it takes for granted. Of course, this does not mean that executive managers can abrogate their management responsibilities. On the contrary, their job becomes tougher as they strive to attain a balance between sensitivity to stakeholders' needs and demands, and demonstrating that they know what they are doing (i.e., that they have a viable strategy which is responsive to stakeholders' aspirations). Only then will management be in a position to secure the necessary support from stakeholders to execute the strategy.

The main purpose of stakeholder management is to rebuild stakeholder confidence at a time when the business has gone through a dramatic decline; incumbent management may be disinclined to face reality; and stakeholders believe their positions to be at risk.

It is rare that either existing or new management teams have the necessary skills to take on the stakeholder management in a turnaround process – because those skills are used only rarely. External advisors are therefore sometimes necessary to help manage the process.

Principles of Stakeholder Management

We have identified eight principles for managing stakeholders:

Think straight – talk straight: Clarity of view and expression is paramount in reducing stakeholders' anxiety. This may well be the first time that stakeholders have received a clear expression of strategy from the business since the original facilities were agreed, and it will be a great reassurance to them. Confusion, however, will lead to antipathy and hostility.

Communicate: In addition to high-quality information, key stakeholders will typically need a large quantity of it; not for its own sake but to satisfy themselves that they are being provided with the means to form their own views about their own positions. Communication really is the heart of stakeholder management.

Be open: Turnarounds need to be managed transparently (in contrast to the norm in ailing businesses) to encourage stakeholder confidence and support.

Manage the information flow: Open, straight-talking communication should never be reckless. Balance candour about facts with discretion about aspirations, and do not weaken negotiating positions through rash disclosure.

Manage perceptions and reality: All stakeholders have perceptions about a business, some of which may not accord with reality. Part of the stakeholder manager's role is to understand where perceptions and reality diverge and to manage stakeholders' expectations accordingly.

Negotiate effectively: Having allayed stakeholders' fears and stabilized management's waning credibility, the stakeholder manager will become deeply involved in negotiations between all the stakeholder groups. Negotiating acceptance of reality and often reluctant support from stakeholders is vital – both to allow the turnaround process to begin and to see the plan implemented in due course.

Manage the people: Stakeholders may be corporate entities in some cases, but every stakeholder is represented by people. Managing people. whether they are management or staff internal to the company, or external stakeholders' representatives, is a development of the communications issues discussed above. All the goals of stakeholder management are reached through managing the people who are or who represent those stakeholders.

Appoint a stakeholder manager: It may be beneficial to use the chairman, a non-executive director or an outside advisor as the stakeholder manager so as to allow the chief executive to concentrate on managing the business. It is too easy for company management to become diverted from their main task of fixing the business when there are others available to take on the stakeholder management role.

What, then, are the qualities required for a good stakeholder manager? We have observed that successful practitioners are normally:

- sensitive
- firm
- experienced
- perceptive
- communicative
- clear
- knowledgeable
- involved
- in control
- a leader.

Leadership is a critical quality because the responsible manager will encounter a variety of challenges to his/her authority, will need to channel the energies of others, and will need to focus all parties on the key issues.

Stakeholder management is rather like engine oil. It is needed from the start to the finish of a turnaround project. It is a vital lubricant without which the project cannot succeed. There needs to be enough of it and it must be at the right temperature and pressure to work effectively. If it gets tired (in a very long-term project), it can be changed! A good recent example of stakeholder management is provided by Eurotunnel, where Sir Alastair Morton, the chairman, performed this role tirelessly as the project lurched from one financial crisis to the next during the mid 1990s.

Stakeholders and Their Aspirations

The principal stakeholder groups, which may be subdivided according to special interests or positions, are:

- shareholders
- management
- employees

- banks
- suppliers/creditors
- customers.

The relative importance of these stakeholder groups will vary from case to case and there will often be a group of key stakeholders without whose support turnaround is impossible.

The banks, creditors and shareholders of a company may be regarded as financial stakeholders, whose principal motivation is to maximize their recovery. On the other hand, management and employees are often driven by a wish to maintain employment. Although financial stakeholders are sometimes more obvious, other external stakeholders such as customers and suppliers should not be ignored.

The most challenging stakeholder group to manage is often the banking syndicate. This may comprise a number of sophisticated negotiators with differing agendas (particularly if there is a complex security structure). There may well be an agent bank, which is more or less successful in controlling the syndicate, but there are likely to be tensions between syndicate members that have little or nothing to do with the turnaround in hand. More significantly, the bankers may have their own advisers and are likely to be the group most demanding as regards information, most critical of its detail, and most suspicious of its veracity. Add to this the likelihood that the banks could be facing greater financial loss than other individual stakeholders, and you have an explosive mixture.

Banks are, however, not always the critical external stakeholders. The position of bondholders, unsecured creditors and the holders of distressed debt can be just as important. As financial instruments become more complex, so the turnaround manager needs to assess quickly which stakeholders can impede the stabilization process.

Other groups of stakeholders to be managed, who may be regarded as secondary but can often have a significant influence over the outcome of the turnaround process, include merchant banks, brokers, solicitors, reporting accountants and turnaround advisers. The aspirations of these secondary stakeholders may not be straightforward. For example, the banking syndicate's reporting accountants may need to score points off the company's turnaround consultants in order to satisfy themselves that they have performed well in the eyes of their instructing bankers. If they are successful, they may be persuaded to support a key plank of the turnaround strategy that, hitherto, the banks have resisted.

Focusing on the needs, both clear and disguised, of the various stakeholders, and satisfying those needs where appropriate, will help the turnaround manager to attain his/her goal. The turnaround manager will find him/herself subject to many pressures, and survival requires gaining a quick appreciation of where the real power lies. It is natural that those with the power will exercise it, but many stakeholders will profess to have power in excess of what they really have.

So what, in practice, does stakeholder management involve during the turnaround process?

The Initial Turnaround Phase

Stakeholder management begins during the pre-mandate appraisal stage of any turnaround assignment. It is important to establish whether stakeholders have an appetite for what is ahead, and that they understand the alternatives. There is no point in proposing a turnaround solution if a key stakeholder has a fundamental and insurmountable objection.

Stakeholder management is fundamental to, but a distinct part of, crisis stabilization. In addition to, say, a cash crisis, a company that is the subject of a turnaround is likely to have some form of stakeholder relationship crisis, most probably a crisis of confidence in management. Stabilizing stakeholder relationships is therefore an urgent task. At this stage, the liaison is likely to be with individual stakeholders, rather than by bringing different stakeholder groups together. Personal attention and avoiding the distractions of third-party stakeholders will help to focus all parties on the key issues.

The next step is to have stakeholders buy into the turnaround process. This really is the bridge between stabilizing stakeholder relationships and rebuilding them to support the turnaround strategy. In order to achieve this buy-in, protocols for the initial planning phase of the turnaround process need to be established and the information flows, which will form a key part of the restoration of stakeholders' confidence, need to be defined.

After establishing channels of communication with key stakeholders, it is often necessary, in order to allow a detailed turnaround plan to be developed, to agree a standstill with key financial stakeholders. Whilst, in effect, this is a part of the crisis management aspect of the turnaround procedure, it will generate the necessary breathing space to allow management to procure the development of a comprehensive business plan (whilst they continue to manage the business). The objective of the support plan is to freeze relationship parameters (e.g., trade terms), and not necessarily to freeze financial exposure levels. The business may be seasonal and the turnaround may have begun in the run up to the company's peak credit requirement. In such circumstances, the support plan will be based on the agreement of creditors to continue to provide increased credit (ideally on previously established terms). A simple example illustrates what we mean. Project Olive was an oil distribution business, where the support plan ran from early December to early February. The key stakeholders were the principal trade suppliers, without whose support, by maintaining continuity of supply, the business could not continue. The company's credit requirement was bound to increase as its customers demanded heating-oil supplies during the winter months. The standstill agreement was therefore based on a forecast requirement, calculated from suppliers' credit exposure in late November of the year in question, increasing in line with the previous year's supply quantity profile (at the current year's prices).

Agreeing a financial support plan cannot be achieved by following a standard formula. It will require a structured but informal process. Too much formality or constraint will paralyse your ability to negotiate with the various stakeholders. Too little structure will make it difficult to bring clarity to the situation and to control unruly stakeholders. In some ways the agreement of a support plan is akin to the London Approach adopted by bankers in multi-banked distressed company situations, whereby UK banks are expected not to act unilaterally whilst a remedy is sought.

Although the support plan concept can be introduced to key financial stakeholders individually, it can only be agreed at a meeting of those stakeholders. This is likely to be the first major meeting of stakeholders in the turnaround process, and the participants will depend on the details of the particular situation.

Not all major financial stakeholders may be able to be accommodated in such a support plan meeting and participate in the agreement. It may therefore be necessary for the relationship with some financial stakeholders to be managed outside the support plan. In many cases, smaller creditors may not need to be made aware of the support plan, which will make allowance for them to continue to be paid on the basis of their credit risk remaining broadly neutral.

The support plan is a non-binding agreement. Its objective is to procure commitment from participating stakeholders – an objective that would fail if the plan were too legalistic. It would be impossible, even at great expense and with the services of many lawyers, to construct a binding agreement adequately representing the views of all parties that fulfilled any useful purpose. There would inevitably be minor breaches of its finer points, and such an agreement would be unworkable. For that reason it is wise to avoid the involvement of stakeholders' lawyers in the process if at all possible. The agreement is designed to represent the commercial aspirations of all parties to find an equitable solution to a common problem. It will not be a legal document that constrains the parties to work to the common good, but instead will follow the commercial imperative of establishing a satisfactory solution. Remember, the prime purpose of the support plan is to give a breathing space to allow the preparation of a turnaround plan.

Following the support plan meeting, a short space of time will need to be allowed to procure the signatures of the participating stakeholders to the support plan document as they will invariably decline to sign at the meeting itself, having not previously seen the document. It should, however, be agreed as part of the plan that the agreement will be announced as effective, by the stakeholder manager, once all the participants have signed it.

The Crisis Management and Business Planning Phase

Once the support plan is in place the business planning exercise can begin – and it will end at the end of the support plan period. This period is likely to last for several weeks or even months. The key stakeholders will need careful management during the business planning and crisis management phases. The key imperatives of the stakeholder management during this period are:

Advising on progress on cash and working capital management: If this aspect has been effectively managed, significant progress will have been achieved and a track record of exceeding targets will have been established. This obviously creates the right climate for positive reception of the business plan and confidence that action steps identified in the business plan can be achieved.

To bring the key stakeholders fully into the process by agreeing the timetable for preparation of the business plan with them, ensuring that the deadlines coincide with any arrangements made with the stakeholders for financial support.

Conducting regular review meetings during the business planning process with key stakeholders. This provides the opportunity for advising on the progress that is being made, the issues and opportunities and, crucially, obtaining the input of the stakeholders and ensuring their concerns are accommodated where appropriate.

During this period, stakeholders will need to be sent regular reports, probably weekly, on:

- cash flows and balances
- performance
- commentary on the above
- commentary on progress of the business planning exercise
- commentary on key external factors affecting the business

- comparisons of key creditor and bank exposures with the standstill opening position and forecasts.

Reports must be clear, concise, well presented and not too glossy. They must, of course, be accurate and must not contain any surprises! (Any surprises should be carefully communicated ahead of the report.)

Whilst this regular reporting regime continues, stakeholders should be integrated into the planning process. It is likely to be important to them that their views are taken into account, and although they must not be allowed to *interfere* with the planning process, they will need to be able to *contribute* to that process if they are to buy into the plan.

Individual and group stakeholder meetings will need to be planned and prepared for. Flexibility of approach and response is critical. Many stakeholders will continue to feel aggrieved about how they perceive themselves to have suffered at the hands of the company and may now be developing strategies of their own to seek to gain advantage over other stakeholders. The integrity of the support plan is likely to be tested as stakeholders reflect on what they agreed and, relying on the non-binding nature of the agreement, seek to manoeuvre.

Managing stakeholders' expectations is crucial. The starting point is a clear understanding of each stakeholder's needs. In communicating information about the company, you should start with the facts and then move on to prospects. A routine of regular, clear reports will assist management in introducing predictability into the company's affairs, at least in the eyes of major stakeholders.

At the end of the business planning phase, stakeholders will have been kept up to date with information about the company's performance and progress in developing the business plan. That plan will then need to be presented (very often by the middle managers who have been most closely involved in the detail of its preparation) at a meeting of the key stakeholders. The initial support plan may need to be extended between presentation and adoption of the business plan, but this second major meeting marks the beginning of the transition towards implementation of the turnaround plan.

It is important that the meeting is tightly focused and controlled, but the objective must be to obtain genuine commitment from the stakeholders. The meeting will need a firm chairman with strong meeting management skills. This could be the company chairman, its chief executive (if s/he has the confidence of the key stakeholders) or the turnaround manager. The management team must be prepared to deal with stakeholders' questions at the meeting in order to demonstrate that the whole team supports the turnaround plan and that it is such a robust plan that it will stand up to a challenge. Again, a short time-limit must be set for adoption by stakeholders.

If the plan has the necessary integrity, stakeholders' expectations have been appropriately managed, and there appears to be a reasonable chance of being successful, the business plan is likely to be approved. The turnaround manager should never allow him/herself to get into a position where the stakeholders do not approve the plan.

Financial Restructuring

Once the business plan and its financing requirements have been agreed, any financial restructuring plan can be finalized. (Financial restructuring is discussed in more detail in Chapter 14.) Assuming that the financial stakeholders have agreed about short-term survival or support financing in the emergency phase, the big negotiation is often reserved for financial restructuring. There are likely to be both inter-group and intra-group conflicts of interest between the financial stakeholders in multi-banking situations. It is always harder to get agreement where there are many classes of debt and a complicated liability structure. Smaller debtors may try to hold out for better terms against the bigger creditors, and may not like the idea of proportional sharing of pain! There is usually a lot of posturing among the banks, and this is not helped by the fact that the banks in a syndicate often change their representatives during the course of negotiations. Each new representative has to be educated about their situation and will often want to flex their muscles, often disagreeing with the previous representative's viewpoint. In the case of the refinancing of WPP, the international advertising group, only the lead bank of the twenty-eight-strong banking syndicate, J. P. Morgan, had the same team in place at the beginning and end of the financing process. Not surprisingly, refinancing can be a long and expensive process for the company, and actually hinder it from getting on with managing the business.

The Implementation Phase

During these later stages of the turnaround process, a clear communications regime remains important. Stakeholders' positions may change, and those managing the turnaround process need to be aware of any such changes. Similarly, stakeholders will have started to become used to regular and consistent information from the company. This must be maintained if stakeholder support is to remain or to increase.

As a result of financial restructurings, stakeholders' interrelationships may need to be redefined. The stakeholder manager will have a continuing important role in such circumstances. As successful implementation of the turnaround plan progresses, stakeholder relationships should develop and form a healthy basis for the future of the business.

Summary

Stakeholder management – managing relationships between the parties with an interest in a distressed company and the outcome of the turnaround process – has at its heart clarity of communication.

In the initial turnaround phase, stakeholder management must first focus on stabilizing the relationship and then on implementing a non-binding standstill agreement or support plan, where the commercial imperative of finding a satisfactory solution is what binds the key stakeholder participants.

During the business planning phase of the turnaround process, stakeholders need clear and concise reports on key performance indicators for the company and on the progress of the planning process. The views of key stakeholders need to be integrated into the planning process and, most importantly, stakeholder expectations need to be managed to ensure that the turnaround plan is not rejected when it is presented.

Clear communication with stakeholders remains important through the implementation phase of the turnaround process as a healthy basis for the future of the business.

9 Developing the Business Plan

This chapter covers the development of the turnaround business plan. Although it may seem an unaffordable luxury to spend time developing and documenting a detailed plan, particularly if the business is in severe difficulties, it is a critical part of the turnaround process. The time invested in producing the plan should be appropriate for the size and complexity of the company: it may be as little as two weeks or as much as six months. However, whatever time is spent will be repaid in the implementation phase, where management activity will be focused on delivering the plan.

The plan therefore becomes the focus for all future short- and medium-term activity of the organization. It provides a clear statement of the recovery strategy for all the employees and managers. Equally, it sets out the rescue strategy for equity and debt providers alike.

By limiting the analysis phase up front, and restricting future action to the priority initiatives incorporated into the plan, management avoid the danger of 'analysis paralysis'. The focus for the implementation phase is on action rather than further analysis, which is so often an excuse for no action.

The development of the plan follows a conventional consulting approach. A central coordination team, typically comprising the CEO and senior management, will manage the activities of cross-functional sub-groups, each focusing on a specific area of the business. The sub-groups are responsible for identifying key improvement opportunities and specify the appropriate turnaround initiatives within their areas, subject to overall parameters set by the coordination group. Typically the coordination group will determine (at an early stage) the overall strategic framework for the recovery plan and focus on integrating the various sub-group initiatives into a coherent plan that tackles the priority improvement opportunities.

We believe that the process for developing the plan should involve as broad a constituency as possible. The overall strategy parameters are likely to be top-down. However, the broad range of tactical and operational initiatives should, as far as possible, be developed by those who will have to implement them; consequently we strongly favour a plan that is both top-down and bottom-up. The process should also incorporate an extensive element of stakeholder review.

Why Write a Business Plan?

There are several reasons why a business plan should be developed:

Focus: It helps the turnaround manager or chief executive to crystallize, focus and summarize the company's strategic direction and the key turnaround strategies and tactics to be deployed in order to return the business to long-term viability.

Process: A business plan is as much a process as a product. The process of developing the plan acts as a catalyst in initiating the cultural and behavioural changes which are essential if the turnaround is to succeed. Developing the plan will force the firm to analyse its corporate goals, business focus, product lines, choice of customers, functional strategies, capital needs and the capabilities of its management team. By working through these difficult issues to the satisfaction of all the stakeholders, the planning exercise alone will significantly raise the chances of success.

Structure: A plan provides a structure for management activity, with actionable steps to be taken in the short- and medium-term.

Performance measures: By identifying and quantifying specific business objectives, a business plan creates financial and non-financial perform-ance measures against which the management team can measure progress.

Finance: A plan provides a persuasive vehicle for attracting capital to help finance or restructure the business during the turnaround process.

What Is a Business Plan?

A business plan is a fundamental document for any business undergoing a turnaround. It is a summary of the business's current state; its strategic, operational and financial plans for the future; and a road map for achieving these plans. It is usually written to meet the needs of a wide audience of stakeholders and should normally include the following:

An executive summary: This provides a concise overview of the important aspects of the plan and it may be the only part of it that some external stakeholders will read. Therefore the summary should cover the purpose of the plan; a brief description of the company, its history and market-place; highlights of financial projections for the period covered by the plan (at least three years); and a summary of any proposed financial restructuring or funding requirements.

History of the business: This should be brief but should point out any past successes, particularly in terms of products or services developed or marketed, which will underpin the company's future. If there are good reasons why past performance is *not* a reliable indicator of future potential – for example, the firm intends to reduce overheads radically or reposition the business – then those reasons should be noted here.

An analysis of the external environment in which the business operates, including the industry, the particular product-market sectors it services, the strength of the competition (both current and projected), an assessment of the threat posed by new entrants or substitute products, and a description of the key customers and suppliers.

A detailed presentation of the business's turnaround strategies: in particular the principal products or services it will sell, the distinctive competitiveness it will develop, the markets it will serve and their current and projected size, and the customers it will target. In addition, other generic strategies to be implemented, such as downsizing operations or significant cost-cutting, should be set out in the plan.

A description of the business's desired end-state or vision (see below).

Operational analysis: The plan should incorporate an assessment of the key strengths, weaknesses and opportunities for improvement in each core business process and each major support function.

Operational action plans: These consist of a series of detailed initiatives that address the weaknesses and opportunities identified in the operational analysis. They 'operationalize' the turnaround strategies, breaking them down into a series of actionable, measurable and quantifiable steps.

Financial projections: These will form the basis of any refinancing, financial restructuring, or negotiations for ongoing financial support from stakeholders. They set out the financial implications of the turnaround strategies and detailed operational action plans, which in narrative form provide the core of the plan.

Implementation process: The plan should include a description of the implementation process to be adopted, including key milestones, key performance measures to be monitored, a timetable for reporting progress to external stakeholders, and an internal communications programme to roll out the business plan throughout the organization.

Risk assessment: For all stakeholders, an assessment of risk will be critical in deciding whether to support the business. It is therefore essential that the question of risk is adequately considered in the business plan.

Who Should Write the Business Plan?

Senior management, and to some degree external stakeholders, should be involved in developing the strategy, articulating the desired end-state, creating the operational action plans and converting these to financial projections. This involvement will generate ownership of and commitment to achieving the plan throughout the organization. If the plan is developed in isolation by the turnaround manager working with a small team, or by external consultants, there is a high risk that it will not achieve buy-in from those who have to implement it. If this is the case, it will ultimately fail, however incisive or appropriate the strategies and plans it contains. Development of the plan is not a peripheral activity; it is the process by which the turnaround is initiated and implemented.

External advisors can play a useful support role, as follows:

- consultants may facilitate the process of developing the plan, challenging management's assumptions and broadening their perspective whilst providing a framework for the plan's development. They can also develop and analyse comprehensive market research, provide an independent assessment of technical feasibility, or provide specific advice or support in particular process or functional areas
- experienced accountants can help to develop or review financial projections contained in the plan
- lawyers can advise on intellectual property, product liability, competition or environmental concerns.

However, it is vital that the plan is 'owned' by management and that it captures the knowledge, enthusiasm and commitment to success of the management team and the wider stakeholders. The style and language should reflect the culture of the business that the turnaround team is trying to create – not the house style of management consultants or other external advisors.

Defining the Desired End-state

Having assessed the industry, competition (both current and future) and product-market segments in which the business currently operates, and reformulated the business's strategy, it is useful to articulate or define the desired end-state for the business *collectively*. The business may already have a mission statement which may be discredited; so this is an opportunity for the management team to set out *their* understanding of the purpose or strategic intent of the business in a way that can be easily understood and absorbed by the other stakeholders.[1] The definition could include:

A statement of the intended product-market positioning of the business: possibly written from the customer's perspective or even in their language, e.g., 'Pre-eminent supplier of building materials to the U K's top twenty national and regional house builders,' or, 'Business X is my first choice for components because their combination of low prices and next-day delivery offers the best value for money in the industry'.

A statement of key strengths or core capabilities: what the business will be really good at in order to achieve its strategic goals, e.g., pre-eminence in design, research and development, low-cost manufacturing, or whatever is essential for sustainable competitive advantage. This should follow the review of core business processes, as described in Chapter 12.

The technology approach: A definition of the technology that will support the business and the direction that technological evolution will take in terms of applications and infrastructure.

A sourcing approach: Based on an understanding of its core capabilities and where it will participate in the value chain, the company must determine which activities will be developed internally and which will be purchased or achieved through alliances with other organizations.[2]

A description of the business's organizational approach: This articulates the critical organizational capabilities required to support the business unit strategy as well as the processes, organization architecture and leadership required to make the change succeed.

A summary of the key human resource policies and principles: e.g., culture, performance measurement, employee development and career progression.

The articulation of the desired end-state − or vision (we dislike the term 'mission statement') − is an iterative process and should be revisited after the market assessment, strategy formulation and review of the business processes. The approaches to be adopted must be consistent with the strategic goals of the business, its planned capabilities, and the actual capabilities it has at present.

Detailed Operational Plans

The next step is to develop detailed operational or action plans which will enable the business to reach its desired end-state. These plans, together with the strategic and operational assessment of the business, form the core of the business plan and implementation process. They might consist of one hundred or more separate, quantifiable and measurable initiatives, which are then reflected in the financial projections. The initiatives must address all key weaknesses highlighted during the diagnostic analysis and process review phases and must deliver the competitive advantages that have been identified as critical to the achievement of the business's strategic goals.

The operational plans should be prepared by the people who will execute them. This is critical to get buy-in from key operational personnel and ownership of each initiative. If action plans are drafted in isolation and handed down to the troops like military orders, they are likely to be regarded as unrealistic, unachievable, or simply be ignored on the grounds that they were 'not invented here'.

In producing the action plans, management must keep an open mind as to what is the best solution to a particular problem. The first idea is not necessarily the only or best idea. Figure 9.1 uses a form of component analysis to show how different ways of reducing raw material costs can be incorporated into operational action planning.

The process of developing focused, realistic but challenging operational plans requires considerable planning, control and coordination. For this reason, it is sensible to form an executive management team, typically including the chief executive and chief financial officer. The executive team's responsibilities include:

Selecting the core implementation team members, each of whom will develop action plans for a critical business process or function. The executive team must ensure that the right depth and breadth of skills have been assembled in the team as a whole. The core team members would normally include senior operational managers and possibly middle managers. The enthusiasm and commitment of the individuals involved are

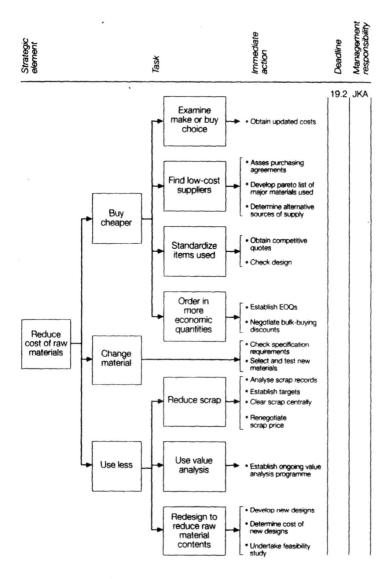

Figure 9.1: **Component Analysis of Cost of Raw Materials**

as important as their functional knowledge and experience. The core team should not include individuals who have a key role to play in crisis stabilization or working capital management. These key activities will run concurrently with the business plan development process and those responsible for the short-term survival of the business should not be distracted.

Establishing and explaining the process of developing the action plans to the core team, including their responsibilities, deliverables and a timetable which meets the overall business-plan timetable.

Agreeing and communicating the desired end-state to the core team. It is vital that each member understands the proposed product-market strategy, core capabilities required and sourcing approach for the business. These must be clearly understood and accepted so that the action plans will lead to the achievement of the desired end-state.

Coordinating the work of the core team, ensuring consistency of approach and identifying and managing any gaps or overlaps in the action plans developed for different processes or functional areas of the business.

Critically reviewing the action plans, financial implications and key performance measures presented by each core-team member and ensuring that these are both achievable and capable of delivering the strategic aims of the business. The review process is described in more detail below.

Integrating the action plans into the overall business plan and drafting the other sections of the plan.

It can be helpful to give the core team a collective identity, such as 'Club X' or 'Team X' (X being the total number of people in the core team). This helps to build team spirit amongst the core team and encourages cross-functional problem-solving and objective-setting rather than isolationist thinking. Each member of the core team should establish their own (small) sub-team, comprising functional expertise and appropriate support resource from other areas of the business.

Kick-off

The process should be kicked off by holding a meeting with the core team. The key purpose of this meeting is to communicate a sense of urgency and to convey the commitment of the executive team to developing and implementing the business plan as an essential part of the turnaround process. The executive team must strike a balance between a 'vale of despair' – a bleak presentation of the business's current difficulties and prospects – and an upbeat, optimistic tone which gives a false sense of security or fails to communicate the need for immediate and perhaps drastic action. If the core team do not share the sense of urgency, the business plan process will appear sterile and unnecessary; but equally they should not be given the impression that they are being asked to fight a lost cause. If it is available, the 'base case' (see below) should be presented to the core team, so that they can appreciate the likely financial consequences for the business if the action plans are not developed and implemented.

It is vital to communicate from the outset that the operational plans must be focused, achievable and capable of measurement, and must deliver quantifiable profit and cash-flow benefits to the business within an agreed time period. It is of little use to the business if the initiatives all require considerable investment, with a three- to five-year payback, as the funds to achieve this are unlikely to be available.

The other key messages to be communicated at the kick-off meeting include:

The short-term vision: A description of the desired end-state for the business and the key turnaround strategies which are to be 'operationalized' in the action plans.

The deliverables required from each sub-team, including timetables for submission of draft and final action plans; level of supporting financial analysis required; time horizon for payback on short- and medium-term initiatives; and types of performance measures expected (both financial and non-financial).

The resources available to each sub-team, including middle management, consultant support, and internal support from finance, HR or IT personnel in developing the financial analysis, reviewing the HR implications of proposed initiatives or actions, and obtaining the information required for developing each initiative.

This meeting should also be used to review the findings of the diagnostic or business process review with the key operational management. Have all the key weaknesses and opportunities been identified? Is there general agreement as to what these are and which team member is responsible for addressing each weakness or opportunity? Are there any ideas which are too good to lose but do not appear to be 'fundable' within the turnaround timescales – if so, capture them in a 'car park' document, to be returned to at a later date. If these ideas are dismissed out of hand, individuals will become de-motivated or reluctant to put forward challenging or groundbreaking ideas which may be critical to the success of the business in the medium or longer term.

Follow-up

It is sensible to have a follow-up meeting with the core team after a few days and ask them to present their outline action plans or key initiatives. The executive team can then ensure that the sub-teams are on the right track and identify any gaps or overlaps in the work of different teams. Most importantly, the core team have the opportunity, through collective and cross-functional discussion, to prioritize and focus on the key initiatives that will have a significant impact on the business. It is essential that this process of focusing and filtering is carried out early on in the development of the action plan, otherwise considerable effort can be wasted developing detailed action plans which will not deliver significant financial benefits in the short or medium term.

Deliverables

It is useful to give each core team member a template to summarize their action plans in order to get consistent presentation. They will, of course, have considerably more detailed working papers which support these summaries, which can be reviewed when they present their plans to the executive committee. A sample template is set out in Figure 9.2.

It is likely that the development of the business plan will highlight certain important issues which cannot be resolved within the time frame of the business plan development process because detailed further work or analysis is required to reach a conclusion. These should be clearly identified as separate initiatives within the action plans. The timetable for carrying out further work and presenting the conclusions or recommendations should be incorporated, along with any anticipated costs, such as consultants' fees.

It is vitally important for the development of robust financial projections that each initiative is properly quantified in terms of its impact on profit and cash flow relative to the base case. Each initiative should have two levels of financial impact, the risk-adjusted benefit, which is certain of achievement, and the target benefit, which has a degree of uncertainty or stretch associated with it. For example, an initiative to reduce unit costs by improving a core process might set a risk-adjusted improvement of 2 per cent but a target improvement of a further 3 per cent, i.e., 5 per cent overall. These can then be incorporated into the financial projections as risk-adjusted/target improvements to gross margin.

Certain initiatives, such as disposal of surplus fixed assets or stock, might have a negative profit impact (if sold for less than book value) but a positive impact on cash flow. Others, such as a redundancy programme, might require up-front cash investment but generate ongoing profit and cash-flow improvements. The acid test is that each initiative must deliver a positive net present value during the period considered by the plan (usually three to five years), with the possible exception of essential research and development, which might have a longer payback period.

Figure 9.2: **Sample Template**

[Ref from strategic plan]	Description of initiative and its objectives	Action Steps	Key perfomance measures	Responsibility for action steps	Complete by	Profit impact RAF* target	Cash impact RAF* target
M 1.01	Consolidate assembly lines on to one site from three and close/ sell two sites to improve assembly efficiency, reduce cycle times and release capital from under-utilized sites and equipment.	1. Complete detailed site assessment and equipment transfer plan. 2. Consult unions/ employee representatives. 3. Execute consolidation during summer shutdown.	1. Assembly cost per unit. 2. Total WIP in assembly. 3. Assembly cycle time.	Operations director.	9/98	£(2.0)m £(1.1)m	£2.1m £3.8m

*Risk-adjusted forecast

Develop Financial Projections

The finance department needs to develop a detailed financial model (or adapt an existing budgeting or forecasting model) which can be 'flexed' to reflect different assumptions and carry out sensitivity analysis. This should be an integrated model, incorporating monthly profit-and-loss, cash-flow and balance-sheet forecasts. There are three key financial scenarios to be developed.

The Base Case

The base case is a measure of the inertia in the business: it is sometimes referred to as 'momentum analysis'. It projects the likely trading performance and financial consequences for the business if no action is taken to address the causes of decline and reverse the current trends. The extrapolation of existing trends usually indicates further deterioration in performance rather than maintaining current levels of profit or loss, as the business is likely to experience a further downturn in sales if its product-market strategy is not reformulated, and costs will remain fixed if no action is taken. The base case is a vital reality check, and all initiatives are then developed and costed with the aim of significantly improving performance relative to the base case scenario. The base case projections will frequently indicate that the business is no longer viable or will become insolvent if current trends are not reversed. For this reason, management teams are often very nervous about sharing the base case with middle management or external stakeholders. However, it is essential that all stakeholders understand the company's true financial position and prospects if no remedial action is taken. If the underlying trends and realistic prospects for the business *in its current state* are not set out and communicated, then stakeholders may have a falsely optimistic view of the business or the time which must be allowed for the turnaround strategies to take effect. If the base case is not sufficiently realistic, the risk-adjusted forecast will be overstated and may not be achieved. This will, in turn, greatly undermine the confidence of all stakeholders in the plan once implementation is under way.

Risk-adjusted Forecast (RAF)

The risk-adjusted forecast builds on to the base case the financial implications of the reformulated strategy and of those initiatives which the core team believe are certain of achievement. The RAF is the appropriate basis for agreeing a refinancing or restructuring, and for setting lending covenants, etc. It is, therefore, the no-fail or minimum level of performance that the business must deliver.

Target

The target financial projections build on to the RAF the financial implications of those initiatives that require additional management action to be taken in order to achieve them. These should contain an element of stretch and may not be achieved in full. However, the business should strive to achieve the target level of performance, and management incentive schemes should be linked to the target rather than the RAF.

The business plan should include analyses which clearly reconcile the improvement in the key financial performance measures – such as sales, gross margin, overheads and net cash flow – from base case to RAF and from RAF to target. An example of such an analysis is set out in Figure 9.3. It clearly links the projected improvements in financial performance to the initiatives contained in the detailed operational action plans. This approach enables both management and external stakeholders to have confidence in the projections, as they are supported by separately identifiable and quantified initiatives which have been developed by the people who will have responsibility for their implementation.

The finance team will also be involved in developing financial models and analyses to support the detailed initiatives, such as manufacturing

Figure 9.3: **Reconciliation of Base Case to RAF and Target**

	Gross profit £000	Gross Margin %	Initiative Number
Base case	**25,000**	**50.0**	
Increased sales at base margin	1,500		S1.01 to S1.04
Procurement initiatives	275	0.5	P1.01 to P1.06
Manufacturing initiatives	1,025	1.9	M1.10 to M1.05
Risk-adjusted forecast (RAF)	**27,800**	**52.4**	
Increased sales at base margin	2,500		S1.01 to S1.05
Procurement initiatives	125	0.2	P1.01 to P1.08
Manufacturing initiatives	1,575	2.6	M1.01 to M1.09
Target	**32,000**	**55.2**	

capacity modelling, breakeven analysis or activity-based costing for process realignment. If possible, the person or persons responsible for the integrated financial model should not be involved in supporting the core team members or sub-teams in this way, as the integrated model requires careful version control and is likely to be re-run numerous times to reflect changing assumptions or sensitivities.

The Integration and Review Process

The Executive Committee

The first level of review is carried out by the executive committee. It is their responsibility to ensure that the detailed operational plans meet the strategic and financial objectives of the business. They must be convinced that each initiative is capable of implementation within the timescales proposed and that the financial costs/benefits are supported by reasonably cautious assumptions and sufficiently thorough analysis. It is likely that each team's plans will be reviewed at least twice, as the first review will highlight areas requiring further consideration. Overall, the executive committee must conclude on the following:

- are the action plans robust and achievable?
- will they deliver the strategies required for sustainable competitive advantage?
- will they build the core capabilities required to deliver those strategies?
- do they contain sufficient 'stretch' to make a significant difference to the performance levels of the organization?
- do they 'right-size' the organization, given the projected levels of revenue, or is further action needed to achieve this?
- are the resulting financial projections realistic but sufficiently attractive to maintain the interest and support of all the stakeholders?
- do the plans include performance measures which will tell us, in a timely and accurate fashion, whether we are on track to deliver the plan?

Once the executive team are satisfied that the plan as a whole and the action plans in particular meet these criteria, they need to integrate the various sections of the plan into a written draft, which can be presented to the board.

The Board

The next step is normally for the executive team to present the draft plan to the board. A timetable should be agreed for board members, particularly those not heavily involved in the process to date – i.e., non-executive directors – to give their verbal or written feedback to the executive committee. This feedback should, as far as possible, be incorporated into the next draft of the plan, so that the board members have participated in the development process and have ownership of the plan. In addition, the board may request further analysis or clarification on key issues, which must be completed before the draft plan can be presented to external stakeholders.

External Stakeholders

The next step is for the board, or their representatives, to present the draft plan to key external stakeholders, such as bankers or shareholders. It is important that the plan is still presented as a draft or work-in-progress. This provides an opportunity to gather feedback from the external stakeholders, to carry out any further analysis that they might request, and to incorporate this into the final plan. Again, this helps the external stakeholders buy into the process and therefore into the resulting plan. If they are presented with a final plan, they might feel that it is a fait accompli, with the implication being 'here it is – take it or leave it', and that they have not had the opportunity to have their concerns heard and addressed. If issues raised by the external stakeholders are documented and addressed in the final draft of the plan, this provides tangible evidence that their input has been heard and taken into account. A key objective for the turnaround manager is to achieve stakeholder support without the appointment of investigating accountants. Bankers are more likely to insist on investigating accountants if they are presented with a fait accompli than if they have ownership of the plan and conclude that it is the result of a logical process and reflects their key concerns.

Finally, the board should formally approve the plan at a board meeting, and this should be documented in the meeting minutes as well as in the plan itself.

Risk Assessment

The assessment of risk is a critical part of the business plan, particularly if the business requires financial restructuring or other financial support from its stakeholders. The discussion of risk demonstrates management's ability to identify and assess risk, to learn from their previous experiences, and to reflect their evaluation of the risks in the financial projections through sensitivity analysis.

Each company has its own unique set of constantly changing business risks. Certain risks will be external to the firm, and many of these will be either difficult or impossible to control, such as competition, financial markets and regulations. Others will be internal, resulting from a company's own organization, processes, products, contractual commitments or relationships with customers, suppliers and employees. Examples of these might be technology (are we using the latest or the optimal?), information (is our information for decision-making relevant, accurate, timely?) or employee satisfaction (are our employees productive; do they represent us well to customers?).

Moreover, each organization's risks change constantly. While reaction is sometimes necessary, detecting and reacting are insufficient ways to manage risk. Every organization must implement effective processes throughout the company so that it proactively identifies, measures and controls business risk.

Effective risk management is a considerable challenge for all businesses, and this challenge is magnified in companies that are undergoing substantial change or transformation, since it is not always possible to apply lessons learned from experience. Indeed, many risks will only become evident after changes have begun. Given the diversity of risks and the difficulties in managing them, it would be useful in the plan to discuss the question of risk in a structured way that all the stakeholders can understand.

The following framework clarifies the various types of risk to which any company is subject. For each of the three categories it should be possible to identify risks relevant to the specific type of business.

Environment risk arises when there are external forces that could either put a company out of business or significantly change the fundamental assumptions that drive its overall objectives and strategies. These forces include the availability of capital, the actions of competitors and regulators, and shifts in commodity or other market prices. Changes in the external environment may present significant threats to a business because they are outside the company's direct control.

Process risk arises when business processes do not achieve what they were designed to achieve. The following are some of the characteristics of poorly performing processes or process risks:

- the process is not effectively aligned with overall business strategies
- the process is ineffective in satisfying customers
- the process does not operate efficiently
- the process is not building wealth
- the process fails to protect significant financial, intellectual and physical assets from unacceptable losses, risk-taking, misappropriation or misuse.

Embedded in process risk is information processing/technology risk, which occurs when the information technology used in a process is not operating as intended or compromises the availability, integrity and security of data, information and other assets.

As with environment risk, constant change has a profound impact on all categories of process risk. The following changes are indicators of potential process risk:

- process re-engineering
- outsourcing
- changes in customer/supplier relationships
- changes in product-line services, revenue categories, etc.
- changes in sales volumes or growth
- changes in organizational structure
- major changes in personnel
- new information systems implementation and/or major enhancements
- new data-processing platforms (hardware) or architectures
- business mergers, acquisitions and reorganizations.

Clearly, a business that is undergoing a turnaround will be subject to many, if not all, of the process risks described above, and plans must be developed that anticipate and control those risks.

Information for decision-making risk arises when information used to support business decisions is incomplete, out of date, inaccurate, late, or simply irrelevant to the decision-making process. Typically, poorly performing businesses have poor information systems and this is a significant risk that must be addressed.

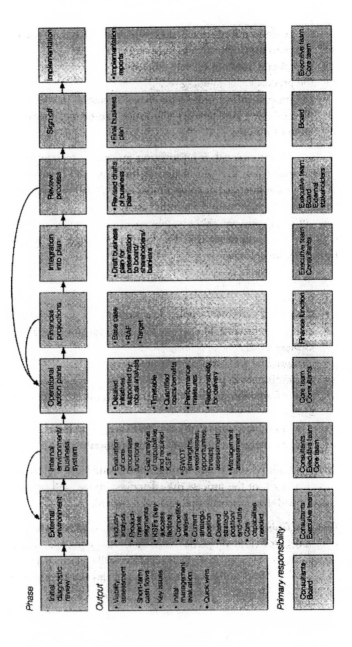

Figure 9.4: **The Business Plan Development Process**

Communication Plan

Finally, the business plan should consider how the executive and core teams are going to roll out the business plan to the rest of the organization. It is vital that the key strategies, the desired end-state and the action plans be explained to middle and junior management as soon as possible, so that the process of implementation can begin. The communication plan might include presentations, a 'road show' to different sites if the business is in multiple locations, workshops, or simply a newsletter that explains the business plan development process and key outcomes. Although it is unrealistic to expect 100 per cent buy-in from the outset, the success of the plan will, in part, depend on the conviction with which it is 'sold' to the organization as a whole.

Summary

This chapter has described one of the key implementation tasks necessary in a turnaround situation – the development of the business plan. The plan contains the generic strategies required to effect the turnaround, as well as the operational action plans necessary to translate the strategies into measurable actions. Figure 9.4 summarizes the process.

Notes

1. G. Hamel and C. K. Prahalad, 'Strategic Intent', *Harvard Business Review*, Vol. 67, No. 3 (May–June 1989).
2. G. Hamel, 'The Core Competence of the Corporation', *Harvard Business Review*, Vol. 68, No. 3 (May–June 1990).

10 Strategic Focus

What Do We Mean by Strategy?

The purpose of this chapter is to explain how we believe strategy should be approached within a turnaround situation. We seek to distinguish the way in which a turnaround leader approaches strategic issues from the approach adopted by a chief executive in a non-crisis situation.

The turnaround leader must approach strategy from an intensely practical perspective, since the strategic issues facing a troubled company are usually straightforward and not overly complex. We stated in Chapter 4 that the difficulty is usually not in the identification of strategic problems nor in the development of solutions to those problems; but in the implementation of the chosen rescue plan. That is not to say that strategy is not important to the turnaround leader. Indeed, we argue very strongly that strategy is one of the cornerstones of a successful turnaround. However, turnaround situations rarely require leading-edge strategic insight, at least in the early phases of the turnaround process.

Consequently we believe that conventional tried-and-tested approaches to strategic management are relevant. Although it may seem somewhat old-fashioned to apply the tools and techniques that were developed by Porter and others in the 1970s and 1980s, our experience is that their practical and relatively simple concepts have very broad application in turnaround situations.[1] We argue strongly in favour of an approach to strategy that is simple, hands-on, and focuses on the critical strategic issues. Some of the more contemporary thinkers address issues that are more relevant for organizations undergoing corporate renewal or seeking global leadership.[2] These ideas have limited relevance for companies that cannot pay next week's wages!

In this chapter we focus on strategy – at both the corporate and business unit levels – as one of the seven essential ingredients of a successful turnaround. Corporate strategy is, of course, only relevant for a diversified organization, and represents an overall plan for such an organization. It addresses the portfolio issue of which businesses the group is in or should be in, and how the portfolio should be managed. Each business unit within the diversified group has its own competitive strategy. The business unit strategy addresses the question of which product-market segments to compete in and how to create competitive advantage in each of them.

Our approach to the definition of a strategy follows the conventional approach developed from classical military thinking. Kenneth Andrews set out one of the earlier but most influential conceptual frameworks for strategy with his introduction to the 'S W O T' (strengths, weaknesses, opportunities and threats).[3] We support his view that strategies should be defined in terms of:

- the range of products or services offered or planned to be offered by the company
- the markets to which the products or services will be offered
- the channels through which these markets will be reached
- a statement of major policies for key functional areas such as marketing, manufacturing and procurement. Today this might be defined in terms of the processes or activities that the company intends to carry out in order to deliver the proposed product range to chosen markets
- high-level financial goals for the organization together with the proposed means of financing them.

We have found that many organizations get extremely confused when trying to articulate a strategy. One source of confusion is nomenclature. Strategies get confused with policies, goals with objectives, programmes with plans, strategic decisions with tactical decisions. For the sake of clarity we follow the simple definitions adopted by James Quinn:[4]

A strategy is the pattern or plan that integrates an organization's major goals, policies and action plan into a cohesive whole. A well-formulated strategy helps to marshal and allocate an organization's resources into a unique and viable posture based on its relative internal competencies and shortcomings, anticipated changes in the environment and contingent moves by intelligent opponents.

Goals or objectives state what is to be achieved and when results are to be accomplished, but they do not state *how* the results are to be achieved. Major goals – those that affect the firm's overall direction, the broad value premises towards which it is striving, and the overall organizational objectives which establish the intended nature of the enterprise – are called *strategic goals*.

Policies are rules or guidelines that express the limits within which action should occur.

Programmes specify the step-by-step sequence of actions necessary to achieve major objectives. They express how objectives will be achieved within the limits set by policy.

Numerous books and articles have been written on the subject of strategy development, and it is not our intention to try to add to that body of work. However, we think it is useful to consider how some of the mainstream tools and techniques are deployed within a turnaround situation.

Strategic Principles for Corporate Turnarounds

Tackle the 'where' and 'how'

It is vitally important for the turnaround manager to articulate clearly the future direction for the company: 'where' the business is going. The vision for the organization must be clearly stated in such a way that it offers hope and inspiration. Troubled companies suffer from poor morale and a history of failure. The employees are looking for a leader who will bring them back from the brink of insolvency into the promised land of profits, growth and success. The turnaround manager's vision becomes a rallying cry for the organization. To make the vision credible and compelling, s/he will also have to spell out *how* it will be achieved. This involves a clear programme of short- and long-term actions and initiatives at both strategic and operational levels.

Sell Into a Need

The way in which an organization's strategy seeks to match its competencies to industry opportunities must always take into consideration both the market demand for the products/services and competitor moves. At the most basic level the organization's products or services must create value (i.e., customer value must exceed cost); and price (which will be determined by the level of competition) must exceed cost.

This simplistic analysis can force companies to consider some very tough questions. Who really wants our products? How much will they pay? Are competitive offers better and cheaper? Why should we exist at all? It is a common mistake for troubled companies to assume they have some sort of divine right to exist. Few companies have that luxury, and the strategy must justify an organization's existence very clearly.

Maximize Strengths

The key to a successful strategy is to exploit one's strengths and minimize one's weaknesses. Competitive advantage can usually be considered in terms of superior skills, superior resources and superior position. Skills encompass the ability of the organization to manage and coordinate its people and processes. Resources include both tangible (physical assets, etc.) and intangible (know-how, patents, brands, customer/supplier relationships, etc.). Position refers to a company's products, markets and competition. It may be based on supplying highly distinctive products, or on capturing a very specific market segment. Irrespective of the source of the organization's strengths, the turnaround leader must find ways of capitalizing on them as a source of differentiation.

Business Focus

Virtually every successful turnaround involves the firm refocusing on selected industries, selected product-market segments or selected activities in the value-added chain. Firms that have little opportunity to refocus themselves usually have little chance of a successful turnaround. Beware of the company that has to grow volume quickly in its existing markets to survive. One aspect of focus important in a turnaround is focusing on fast-response sectors or segments, where new initiatives will have a quick impact on profits and/or cash flow.

Be Radical

'Twiddling the knobs' rarely works in strategy and certainly almost never in a turnaround situation. Experienced turnaround managers know that when they take over from a chief executive who has tried and failed, they have to be more drastic than the previous incumbent. A good example of being radical was the decision by Stuart Wallis when appointed chief executive of Fisons to sell off its research and development laboratories as part of a turnaround strategy − a brave move for an ethical pharmaceuticals company.

Stretch, But Not Too Much

Turnaround situations require radical improvement. Without a quantum leap in performance improvement, it is unlikely that the organization will survive. Stakeholders are unlikely to support a recovery strategy that shows only marginal recovery in the medium term. The risk of investing further money and the hassle of being involved in the recovery process are only acceptable if the rescue offers significant upside potential. Consequently the strategy must stretch the organization. However, it must also be credible in the context of the strengths and weaknesses of the company and the opportunities and threats from within the industry. It must be feasible when viewed against the physical, human and financial resources available.

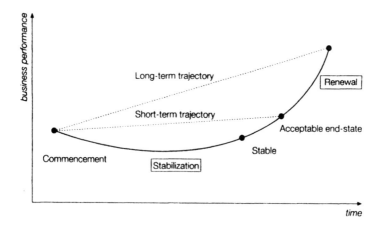

Figure 10.1: **Short- and Long-term Trajectories**

Cash Is King

In the same way that many organizations demand that their constituent businesses must at least generate a return on capital employed (ROCE) that exceeds their cost of capital, positive cash flow becomes the key policy in many turnaround situations, particularly in the early stages. Inevitably there will be trade-offs in favour of cash flow and against profit, but until the funding position is secured an emphasis on cash is critical. This may mean, for example, that within a diversified situation a CEO will be forced to sell the group's most attractive businesses or assets ('the crown jewels') in order to keep the whole organization alive.

Learn to Walk Before Learning to Run

The turnaround manager will often face a conflict between short- and long-term strategic priorities. Short-term priorities may have to take priority over longer-term objectives in order to ensure survival. In the short term (six months to a year), the turnaround manager may have to pursue an emergency stabilization trajectory (see Figure 10.1). This is likely to involve a series of strategic initiatives designed to secure the near-term future. The priority is to achieve stability. This is likely to involve a focus on cost reduction, restructuring, squeezing more out of the business, etc. Very often this can be characterized as 'doing things better' rather than 'doing better things'. It may not be possible to focus on the desired end-state (a profitable, viable, independent business); the company doctor may initially have to aim at a less ambitious target, the acceptable end-state (i.e., merely stable). Having passed the point of stability during the first year or so of the turnaround, the turnaround leader can then move to refocus the business on the desired end-state. This is a substantially more ambitious target and is likely to involve a focus on revenue growth. This phase may involve 'doing better things' rather than 'doing things better'.

Urgency and Action Bias

The danger with any strategic planning exercise is that it becomes an endless exercise that is never implemented. Turnaround leaders do not have that luxury. The exercise must be completed quickly and lead to immediate action.

Focus on Key Strategic Issues

In any business there are only a few key strategic issues. It is important to focus on these fast. Analysis at the corporate level should quickly identify the problem businesses, while analyses at the business-unit level should identify the critical product and customer segments causing poor performance, and those segments which have the potential to generate short-term profitability.

Corporate Strategy

The management writer, Henry Mintzberg discusses generic corporate strategy in terms of either extending the core business or 'reconceiving' the core business.[5] We find both of these strategies present in turnaround situations, although the latter dominates.

Redefining the Core Business(es), and Divestment

One of the first questions to be addressed by a turnaround manager tackling a sick diversified group is, 'What businesses are we in?' and more importantly, 'What businesses should we be in?' One of our key themes throughout this book is the issue of focus. Troubled companies have limited financial and management resources, and these must be directed at the most critical areas. This is particularly the case for a troubled conglomerate, which typically comprises a sprawling mass of unrelated businesses in varying degrees of corporate health.

The key therefore is to rapidly choose the core businesses to focus on, and to divest/exit the remainder as quickly as possible. By focusing on a manageable number of priority businesses, and selling everything else, the turnaround leader frees up cash (and thus reduces debt) and frees up management resource (thus reducing complexity). Two related but distinct generic strategies can be identified: redefinition of the core business(es) and divestment.

Redefining the core business(es) in a turnaround situation usually involves a fundamental change in the future direction of an organization and a radical restructuring as large chunks of the business are sold off. In the case of the turnaround of a diversified organization, it usually involves reducing the cope of activities and focusing on a specific area. One way of achieving this is through industry focus. For example, a diversified industrial conglomerate may refocus, as did British Aerospace between 1992 and 1996 (see box).

British Aerospace

In 1992 British Aerospace stood on the brink of failure. The company was Britain's biggest exporter, the maker of Rover cars and Tornado fighters, and a partner in Airbus. It had a turnover of £10 billion per year, yet it was almost Britain's biggest-ever corporate collapse. Today British Aerospace is one of the strongest aerospace companies in Europe and appears to be leading the consolidation of the European defence industry. This remarkable transformation has required a huge restructuring of BAe's operations. This classic turnaround provides an excellent example of the way in which divestment is used to stop cash outflow and generate cash inflow.

The management team quickly recognized that the longer-term strategy was to focus on the defence business, which was profitable and which the company understood, and to restore the civil aircraft business to profitability. To release cash, everything which was not central to the defence and civil aerospace business was put up for sale. Corporate jets, which needed a heavy investment for a new generation of products, went to Raytheon; Ballast Needham – a Dutch construction company no longer needed for large projects in Saudi Arabia – to a consortium led by ING Bank; the satellite business to Matra Marconi. Arlington Securities (property, business parks, etc.), which could not realistically be sold in the short term, was run to generate cash. Rover was sold for £800 million to BMW in 1994. The final major development was the disposal by way of flotation of BAe's stake in Orange, the cellular phone network, in 1996.

A second route to focus is by breaking up vertically integrated organizations and focusing on fewer businesses within the enterprise system – i.e., the reversal of vertical integration. Many businesses can be positioned within an enterprise system that links upstream industries to downstream industries as follows:

Extraction Processing Fabrication Assembly Wholesale distribution Retail distribution

A diversified group that operates businesses in, for example, the first three stages may be refocused on fabrication by selling all operations in the extraction and processing areas. Lonrho Textiles' decision to get out of retailing and focus on manufacturing is a good example of this strategy (see box). Laura Ashley are doing the opposite by getting out of manufacturing and focusing on retailing.

A third way of achieving focus can be geographical refocusing. Many successful domestic organizations hit trouble when they move overseas, and the solution frequently involves a repositioning of the group away from international operations towards a domestic business.

Whichever way of achieving focus is chosen, the turnaround leader will deploy the two key generic strategies of business redefinition and divestment. In the first instance, s/he will identify the future area of focus for the group, and this will be followed by the rapid divestment of non-core businesses. This approach begs the question, how does the turnaround leader establish which businesses to focus on? In many situations the answer is straightforward, and is based on the very simple expedient of keeping the good businesses and exiting the bad. Speed of analysis is critical, and therefore it is important not to over-complicate matters. Good businesses are profitable and generate positive cash flow; are led by a strong management team; have growth potential; and are based on genuine competitive advantage.

We have found that a 'quick and dirty' portfolio analysis is often a helpful tool because it can distil a relatively complex situation into a single graphic image. The old directional policy matrix, originally developed by General Electric and Shell to address the strategic challenges of managing a diversified group, is still useful in helping sort the good from the bad and the indifferent. Businesses are plotted on a two-dimensional matrix with market attractiveness on one axis and relative competitive advantage on the other. Businesses in an unattractive market without a competitive edge are, prima facie, candidates for divestment (and vice versa). An alternative portfolio matrix, using strategic viability and short-term cash flow, was used in a turnaround analysis of a UK clothing company, Hamlet International (see box).

Lonrho Textiles

In 1995 Lonrho plc appointed a new CEO, Paul Bridges, to their loss-making subsidiary Lonrho Textiles. At the time Lonrho Textiles was a manufacturer and retailer of household textiles (bed linen, etc.) with an £80 million turnover. The company operated a fully integrated manufacturing facility in Newcastle and distributed the majority of finished products through its own retail businesses, Brentfords (a group of eighty high street stores) and Accord (a group of eighty department-store concessions). Turnover was split approximately equally between manufacturing and retail.

Retailers and manufacturers argue convincingly both for and against vertical integration. In this case the benefits of integrating the manufacturing and retailing businesses had been substantially lost over time and had been replaced by substantial disbenefits. The manufacturing arm was failing to deliver flexible supply, short lead times, etc. The retail arm was failing to deliver a reliable high-volume distribution channel. Both sides blamed each other for the operational problems.

Following a rapid strategic analysis of the business, Bridges moved quickly to split the business in two by closing the retail arm and focusing the turnaround on the manufacturing operation. Within three months of his appointment, Bridges had disposed of the majority of the Brentfords stores; the Accord business was subsequently sold and the remainder of the Brentfords shops closed or sold on a piecemeal basis.

The rationale for Bridges' decision was straightforward. The majority of the trading losses were incurred on the retail side; the scale of investment to turn around the manufacturing operations was considerably less than the funding required for a retail turnaround; and there was a ready purchaser for the stores.

Hamlet International

Hamlet International was a struggling group of businesses primarily operating within the clothing sector. The company, which was quoted on the London Stock Exchange and had a turnover of approximately £100 million, ran into serious cash-flow difficulties in the summer of 1997. A firm of turnaround consultants was hired to advise the board on the options for the group. Following their review the consultants presented the following summary matrix (simplified) to management:

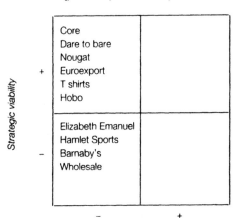

12-month cash flow

The message was pretty bleak. All ten trading businesses were forecast to be cash-absorbing during the next twelve months, and of these only six were considered to be viable in the medium to long term. The consultants were unable to find any evidence to suggest that the remaining four businesses could be restored to profitability. A successful turnaround was not possible, and the company went into receivership.

In a turnaround situation, however, particularly during the early days, the critical constraint is usually cash. The less attractive businesses may not be readily saleable, in which case one of the better businesses may have to be sold. This happened at Stakis Hotels. Stakis had grown fast during the latter part of the 1980s, and diversified into property development, nursing homes and casinos. The turnaround business plan called for keeping the hotels and nursing homes and divesting the casinos. When the turnaround manager tried to implement this plan, he found that he could not sell the casinos but was able to sell the nursing homes.

Growth via Acquisition

Acquisitions are most commonly used to turn around stagnant firms – firms not in a financial crisis but whose financial performance is poor. The benefit of growing by acquisition rather than organically is the faster speed at which turnaround can be achieved. It is a strategy available to few firms in a crisis situation: most lack the financial resources to make an acquisition, although once survival is assured, acquisition may be part of the strategy to achieve sustainable recovery. Westinghouse Electric Corporation (see box) is an interesting example of divestment followed by acquisition.

The acquisition of related businesses permits the organization to acquire firms that complement existing operations. The acquired firm may, for example, permit the acquirer to implement a product-market reorientation. At other times, acquisition may improve the turnaround firm's competitive advantage or reduce its competitive disadvantage by providing, for example, access to new distribution channels or new technology, or the opportunity to gain economies of scale by combining operations.

Diversification via the acquisition of unrelated businesses provides the means for entering product-market areas where the profit and growth opportunities are better for the turnaround firm. Many turnaround firms are in highly competitive or declining industries where

Westinghouse Electric Corporation

Westinghouse provides a good example of the application of both divestment and acquisition as generic turnaround strategies. By the end of 1992 the organization was in serious trouble. The sprawling US conglomerate that traced its roots back to the earliest days of power generation and broadcasting was weighed down by a mountain of debt that had been used to fund an ill-fated expansion of its financial services business.

The immediate priority in 1993 was to refocus the business, liquidate non-core assets and reduce the bank debt. Under a plan drawn up in November 1992, the group planned to exit financial services, DCBU (distribution and control) and WESCO (electricity supply). Financial services comprised $9 billion of assets; management proposed to dispose of the real estate and corporate finance assets over a three-year period, and continue the lease book until 2015. DCBU was sold for $1.1 billion in January 1994 and WESCO for $340 million in February 1994.

Plans for the second phase of major divestments were drawn up in 1995, resulting in the subsequent sale in 1995 and 1996 of WCI Communications, Knoll (office furniture) and the defence business for approximately $4.5 billion. This second phase of disposals was accompanied by a strategy to aggressively grow the media business via acquisition. The success of the first-phase disposals had rebuilt balance sheet strength, and the more focused group was able to borrow extensively to fund the $5.4 billion acquisition of the CBS TV and media business in August 1995. A further $1.5 billion acquisition of two major networks, The Nashville Network and Country Music Television, followed in February 1997.

At the time of writing the turnaround is continuing. Management have recently announced their intention to split the group into two separate businesses. The power business is to be named Westinghouse Electric Corporation, and the media business CBS Corporation. Thermo King, the refrigerated distribution business, will be initially retained by CBS with a view to disposing of it soon after the separation.

the long-term choice for management is either survival by diversification or allowing the firm to die. There have been a number of studies to show that diversification as a business strategy does not pay off for the shareholders and that the financial benefits accruing at acquisition go to the vendor shareholders not to the acquirer. None of these studies, however, has looked explicitly at turnaround firms, and intuitively it seems reasonable that the results might be different for such firms.

Michael Porter argued that three conditions must be satisfied if diversification is to create shareholder value:

The attractiveness test: the business to be acquired must be in a structurally attractive industry.

The cost-of-entry test: the cost of entry must not capitalize all future profits.

The better-off test: the new unit must gain competitive advantage from its link with the corporation, or vice versa.[6]

Perhaps because of the difficulty of passing these tests, it is rare in our experience for a turnaround situation to involve diversification.

The dangers of growth by acquisition are essentially the same for turnaround firms as for healthy firms making acquisitions: the acquisition price is too high, post-acquisition management is poor, the acquired firm's financial or market position is weaker than anticipated, etc. The danger of making a single, poor acquisition, however, is usually greater for a turnaround firm, where gearing is usually high and the financial resources available in an emergency rather thin. On the other hand, the danger of poor post-acquisition management may be reduced by management's familiarity with the turnaround process. But the opposite may also happen. If management has once been successful in pulling a firm out of a crisis by introducing tight management control, cost and asset reduction strategies, etc., it may take on a false sense of belief in its own abilities to turn around acquired firms.

Too Little Too Late

Before leaving the issue of corporate strategy within a turnaround context it is worth considering the case of Sears plc. Sears offers an interesting example of a management team who attempted a major strategic repositioning of a sprawling diversified retail group, but who ultimately failed because their restructuring was 'too little and too late'.

Sears is a company that was initially built up by Britain's first takeover king, Sir Charles Clore, during the 1950s and 1960s. At its peak it operated almost 4,000 outlets, owned businesses as diverse as jeweller Mappin & Webb and bookmaker William Hill, and made more sales than department stores Marks & Spencer and Woolworth's combined. But by the autumn of 1998 Sears had a market capitalization of £230 million, whereas Marks & Spencer's was £12.4 billion.

The group was in serious trouble in 1991. Turnover was flat, at about £1.8 billion, and the loss for the year was £70 million, compared to a prior-year profit of £12 million. The board was forced to reduce the dividend by 35 per cent and bring in a new CEO, Liam Strong.

The situation that confronted Strong was a mess. The group's activities spanned retail businesses covering footwear, childrenswear, womens-wear, menswear and sport/leisurewear, operating from more than 2,000 shops in the UK. Other activities included a home shopping business (catalogue/mail order), an upmarket department store (Selfridges), Asprey's the jeweller, a housebuilder and a European retail joint venture. The group had multiple brands and trading names and employed 44,000 people.

Strong's strategy was to focus on achieving leadership in specific market segments within the mass-market clothing and footwear retail sectors by offering distinctive merchandise, excellent value and out-standing service, and by building exemplary operating practices.

The initial phase of the turnaround appeared to be successful. Within the first year, the menswear business and the housebuilder were sold and a provision of £30 million was taken for the proposed restructuring of British Shoe Corporation, the group's footwear retail division.

The following year saw the sale of Asprey's, closure of the Dutch mail-order business and the expansion of the new shoe retail format, Shoe Express. Financial performance appeared to be improving and trading profits were reported as up by 75 per cent. The positive developments appeared to continue in 1994 as the group exited its joint-venture business in Germany, took full control of its (joint-venture) footwear retailing business in the Netherlands, rolled out a new retail concept for kidswear, and sold part of its sport/leisurewear business. Trading profits were reported as 23 per cent up on the prior year.

However, by 1995 the business went into decline again as the group reported a loss after tax of £107 million, and a decline in cash and cash equivalents of £195 million. At the time Strong admitted that in three key areas the turnaround initiatives had not been pursued far enough or fast enough. The core problems were a proliferation of brands (despite recent disposals, Sears still had twenty-four trading names at the start of 1995), continuing problems at British Shoe Corporation, and a lack of progress in achieving group-wide operational efficiencies.

Strong reacted by pursuing a policy of continuing divestments with the sale of the sports and leisurewear retailing business, the partial disposal of the footwear business to Facia, and the sale of the Dutch footwear business. The corporate strategy remained broadly unchanged: focus on achieving leadership within a limited number of retail sectors in the clothing and footwear mass market. The slimmed-down footwear division would concentrate on four key brands and the clothing business on five principal trading facias.

Selfridges, the department store business, would continue to be grown aggressively and the home-shopping business (a distant number three in its market) would be managed for cash until it could be sold. In order to achieve a quantum leap in operational efficiency, Sears signed a major ten-year outsourcing agreement covering accounting, information technology and logistics.

By early 1997 Strong was under intense pressure. The share price had continued to under-perform the market substantially. Two attempts to sell Freemans, the home-shopping business, had failed. Facia, the purchaser of a major part of the shoe business, collapsed into receivership with the result that the leasehold interests in the shops reverted to Sears.

The City was also getting increasingly nervous about the lack of progress being made in the core footwear operations.

In April 1997 Strong stepped down from the board. For the preceding five years he had been attempting to lead Sears through a major turnaround. At the time of his departure he said that although he had been successful in strengthening the clothing business and substantially improving Selfridges, he had failed to sort out the serious problems in the footwear business and failed to conclude a sale of the home-shopping business.

Since his departure a sale of Freemans has been conditionally agreed, a new CEO/company doctor (David James) brought into British Shoe Corporation, and the proposed demerger of Selfridges announced. Following a strategic review, David James has announced that the footwear business will be put up for sale forthwith, with any unsaleable part being closed down. Following the restructuring, the remaining business will comprise a leading clothing business focused on five strong brands within the childrenswear and womenswear mass markets.

With the benefit of hindsight, we can draw a number of valuable lessons. It is clear that the initial turnaround effort failed to address the very serious problems within the footwear business. Management's initial plan for the footwear business did not appear flawed at the time; perhaps the problem was underestimating the scale of the task ahead. We might also speculate that the plan for the footwear business might have worked if it had been pursued to the exclusion of everything else. It is at least arguable that an alternative route for Sears in 1991/2 would have been to focus exclusively on either footwear or clothing and divest everything else much more rapidly.

Competitive or Business-unit Strategy

The fundamental strategic principles that we set out at the beginning of this chapter also apply at the business-unit level. In turnaround situations successful strategies are based on a mixture of intuition and analysis. The emphasis must be on speed of analysis and a rapid move towards implementation. Generally, it is better to get to 80 per cent of the answer within a month than spend six months getting 100 per cent of the answer. This approach necessitates simplicity and a focus on the key issues.

The critical issue in evaluating any firm's competitive strategy is to ensure that the firm can make money in its chosen areas of business focus. The starting point is to define which products or services the firm is selling to whom and in what part(s) of the value-added chain the firm is competing. This is not as easy as it sounds, because breaking a business down to its component segments and activities requires careful segmentation analysis. The aim is to determine whether the firm's current product-market segments and activities are the correct ones, given the firm's resources and the characteristics of the external environment in which it operates.

Detailed profitability analysis (including allocation of overheads) by product and customer segments is necessary. This internal analysis has then to be put together with the external industry analysis to identify viable product-market options. The criteria for choosing product-markets are segment attractiveness (based on industry analysis), the extent to which the firm has a competitive advantage or disadvantage, and the extent to which it is capable of implementing its chosen strategy. The reader is referred to the classic textbooks on competitive strategy for more details.[7]

Product-market Refocusing

Where one of the major causes of a firm's decline is lack of competitiveness in one or more of its product-market segments, it is imperative that the firm refocus its overall product-market strategy if sustainable recovery is to take place. Refocusing may also be necessary where the cause of decline is rapid growth. When profits decline as sales continue to grow, there is usually a need to refocus the firm's product-market strategy, since much of the marginal business the firm has obtained is unlikely to be profitable. Refocusing may involve any or all of the following:

- addition or deletion of product lines
- addition or deletion of customers (by customer type and/or geographical area)
- changes in the sales mix by focusing marketing efforts on specific products and/or specific customers
- complete withdrawal from a market segment
- entry into a new product-market segment.

In the short term the firm's choice of business focus is constrained by its history and lack of financial resources. Where survival is a key issue, the short-term horizon means that product-market decisions are often of a surgical nature. The firm pulls out of complete business areas – either by closure or divestment – and cuts out product lines and/or customers that are unprofitable or where the return on capital employed is too low. The emphasis is on cutting back the business to its profitable core. This is easy where the core is strong and only the firm's peripheral activities are weak. It is more difficult to achieve where the core itself is non-viable, in which case the chances of a successful turnaround are slim and the firm is likely to fail eventually.

Slightly less drastic are strategies that involve a shift in the sales mix by concentrating marketing efforts and manufacturing or operating priorities on selected products or customer groups where the short-term profit potential is greatest. This does not necessarily mean focusing on those products or customers that show the highest percentage gross-profit margin, since higher profit margin items might have long lead times between the time marketing effort is increased and the product or service is finally delivered. Criteria for selecting specific products chosen for emphasis include:

Sales volume: generally, bigger-selling products are more attractive due to the greater opportunity they provide for leverage.

Growth rate: declining products are generally unattractive as their competitive position is usually weak – although this is not always so, and a declining product with strong brand loyalty can often be milked for cash.

Gross margin or contribution: products with a higher gross margin are more attractive, all other things being equal.

Speed of buyer response: consumer goods are usually more susceptible to a rapid sales increase through increased marketing effort than are industrial goods.

Seasonality: this demonstrates at what time of the year certain products can be emphasized.

Length of manufacturing cycle: the shorter the cycle, the quicker sales action translates into profit and cash flow.

The criteria are *not* mutually exclusive, and trade-offs may have to be made – e.g., products sold primarily for consumer use may have to be emphasized over industrial-use products, in spite of their having a lower gross margin, due to the consumers' faster response to marketing effort.

Selecting customers is much the same process, and many of the same criteria apply. The key difference with customers, however, is the need to determine customer profitability – something which is usually missing in most management accounting systems and almost never found in a turnaround situation. The need arises because the firm's largest customers are not necessarily the most profitable. The objective of customer profitability analysis is to determine the contribution provided by each customer after deducting the overhead costs (usually technical and marketing costs) associated with that customer (e.g., distribution costs, selling, after-sales and servicing costs) and interest charges on the working capital tied up in debtors and inventories for that customer. Ideally, customer profitability analysis is undertaken on a customer-by-customer basis. If there are few customers, this may be possible, but where there are many this will not be possible until the firm's information systems have been improved, and even then it may be impractical. More commonly, the firm's customers are segmented into groups, based on the nature of their business, size or location. The danger of grouping customers together is that the resulting 'contribution before unallocated overheads' is an average marginal contribution figure and may hide unprofitable accounts. Such an analysis involves a number of assumptions with regard to allocating overheads and the appropriate grouping of customers; but whatever assumptions are used (and several alternatives should be used, particularly in regard to customer segmentation), startling results may emerge.

The reader should now be able to appreciate that it is not always wise to focus on the largest customer; and how important it is to have reliable information on which to base decisions. If volume is required, and the large customers are profitable, the greatest profit leverage is obtained by concentrating on those customers – but this is not always the case. Many companies have failed because of inadequate analysis and understanding as to where profits and losses are being made. In the emergency phase of recovery, accurate information is unfortunately not always available for undertaking anything but an extremely crude customer or customer-segment profitability analysis.

Having chosen the products and customers on which to concentrate short-term marketing efforts, the company must then shift its marketing resources to these customers. The primary means of implementing this is by targeting selling and promotional efforts, topics which are covered in Chapter 12.

In his book *Competitive Strategy*, Michael Porter identified three generic strategies which can be used successfully to protect a firm against the forces that drive competition in an industry: cost leadership, differentiation and focus.[8] The latter involves the firm in selecting a narrow product-market segment in which it competes on the basis of cost leadership and/or product differentiation. It involves focusing the firm's limited resources on one or a few product-market segments. This is usually the only strategy that is available to the turnaround firm in the short term, since it is unlikely to have the large financial resources required for industry leadership based on either cost or product differentiation factors. If the turnaround firm is in an industry where a cost leadership strategy is the only one open to it (due to the commodity nature of the product), then the situation is usually not recoverable. Where strategies based primarily on product differentiation are possible, the adoption of a more aggressive marketing strategy may help the turnaround firm improve its short-term market position, providing the product is not obsolete and aggressive selling rather than aggressive advertising is the key factor for industry success. If a considerable amount of new product development is required or large amounts of advertising money are required, a product differentiation strategy is possible only *after* survival has been assured.

Where the diagnostic review shows that the firm cannot be made more profitable at current or lower sales volumes by a combination of focusing and cost reduction strategies, turnaround is only possible via sales growth. This may be possible if the company's problems are operational in nature and only require some relatively easy improvements to critical processes (e.g., the hiring of new salesmen). However, the turnaround firm is usually no better than a 'me too' player in a mature and unattractive market, in which case sales growth has to come from increased market share. Increasing market share usually requires a significant competitive advantage, which is usually missing in a turnaround company; on top of which it is also likely to require investment in additional revenue costs and working capital. Not surprisingly, most such strategies fail.

The adoption of a focused strategy may of itself lead to a sustainable recovery, particularly if the chosen product-market segment is too small to be of interest to the industry leaders, or if the turnaround firm is better able to service customers' needs because the industry leaders are too diversified, too large or too bureaucratic. At other times, a focused strategy will provide the turnaround firm with 'breathing space' at a time when it lacks competitive advantage vis-à-vis the industry leaders.

There are two dangers, however, in adopting a focused strategy. First, it may cause the firm's unit cost structure to deteriorate as volume – and hence economies of scale – are reduced. Both variable and fixed unit costs may increase. For example, variable costs may increase as purchasing power declines, and unit overhead costs may increase as fixed costs fail to decline in proportion to the reduction in sales volume. Second, the firm may find that a focused strategy is not a defensible strategy in the long term. This is often the case in those situations where focusing means adopting a segment-retreat strategy: a strategy under which the firm pulls out of the high-volume, price-sensitive segments of the market and concentrates on the least price-sensitive segments, where having lower unit costs than one's competitors is not so critical for success. The history of the British motorcycle industry in the 1960s and 1970s provides a classic example.

As Japanese competitors – Honda, Yamaha and Kawasaki – attacked the high-volume, price-sensitive, small-bike segment of the motorcycle market in the 1960s, British manufacturers phased out that segment and concentrated on bikes with larger engine capacities. The Japanese, however, then attacked the 250–500 c.c. segments, causing the less efficient and less marketing-oriented UK manufacturers to retreat to the large bike (over 500 c.c.) segment only. By the mid 1970s, the British were left as competitors only in the superbike segment (over 750 c.c.), but that area proved indefensible. The Japanese were by now many times the size of their UK competitors and over the years had been working hard to build up product differentiation advantages in the form of good brandnames, superior quality and good distribution networks. A similar story has occurred in many other industries.

Clearly, the adoption of a focused strategy will not guarantee recovery. The viability of a focused strategy depends on the characteristics of the industry and the firm, and it may provide nothing more than a breathing space while the firm works on developing a growth strategy aimed at sustainable recovery. Some firms adopt a focused strategy and fail because their strategy implementation is too slow. By the time they have actually focused their resources, any competitive advantage they might formerly have had in the segment they are focusing on has been eroded, or their resources have been so depleted that focusing means that no additional resources are available for implementing the focused strategy.

The choice of products and customers made in the emergency phase of recovery may not be appropriate for the subsequent growth phase, at which time a more fundamental shift in the firm's product-market strategy may be appropriate. Growth-oriented strategies are only possible once survival is assured, or in turnarounds of stagnant firms where there is no financial crisis. The time horizon required to implement growth strategies is usually considerably longer than that required to drop products and customers. The major growth strategies which involve a change in product-market focus are new product-development strategies (introducing new products to the firm's existing customer base), market-development strategies (introducing existing products to new customers) and diversifications (entering totally new areas of business). These strategies rarely work in a crisis situation. They divert management's attention from the problem at hand and often result in considerable investment in fixed assets, working capital and revenue expenditure (e.g., in marketing and research and development). The German underwear manufacturer Bruno Banani is a successful example of such a strategy (see box).

Bruno Banani

At the end of the 1980s, the small town of Mittelbach in Saxony could claim to be an essential part of communist Europe. In a modest red-brick local factory, VEB Trikotex manufactured much of the underwear worn in the Eastern bloc.

Mittelbach still turns out underwear, but under a different guise. The factory that once housed VEB Trikotex is now the headquarters of Bruno Banani, one of Germany's leading makers of designer underwear. It represents an instructive as well as a successful example of a company turnaround in the former East Germany.

Mittelbach once made standard bras by the million for the Soviet Union's mass market. Now it makes 'active wear' bodies – sold under the motto 'Not For Everybody' – for the designer boutiques of western Germany's wealthier cities.

Bruno Banani was formed after privatization by Mr Wolfgang Jassner, CEO and majority owner. Mr Jassner came to Mittelbach shortly after the fall of communism as a consultant, to advise Trikotex on how to adapt to capitalism. At the time, the Treuhand privatization agency was unsure what to do with the company, which once employed 2,500. Like many East German companies, Trikotex had skilled workers, but its machinery was outdated and the company found it difficult to compete with more sophisticated Western competitors. Trikotex had won a few contracts to supply west German companies, but knew there was little future in being a piece-work operator in a mass market.

Mr Jungnickel (Trikotex's business manager and now managing direc-tor of Bruno Banani) says, 'We were very ambitious and were determined continually to raise the quality of our output.' He was interested in establishing Trikotex as a brand, but lacked the knowledge of how to go about doing so. The arrival of Mr Jassner, who has a background in marketing, was highly fortuitous. In the first three years, DM 4 million was invested in the company. Much of this went into new machinery, but there was also heavy expenditure on marketing. An advertising agency was called in to advise on giving the company a new image – starting with a new name. Freelance designers, mostly in west Germany, were commissioned to design new ranges with an emphasis on the body-hugging and sporty. Every forty-five days a new range is launched to sit alongside the basic lines. Both are backed up by slick promotional material. Mr Jungnickel says the heavy emphasis on image is necessary to distinguish the product: 'In the end, all we are talking about is a pair of underpants.'

On the distribution side, the company has concentrated on upmarket outlets in good locations. It is there, says Mr Jassner, that the ideal customer – sporty, image- and quality-conscious – can be found. Most of Bruno Banani's 700 stockists are in west Germany, though recently the company has started to export as well. Products are priced to be at the lower end of the designer underwear market.

Outsourcing

In the context of business-unit strategy, we mean the outsourcing of one or more business processes. Deciding whether or not to perform a specific major activity is fundamentally a strategic issue, and we have therefore covered outsourcing in this chapter. Outsourcing is one way for an organization to achieve a quantum leap in performance improvement, and it therefore has wide application within the turn-around environment.

Activities are outsourced to achieve an improvement in cost, quality or time. The activities that can be outsourced are either core or support. Traditionally, outsourcing has been applied to non-core support processes with a heavy emphasis on management information systems (MIS). Increasingly, however, it is being applied to core functions and processes. The starting point for analysis is a detailed cost analysis of the activities that make up the value chain to identify where the firm does and does not add value.

Consider, for example, the hypothetical case of an under-performing company manufacturing and distributing branded jeanswear. We might simplistically illustrate the primary activities of the business as follows:

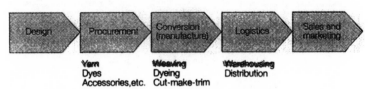

Yarn
Dyes
Accessories,etc.

Weaving
Dyeing
Cut-make-trim

Warehousing
Distribution

The company has its own in-house design team, which designs a new range twice a year. Key inputs into the manufacturing process are yarn, dyes, fasteners and buttons. The manufacture involves the weaving and dyeing of the denim cloth, which is then cut and sewn to form the finished product. The company manages its own warehousing for both new materials and finished goods, and runs its own truck fleet distributing products to a wide range of retailers. The primary tasks for sales and marketing are brand management, advertising and promotions.

Analysis reveals fundamental problems in design, conversion and logistic functions. The design group is 'fixed', lacks inspiration, and rehashes old ideas. The conversion operations are not cost competitive with imported finished products, and the logistics function is unable to provide the retailers with the flexibility and quality of service they require.

In the short term the CEO may be able to make some progress by focusing on design and logistics. It may be relatively straightforward to hire a design boutique to provide additional product design and range-planning support to the existing in-house design team. Equally, there are a wide range of logistics companies that will take over the warehousing and distribution activities. It may be possible to move gradually towards outsourced production by initially buying in low-end product and focusing in-house manufacturing on more expensive, higher-quality items.

The longer-term solution may be the radical restructuring of the entire business, involving a transformation from a manufacturer and supplier of jeanswear to a brand holder. The business would exit from design, procurement, conversion and logistics and focus entirely on sales and marketing. This may seem extreme, and in practice it may not be achievable, but there are many successful leisurewear companies that are little more than brand holders; they focus on a single functional area and outsource everything else.

Notes

1. See, for example, M. Porter, *Competitive Strategy* (Free Press, New York, 1980).

2. See, for example, G. Hamel, *Competing for the Future* (Free Press, New York, 1994).

3. K. R. Andrews, *The Concept of Corporate Strategy* (Dow Jones – Irwin, New York, 1971).

4. J. B. Quinn, *The Strategy Process*, second edition (Prentice Hall, New Jersey, 1993).

5. H. Mintzberg, *Strategy Process: Concepts and Contexts* (Prentice Hall, New Jersey, 1992).

6. M. Porter, 'From Competitive Advantage to Corporate Strategy', *Harvard Business Review*, Vol. 65, No. 3 (May–June, 1987).

7. See, for example, G. S. Day, *Market Driven Strategy* (Free Press, New York, 1991), and R. Grant, *Contemporary Strategy Analysis*, second edition (Basil Blackwell, Oxford, 1995).

8. See Note 1, above.

11 Organizational Change

Nearly all successful corporate turnarounds involve significant organizational change – change to organizational structure, people, processes and systems – brought about by the strong leadership of the top management team. The best thought-out turnaround plan will never succeed unless appropriate organizational changes are made to allow effective implementation of the plan. The starting point for organizational change is the appointment of a suitable turnaround manager and team as discussed in the previous chapter. There are four components of organizational change that the turnaround manager needs to consider:

- organizational structure
- people
- building capabilities
- terms and conditions of employment.

The combined effect of strong leadership and changes in the four components of organizational change will bring about a new organizational culture: in the short term, a change in behaviour, and in the longer term a change in corporate values.[1] We believe that a changed organizational culture is the end-product of organizational change, not the starting point.

The Organizational Structure

Organizational change should not be contemplated as a short-term turnaround strategy except under special conditions. It is often said that organizational change is riskier than strategic change, and this is never so true as in a turnaround situation, where it can direct attention away from the economic problems facing the business. The reasons for this are:

A new product-market strategy comes first: The appropriate organizational structure for a firm is determined at least in part by the firm's product-market strategy. Until such a strategy has been formulated, major organizational change is usually premature, even though analysis of the firm may indicate the existence of organizational problems such as lack of coordination, poor communications, or too wide a span of control. Organizational problems are often *symptoms* of strategic problems, with the result that reorganization has little or no effect on the firm's performance except to cause confusion and mask the real problems facing the firm. We often refer to organizational change as the 'aspirin effect': it attacks the symptoms and not the causes.

It requires in-depth understanding: A new chief executive knows neither the strengths and weaknesses of the individuals in the firm nor how the informal organization structure works in the early days of a turnaround. It is totally inappropriate to design an organization based solely on what arrangement of boxes would, in theory, optimize coordination, communication and motivation. One cannot draw boxes and put people in them; one needs to balance the need for a logical structure against the personal and professional characteristics of the available management. Furthermore, one needs to know how the organization actually works in practice. Formal reporting relationships often bear no relation to reality, and it is more important to understand who lunches with whom, or who plays golf with whom, if one wants to understand how decisions are actually made. The new turnaround manager, however perceptive, cannot have the in-depth understanding needed to make the correct decisions within days or even weeks of his/her arrival.

It requires considerable time and effort: Changing the organization is not merely a question of drawing up a new organization chart, writing new job descriptions where appropriate, and informing everyone of the changes. If this is all that is done, it is quite likely that the organization will either be totally confused or will continue to operate in exactly the same way it did before the changes were announced. Organizational change requires a considerable amount of learning on the part of the firm. This takes considerable management time and effort, something which is likely to be scarce in the early stages of a turnaround.

There are however two situations when it may be useful for the turnaround manager and his/her team to change the organizational structure in the early days of the turnaround:

- to help gain management control
- to support cost and asset reduction strategies.

These two exceptions to the rule of minimizing organizational change in the early days of a turnaround involve structural changes only at the highest management levels. None of these exceptions involves changing the organization at middle-management levels and below. At a later stage, when the turnaround is under way, more fundamental changes to the organizational structure can and should be contemplated – particularly those that will lead to increased operational efficiency through decentralized decision-making.

Gaining Management Control

It is crucial – as we saw in Chapter 5 – that the turnaround manager gains management control over the business as soon as possible. S/he needs to gather information quickly about how the firm operates and to ensure an adequate system of controls is in place which will allow the turnaround manager to influence results.

One common organizational change that may take place almost as soon as a new turnaround manager is appointed is a *widening* of the span of management control at the top of the firm. Whether this occurs depends on the management style of the turnaround manager, but if s/he exhibits the typical characteristics discussed in the previous chapter, s/he will want to operate in a power culture and gain management control rapidly. In large, divisionalized companies where there are main board directors acting as divisional heads (to whom a number of managing directors or chief executives of operating companies report), it is quite common to see a turnaround manager bypass the divisional chairman. S/he does this either by formally changing the role of the divisional head so that the chairman is now 'part of head office', or by making it clear by his/her actions that s/he is going to manage the operating company heads directly. In both cases the structure stays in place but now operates in a different way than it did before. Whenever this approach is used it is quite common for some of the divisional heads to quit or lose their jobs in the ensuing months. If, however, the turnaround manager removed the divisional heads immediately, s/he would be faced with the short-term management problems described in the previous chapter.

A second type of structural change is that found in situations where the new team find it necessary to sideline but not remove senior executives. Organizational changes of this type are often found to be necessary when the turnaround firm is owner-managed or family-dominated, or where some manager has been running part of the firm as a private fiefdom. In these situations it may be impossible for the banks or minority shareholders to force out the chief executive or a particular family member completely. In fact, it may even be part of the negotiations with the bank (or whoever else is triggering the turnaround mechanism) that a turnaround manager will only be allowed in on the condition that Mr X remains in his job. Another situation in which a particular director – whom we will refer to as Henry – could not be fired was in the turnaround of a photographic equipment company, where Henry was the agency director who had close personal contacts with the overseas principals. The turnaround was an acquisition situation and all the agency agreements had become voidable, with the obvious danger that Henry, if fired, might be able to persuade the principals to sign new agency agreements with him personally or help them to set up their own UK distribution company. Although Henry was totally uncooperative with the turnaround team, the turnaround manager thought it was unwise to fire him; instead, he was removed from day-to-day operations such as purchasing and pricing, and given a staff position as Director of Agency Relations! The solution adopted in most situations is to push the former management 'upstairs' or 'sideways' so that the turnaround manager can take over effective day-to-day management of the firm, division or department.

The need for structural change to gain management control is, as might be expected, more common in large firms. At the top, the changes might be quite fundamental and have a big impact on the role and responsibilities of existing senior management. The appropriate type of organizational change requires careful analysis of the issues but we have found three types of change particularly common in turnaround situations – decentralization through divisionalization; centralization of key functions, and the development of a superstructure on top of the existing structure.

Many successful turnarounds are characterized by decentralization of decision-making to the general managers of operating units, while at the same time maintaining strong central financial control. Decentralization may occur without any change in the organization structure, but divisionalization may have to precede or accompany decentralization if the organizational structure of the firm is highly centralized to begin with (which, we say in Chapter 2, is a common characteristic of declining firms). Divisionalization (or breaking up the firm into operating units, each under the profit-and-loss responsibility of a general manager) is usually both necessary and possible in anything but a very small firm with only a few hundred employees. Most firms that have grown beyond the entrepreneurial stage are somewhat diversified and present opportunities for divisionalization. The optimum size for an operating unit will depend in part on the industry (the minimum efficient plant size, for example); but an increasing number of professional managers have come to believe that an operation with more than about 400 people is unwieldy from an organizational point of view. At that point or thereabouts, the chief executive loses touch with the workforce.

Divisionalization and/or the establishment of clear profit centres, is particularly appropriate in turnaround situations where one so often finds confused organizational structures and a lack of clearly defined accountabilities and responsibilities.

At the same time as establishing decentralized profit-and-loss responsibilities, certain parts of the organization structure may be centralized to give more power to the turnaround manager. This is particularly true where the distressed company already operates a highly decentralized structure without adequate control systems in place. Such organizations are often almost anarchic, and run as a series of near-autonomous fiefdoms. All the information the turnaround management team needs to evaluate the business is deep in the bowels of the organization, and structural change may help to extract it. In these situations, centralization usually means establishing a more functional structure at the centre. So for example, instead of each operating unit having its own functional directors responsible to the operating company, some or all of these functions are now managed from the centre (at least in the short term).

Finally, but perhaps less common, is the imposition of a superstructure on top of an existing organizational structure. We sometimes find this situation where a big group acquires an under-performing business, or in a management buy-in (MBI) situation. A new top management team is 'parachuted' in to sit on top of the existing management structure. This rarely lasts for long – but just long enough for the new team to assess the business before firing most of the incumbent management team.

Supporting Cost- and Asset-reduction strategies

Changing the firm's organizational structure often occurs as part of a cost- or asset-reduction strategy. Pyramid organizational structures are still characteristic of under-performing companies, and the immediate removal of one or more layers of management can save overhead costs at the same time as shortening lines of communication within the firm. When the UK food and drinks group Diageo bought Burger King as part of its acquisition of Pillsbury in the USA, they found seventeen layers of management in Burger King! By removing unnecessary layers of management in an organization, top management is also more likely to receive accurate information about the state of the business.

A key part of most cost-reduction strategies in larger organizations is a reduction in the size of head-office staff. The role of corporate head offices is now much better understood than it was even ten years ago. It is very rare to find head-office functions creating value for shareholders in a turnaround situation. Most likely they are destroying it. Staff functions such as personnel, training, corporate marketing, strategic planning and public relations are just a few of the non-productive head-office functions that are commonly cut back or eliminated altogether as part of a recovery strategy. In the large firm these functions are often second-guessing divisional management and rarely, if ever, assisting them to make better decisions. The head-office specialists are rarely cost-effective and are not needed if competent management is hired to run the divisional business units. Most of the work undertaken at head office is better carried out at the divisional level. It is no accident that the most successful diversified firms operate with very small numbers of people at head office. The only head-office function of any size in a turnaround situation should be finance – which would consist of a treasury function, dealing with the firm's financial requirements (managing cash and dealing with the banks), and a financial control function, responsible for monitoring the business units and consolidating group financial results.

Less common but not unimportant is the use of organizational change to facilitate the divestment of part of the business. It is generally easier to sell what appears to be a division or a stand-alone operating unit than a product line or part of an existing division or operating unit.

Decentralization to Improve Operational Efficiency

Most turnaround situations need to improve their operational efficiency in terms of lowering costs and improving customer service. While some early wins may be possible, a real turnaround in performance often requires deep-rooted changes to the way the organization operates. More often than not, decentralization by a group chief executive in a turnaround situation stops at the next level down in the hierarchy. Most firms, however, have only been successful in improving productivity by flattening their organizational structure at middle- and lower-management levels and by giving more real responsibility to their supervisory and first-line management personnel. The result is greater job satisfaction for first-line management, more efficiency on the production line, better customer service, and fewer layers of middle management. Information flows are improved both up and down the organization because lines of communication are shorter. For decentralization of this nature to work effectively, management must adopt a policy of frequent and open communication with the workforce and must also invest heavily in training, both of which are discussed later in this chapter.

British Airways provides a classic example of how this was accomplished in a service business in the 1980s, and Rolls-Royce Motors provides a good example of improved productivity through decentralization in the 1990s.

The People

At the same time as the turnaround manager and his/her team are determining the appropriate turnaround strategy, they need to evaluate the firm's senior and middle management because it is this group who will be required to implement the turnaround strategy. It is vital that both the capabilities and attitudes of the management are assessed, since one without the other is no good. Too often in a turnaround situation, we encounter managers who, if given the right direction and control from top management, are capable of doing a competent job, but their attitudes to change are such that they resist and block all or part of what top management tries to do. These are often bright, intelligent people who can understand why the business needs to change but cannot bring themselves emotionally to go along with the necessary actions. At the other end of the spectrum we find managers willing to change but who just do not have the capability required to come up with solutions and implement them. It is often not their fault: they have been over-promoted by previous top management.

The big question for the turnaround team is which (if any) managers should be changed and how soon. There are two major schools of thought which reflect the different styles of turnaround managers. On the one hand is the tougher school which says 'if in doubt have them out', and involves significant personnel changes; while on the other hand is the view that 'you have to make do with what you've got'. There is a spectrum in between.

Assessing the People

The experienced turnaround manager is often asked how s/he assesses management. The reply is usually fairly short and simple. A well known company doctor recently told a class taught by one of the authors at the London Business School that it takes him about two minutes to decide: 'I look them in the eyes and decide if I can work with them.' This may sound somewhat superficial, but in reality many senior managers in business operate on gut feeling or instinct when making decisions about people.

Other managers take a slightly more objective approach and rely on one or more of the following four methods of assessment:

Interviewing and observing: the turnaround manager and/or his/her team may conduct formal one-to-one interviews with managers, but are more likely to build up a picture of an individual's capabilities and attitudes from a series of meetings. These meetings may be one-to-one discussions, subsidiary board meetings, departmental meetings, presentations to top management or even social occasions. In the early days of the turnaround process, every existing manager is being constantly assessed. The kind of questions that will be going through the minds of the turnaround team are:

- does the individual have their business/function/department under control?
- do they know what is happening in the area for which they are responsible?
- do they understand the critical issues facing them and do they have any sense of urgency or priorities?
- do they know their customers and competitors?

- are they negative about change?
- do they have realistic solutions to their problems?
- how is the individual perceived by his/her peers, superiors and subordinates?

The list can go on and on. The assessment process is primarily one of questioning and listening; but observing the individual's behaviour is also part of it. How does the individual respond when challenged? How does s/he contribute in a meeting? What are his/her presentational skills like? How does s/he deal with subordinates? What about body language? And so on.

Look at results: If a manager is delivering consistently good results in the part of the organization for which s/he is responsible, prima facie the manager is competent. Providing the manager is outwardly cooperative with the turnaround team, s/he is probably judged satisfactory or better. Similarly if a manager is given a task to do by the turnaround team and s/he does it well and on time, a favourable impression will be built up. Turnaround managers are strongly influenced by results and will quickly see through the big talkers who do not deliver.

A view from third parties: Comparing their own views about key individuals with those of outsiders can often provide a useful check for the turnaround team. Customers usually have a view about a firm's senior managers, as may outside consultants and other suppliers. Management consultants and turnaround consultants are nearly always asked their opinion about individual managers, and sometimes about the effectiveness of whole management teams. As consultants, we interview managers; facilitate workshop and team meetings; work in implementation task forces with clients; review draft plans critiquing managers' analysis, conclusions and recommendations; and lunch and dine with the managers. Add to this our experience of working with many companies in many industries, and we are able to provide the turnaround team with a useful perspective on the capabilities and attitudes of the people they are dealing with.

Formal external assessment: Formal assessment of managers using a battery of tests – intelligence tests, reasoning and logic tests, and psychometric tests – has become increasingly common in large companies over the past twenty years. In the turnaround arena, fewer company doctors are prepared to spend the time and money testing all their senior management. There are, however, exceptions. Twenty years ago, when Sir Michael Edwardes was attempting to turn around what is now the BMW-owned Rover Group in the UK, he employed a psychologist to assess each of the managers as part of the evaluation process. More recently, the Varity Corporation used external head-hunters to interview and assess the top 200 managers in Lucas as soon as it acquired the company.

Few top managers would rely completely on outside assessment methods, but the growing use of such approaches testifies to their value. They have the added benefit of appearing to be objective – although there is little consolation for those who lose their jobs. One word of warning, however, about formal assessments: they tend to show only the good, average and poor performers relative to each other. The turnaround firm's good performers may be worse than the average performers in competitors' organizations!

How Many Should Be Changed?

It is likely that most assessments, whether done by the turnaround team alone or with the help of outsiders, will show a normal (bell-shaped) distribution curve of managerial talent. The question still remains, how many should go and how soon? The tough school will point to the one-third rule that Stuart Slatter first put forward in *Corporate Recovery* (the predecessor to this book) in the early 1980s: one-third should go immediately; one-third will be as good as any external manager given the right direction and culture; and the remaining third should be replaced over time. There are many examples both in the UK and overseas of firms following (probably unconsciously) this rough rule of thumb. In firms which catch the crisis early, it may be 40:40:20 because the best people have not had time to leave, but in some of the fragile professional service firms, turnaround has often involved replacing 50 per cent of the professional staff.

The opposing view is that while many managers may have to go due to overmanning – in which case the poorest performers should obviously go – managers surviving the cull should not be replaced. Instead, exceptional leadership should take the average performers and obtain better-than-average results from them. In many instances the turnaround manager has no choice but to go down this route, particularly in the short term. Firstly, many of the managers that one would like to change in an ideal world have a lot of know-how and information which the new team needs to keep the business going. Act too quickly and there may be a short-term cost while new management goes down the learning curve. Secondly, it is not easy to recruit good-quality managers. This is particularly true for smaller companies in crisis: who wants to risk a successful career to join a high-risk situation? The recruitment process usually takes a long time and may often stumble at the last hurdle. The search and selection process may have narrowed down potential new recruits to a shortlist; extensive interviews and reference checks have been undertaken; the preferred candidate offered the job; and then s/he eventually declines. In the meantime the other short-listed candidates have disappeared and the process must start all over again. This is extremely time-consuming for top management – time which could perhaps be put to better use dealing with the problems facing the business. Even if a new manager is recruited, there is always a strong risk that the new individual may be the wrong person for the job or may leave for new pastures before contributing to the turnaround.

An obvious alternative to external recruitment is promoting young talent. Many turnaround managers agree that once they peel away the layers of management there is usually talent that can be promoted from within. However, inexperienced internal talent, while right for the longer term, may not be able to achieve what is required in the critical twelve- to eighteen-month turnaround time frame.

Thus doing a turnaround with existing management may well be the preferred route. However, even with strong leadership, culture change without introducing a cadre of new managers is likely to be very slow in large organizations. Just a few new people will not be enough – they will become frustrated and leave. Some 20–25 per cent of the senior/middle management group needs to be brought in from outside before there is enough of a critical mass to shift the old culture.

Thirdly, and perhaps most important in a turnaround situation, is the fact that the firm cannot afford to make people redundant. Redundancy can be expensive and involve an immediate one-off cash payment, which may not be possible in a severe cash crisis. Furthermore, if the firm is planning to replace an existing employee with a new recruit then the employee is not redundant and could make a claim for unfair dismissal if the firm has not gone through the correct dismissal procedures. These procedures involve verbal and written warnings and elapsed time for an individual's performance to improve. In a turnaround, time is precious and so the experienced turnaround manager will either change the organization structure to make the individual technically redundant, or play 'hardball' with the individual. This entails making an offer to the employee of compensation if s/he agrees to leave immediately and forgo any further claims against the company, or s/he will be summarily dismissed with no immediate compensation and left to fight in court. When faced with this choice, most employees take the money.

There is clearly no one answer as to how many people should be changed: it depends on the situation, and requires considerable judgement. Experienced company doctors (even those from the 'if in doubt' school) nearly all agree that they tend to give people the benefit of the doubt too long. A year into the turnaround they look back and wish they had been tougher than they were. Managers and key people about whom they had initial doubts but decided to keep (for whatever reason) usually fail to deliver and are eventually replaced. The turn-around manager has lost valuable time which cannot be regained.

Building Capabilities

Having capable people in an organization is a prerequisite for implementing change. Motivation is of course an important ingredient, but however motivated the management and staff may be, there is no substitute for capable people. What do we mean by this? These capabilities – or competencies, as they are sometimes referred to – comprise the set of technical, business and behavioural skills needed to implement the recovery strategy. Many distressed companies lack key capabilities. External recruitment and internal promotions may solve some of the capability gaps identified by the turnaround manager. However, the success of the turnaround will nearly always depend to a large extent on the incumbent management and staff. More often than not incumbent staff possess key technical knowledge and skills, but lack business skills and some of the softer skills that may be required to succeed in the marketplace.

At senior management levels the turnaround manager will often find that there is little understanding of how to formulate strategy; what it means to be a performance-oriented company; how to manage change; how to analyse financial information, etc. The incumbents' knowledge of the business and customer relationships means that changing the senior management may not be the preferred option, even before taking account of the cost of redundancy. However, without some of the basic management skills in place, it will be hard for the turnaround manager to implement change. There are two reasons for this. Firstly, it is easier for senior management to see the need to buy in to change if they understand basic management frameworks; and secondly, implementation is likely to require senior management to do things differently, which in turn requires new knowledge.

While coaching, on-the-job training and peer pressure will all be used as part of the process of building new capabilities, management education and training can be an important catalyst for change. Tailored in-company management development programmes or workshops, which combine intellectual frameworks with practical application and discussion sessions about the turnaround firm's problems, can deliver significant benefits. The need to understand from an analytical perspective why change is required, and the opportunity to debate and discuss this with one's colleagues, are never more obvious than when one is dealing with highly analytical and technical people. Communicating new strategies to such individuals does not work; they do not accept them at face value. The other benefit of this approach is that it can provide a much-needed overall perspective which is often missing to all but those in the top team. There are usually so many initiatives or actions taking place simultaneously in a turnaround that even senior management often fail to see how the whole picture fits together. When they do, it is surprising how their awareness and commitment to change increase.

At middle management levels some of the same issues emerge, but at these levels implementation of some of the critical process improvements (discussed in the next chapter) is likely to require significant change to operating systems and working practices. Too many turnaround managers neglect the need to build middle management capabilities, and yet this is often the critical level responsible for implementing change.

Below the senior and middle management levels, staff capabilities and motivation to change are also key organizational issues. It is interesting to see just how often extensive staff training is an integral part of a turnaround strategy. In today's world skills and capabilities can be out of date relatively quickly, and yet people's skills are the source of a firm's competitive advantage.[2] Building new capabilities and skills is often crucial to turnaround success. Training, if undertaken on an in-company basis, can also be a useful way of changing and/or reinforcing new behaviours and attitudes which are important to longer-term cultural change.[3] A good example of this in practice was British Airways in the 1980s, where all staff were involved in a series of customer-service workshops. We also see a lot of staff training taking place in the turnaround of retail store chains. Improving customer service is a high priority in most turnaround situations today and cannot usually be achieved without investing in training.

Terms and Conditions of Employment

Under this heading we refer to changes to reward structures, changes to contracts of employment and changes to union agreements. All of these mechanisms are tools of organizational change widely used in managing corporate turnarounds.

Reward Structures

When we talk about rewards we usually mean the full range of money, perks and status, and even psychological rewards that employees may receive. In turnarounds it is usually pay structures that are changed. On occasion, boards of directors agree to cut their own salaries as a gesture, although the impact of this on costs and as a signal to the rest of the workforce is usually minimal. Sometimes approaches are made to employees which give them the option of redundancy or accepting lower pay. More commonly, though, pay structures are changed to link pay more directly with performance. Many turnarounds in the retail sector have involved adopting new structures that link pay to sales, and in manufacturing businesses new pay structures are often linked to productivity targets. The important point is to link rewards to the key performance indicators.

Contracts of Employment

Many companies in distress are characterized by onerous terms and conditions of employment which arose during the days of union power and high taxation of the 1960s and 1970s. Many of these contracts have by today's standards over-generous terms relating to notice periods for termination, pensions, cars and redundancy terms. Changing terms and conditions of employment requires expert legal advice and is beyond the scope of this book. It also usually involves a short-term cost to the firm and so this option may not be readily available to a firm in a deep cash crisis.

The reason for changing contracts of employment is usually more about gaining control and flexibility than cost-cutting. Although not in a turnaround situation, the new principal at the London Business School in 1990 changed faculty contracts to limit external consultancy work by faculty and introduce performance-related pay, in return raising salary levels well beyond normal university levels. Those few who did not sign the new contracts were left on the old pay scales and their careers in the institution were effectively ended. The same applies in turnaround situations.

Union Agreements

Many turnaround managers inherit union agreements that severely restrict their chances of improving operational effectiveness. Old union agreements are often full of restrictive practices which limit the introduction of new working practices, particularly multi-skilling and teamworking. One of the best examples of this occurred in the early 1990s with Rolls-Royce Motors. The company had lost 50 per cent of its volume in a twelve-month period as the recession took hold. If it had not been a subsidiary of a larger group (Vickers plc) it would probably have become insolvent. Crucial to the turnaround was a complete change in working practices, which could only be brought about if the existing rule book (the 'Red Book'), which contained the union agreement, was torn up. The situation was so bad that management told the unions that they would close the company down if they did not agree to tear up the Red Book. The outcome was a completely new agreement, which allowed Rolls-Royce to establish a cell manufacturing system with multi-skilled teams.

Many of the ex-British Rail companies sold off by the government are currently attempting to renegotiate union agreements to allow them to increase productivity over and above what can be achieved by reducing overmanning. Unless these firms are successful they may find it very difficult to compete in what are becoming increasingly price-competitive markets.

Notes

1. For a discussion of corporate culture, see J. P. Kotter and J. L. Heskett, *Corporate Culture and Performance* (Free Press, New York, 1992).

2. See, for example, J. Pfeffer, *Competitive Advantage Through People* (Harvard Business School Press, Boston, 1994).

3. F. J. Gouillart and J. N. Kelly, *Transforming the Organization* (McGraw-Hill, New York, 1995).

12 **Critical Process Improvements**

The breakdown or malfunctioning of the key processes that a company has developed and relied upon to enable it to meet delivery promises on time and to cost is a common symptom of distressed companies. If untreated, as it often is, it becomes a cause of decline and plays a key role in developing the negative spiral that we often see in troubled companies. This neglect is not wilful, but results from a change in emphasis by management as decline takes hold and financial considerations become paramount. It is because of this that effective turnaround plans have to include doing things better (process improvements) as well as doing better things (redirecting strategies). It is also because of this that it is rare to find a viable quick fix – an elastoplast solution.

Process improvements in turnarounds are aimed at:

- the demand generation process – primarily improved sales and marketing processes, which better meet customers' needs
- the demand fulfilment process – primarily improved operational efficiency in the supply chain, leading to cost reduction, improved quality and improved customer responsiveness
- key support of infrastructure processes, with improved management information and cost management systems being the priority areas for attention.

We have chosen critical process improvements instead of the more generic strategies of improved sales and marketing and improved operational efficiency as one of our seven key ingredients because the typical turnaround company is characterized by the classic 'silo mentality' whereby the functional departments operate in isolation from each other. There is nearly always a blame culture, where poor sales performance is the fault of operations and vice versa. Functions measure themselves in isolation from the rest of the organization, usually demonstrating they have improved their performance! Solutions to the company's operational problems typically require cross-functional teamwork and therefore the concept of processes is useful in helping managers understand that operational efficiency and effectiveness is about getting key functional departments to work together.

However, the reader should understand that we are not talking about classic business process re-engineering (BPR).[1] We are talking about focusing on a few critical processes where change can be implemented quickly and have a big impact on cutting costs, improving quality or improving responsiveness to customers' requirements. Our focus is therefore somewhat more functional than may be found in a corporate transformation or at a late stage of the turnaround process. There are some real dangers in adopting the classic textbook approach to process improvements.

We have seen turnarounds fail because the turnaround manager knows how the business ought to operate and sets out immediately to introduce changes and processes to develop a business that would be the best in its class, or at least as good as his/her best experience, if all the improvements were successfully implemented. A feature of a turnaround, however, is considerable turbulence at all levels in the organization; and it is not uncommon to find that the support required to render these improvements effective has been wasting away while the crisis has developed. Depleted resources render widescale process change risky, and the turnaround manager must ensure that adequate support is in place to implement change. This wasting away of support may not be obvious to the outside world until the point has been reached where it consistently and adversely affects the ability of the enterprise to meet delivery promises. The most common areas of support that begin to deteriorate are cash and staff. As support dwindles it is harder for the residual staff to operate at required levels, and this feeds the downward spiral.

We have indicated earlier in the book that crisis stabilization is critical to survival, and that cash control is critical to crisis stabilization. If the turnaround manager is not careful, his/her enthusiasm for adopting the crisis management procedures set out in Chapter 6 can give the impression of early wins, but at the expense of accelerating the downward spiral through further attacking the critical support essential for processes to operate. The end result of this is a breakdown of the business system; in which case insolvency is inevitable and the turnaround has failed. During the period prior to failure, more cash than was expected may have been released from the business – but at the cost of the survival of the company. This is a process that is some-times referred to as a 'soft receivership', whereby the business is main-tained for the purpose of achieving better asset realizations than would occur if trading were to cease. Such an outcome rarely fulfils the expectations of all stakeholders and cannot truly be described as a turnaround procedure. In such circumstances the main beneficiaries of the turnaround manager's efforts are those creditors who enjoy preferential treatment in an insolvency.

The other key support to business processes is people. We have commented in Chapter 3 that a feature of decline is the loss of key people. A feature of early crisis management is cost reduction, and often the most effective way to cut costs is to cut heads. Such procedures are, of course, totally applicable to turnaround situations, but where the axe is wielded too early and without being part of a structured process improvement plan, this can lead to a further acceleration of the downward spiral.

The turnaround manager is often faced by a dilemma. S/he is under pressure to act, but this can result in a hasty response which incurs considerable severance costs and subsequently leads to considerable re-hiring costs. The successful turnaround manager will make changes as soon as possible but not too soon.

If you read in the headlines that so-and-so has been appointed on day one, and by day seven major changes have been announced, be wary; and if the subject interests you, keep a look-out for how the company is doing in, say, a year's time. It may well be a different story to the one predicted, because the complexity of most business organizations only render them responsive to radical change that is in line with a well-thought-out plan for the fulfilment of a viable strategy. Beware the fast shooter!

Critical Ingredients

The aim of any process improvements developed and implemented in a turnaround situation should be to meet promises made to customers at the least cost to the organization while conserving cash. Improvement will usually take place along the following three dimensions:

Cost improvements: Enduring cost improvements generally result from taking steps out of processes, in order to reduce the direct costs of carrying out a particular activity. In a turnaround situation the initial focus will be on taking out non-value-added activities from the business system. Assuming that a cost-reduction strategy obtained some quick savings in the crisis stabilization phase (see Chapter 6), later actions to reduce costs typically require considerably more analysis and more involvement of staff down the organization. It is at this stage that activity-based costing is introduced and firms employ zero-based or priority-based budgeting techniques.[2] The opportunity to simplify business processes and save costs is often quite apparent as soon as the turnaround team start to map work flows in the organization.

Quality improvements: This is concerned with reducing network loops, systematically analysing the reasons for non-conformance, and putting in place corrective actions to improve processes. Quality improvements also arise from buying the appropriate raw materials and components so that quality is built in rather than bad quality being inspected out. Where poor quality is clearly a cause of decline – customers will be quick to tell you – improving quality must take priority over cost reduction. In the medium to long term, improving quality reduces costs since it is not uncommon for the cost of quality in a manufacturing business to be as much as 25 per cent of the total manufacturing cost.

In the short term, however, additional costs may be required to solve quality problems. Unless the firm can deliver acceptable quality products (or services), the turnaround is likely to fail.

Time improvement: Typically this is about making the organization more responsive to the marketplace by reducing the time taken to bring new products to market, or reducing manufacturing lead times. Changes of this nature also tend to reduce the number of steps within a process, which can reduce the indirect costs of managing or supervising the process; and reduce the 'inventory' within a process, which can significantly reduce funding requirements.[3] The situation is similar to that with quality. Customers' delivery requirements have to be met – and the turnaround manager may find that additional short-term costs are necessary to avoid losing profitable customers. The solution is often the introduction of an improved production planning function.

The critical ingredients of a successful process improvement plan require:

- understanding and buy-in from those who are going to implement them
- behaviours that give priority to corporate objectives even where these may conflict with departmental objectives
- improvements that are susceptible to measurement through key performance indicators
- improvements to processes that are aligned to the recovery strategy
- focus on processes that are critical first for survival and then for rehabilitation.

Prioritizing process improvement activities is crucial. The turnaround manager should adopt a phased approach to process improvements. In the early days s/he cannot be too radical without the 'train coming off the rails'. The turnaround manager is advised to keep his/her own counsel and not be too quick to say all the things s/he wants to achieve. Staff can quickly show signs of battle fatigue!

Sales and Marketing

When reviewing a troubled company's sales and marketing function we expect to find all or some of the following:

- the firm is out of touch with its customers, being driven instead by internal preoccupations
- little real knowledge of competitors
- a focus on volume rather than profits, compounded by poor information systems
- a large, fragmented and ageing product line
- turf wars between sales and manufacturing
- inconsistent pricing
- poorly defined incentives and over-optimistic targets
- poor understanding of which products or services to sell to generate highest profitability
- ineffective or non-existent sales targeting
- a poor-quality sales force, poorly managed
- lack of consistent performance measures
- slow response to customers' enquiries.

Many sales and marketing improvements can be implemented relatively quickly, and therefore lend themselves to the emergency phase of recovery. The major actions involve:

- understanding customers
- changing prices
- improving the sales process
- product-line rationalization
- improving the cost-effectiveness of the marketing effort.

A word of caution is needed before we start to discuss these actions. Whereas the implementation of cost- and asset-reduction strategies can be achieved without making a major impact on customers, great care should be taken when implementing marketing changes. It is one thing to upset the organization, quite another to upset one's customers! The company is more often than not in a position of weakness in the marketplace, therefore the turnaround manager must think very carefully about the consequences of any actions that are likely to have a negative impact on customers. Consequently we believe the first step is to understand customers' needs and perceptions.

Understanding the Customers

Corporate decline focuses companies in on themselves, and by the time the turnaround manager arrives, there is little talk inside the company about customers – who are ultimately the only reason the company exists at all. Senior and middle management have often lost touch with them. Understanding their needs, their buying behaviour, and their perception of the turnaround firm and its competitors, is crucial information for the preparation of the business plan. It is the starting point for both strategic analysis and analysis of critical process improvements.

In some instances it will be necessary to obtain independent market research, but in most cases there is good information buried inside the organization, inside people's heads. Typically the salesforce and customer service departments have most information, but it is not uncommon to find a few technical staff or manufacturing people with a good understanding of customer needs. The turnaround manager will also want to visit key customers. The internal and external sources together should provide enough information for the emergency phase of the turnaround. In the longer term, more detailed market research may be necessary.

Changing Price

Increasing price is a common and effective turnaround action in many instances. It can be implemented more quickly than any other strategy available to the turnaround manager. Price increase can be achieved by raising list price or by reducing discounts, or both. Price decreases, on the other hand, are usually implemented by offering large discounts or by holding prices while cost inflation continues.

Raising List Price

This is the quickest and safest method of increasing price, since changing discounts is more complex, has a greater impact on distributors, and requires more detailed cost and market information than is often available at the start of the recovery phase. There are three questions to consider:

On which products should the price be raised? The same percentage price increase on all product lines is unlikely to be appropriate unless the range is very narrow. Management therefore needs to assess the price elasticity of demand for the firm's major product lines, paying careful attention to its competitive position vis-à-vis competitors. Competitors' prices should be quickly collected (if not already known), and managerial judgements will have to be made about product comparability and price elasticity. It is unlikely that management will be able to determine how much volume will be lost for a given price increase with any degree of accuracy, since neither historical information nor the time required to undertake a market study is likely to be available. In the final analysis, the decision will rest on the argument: 'If I raise the price *x* per cent, I can afford to lose up to *y* per cent in volume for the net profit effect to be beneficial. Does it seem reasonable to think I will lose less volume than *y* per cent?' Some of the factors to take into account when assessing price elasticity include:

- products that already have high margins can often stand a further price increase more easily than low-margin products, since their competitive position is likely to be stronger
- infrequently purchased consumer goods tend to be less price-sensitive, since the user often cannot remember how much s/he paid on a previous occasion
- if there are few sources of supply for a product or few comparable products on the market, price increases are usually easier to implement
- high switching costs and fragmented buyers also lead to price inelasticity.

How much should the price be raised? Again, this is dependent on the shape of the price–demand curve; but for nearly all products there is a price premium above which demand falls off very strongly. The potential premium that can be charged over the mean market price must depend on the nature of the product and competition, but 10–15 per cent would appear to be at the high end of the spectrum. Consumers are often relatively price insensitive within a certain price range. Thus, they may decide they want to spend about £50 on buying a camera, in which case raising the price from £47.75 to £52.95 may have almost no impact on sales volume. Unless the firm has a tremendous order backlog and wants to discourage more orders, there is probably a limit to the extent to which price can be increased at one time without losing customer goodwill.

What is the best time to raise prices? Most firms' terms of trade explicitly state that prices can be raised at any time, and legally management can raise prices on any orders which have not yet been dispatched to the customer. Adopting this tactic, however, can aggravate customers unnecessarily and it is usually preferable to make price increases effective only on new orders taken from a specific date, even though the full impact of the price increase will be delayed. If the firm has excess inventories and desperately needs cash, it may wish to give customers advance warning of the price increase, in the hope of liquidating excess inventory, but the benefit of increased profits, and hence increased cash flow, in the future must be balanced against the short-term need for cash.

Another timing issue relates to the length of time elapsed since prices were last increased. If the last price increase was more than twelve months ago, there is no problem; prices should probably be increased automatically, to take account of inflation. If less than twelve months has passed, it is harder to justify another price increase, particularly if inflation is relatively low compared with historical levels. Adverse movements in exchange rates and other external shocks may warrant more frequent price adjustments.

What should be done about contracts? Today's turnaround firm may have escalation clauses built into its contracts, having learned from the lessons of others. However, even if escalation clauses are included, previous management may have totally miscalculated its costs of performing the contract, and the increased costs that may be recouped under the escalation clause will be narrowly defined. In these circumstances, new management should always attempt to renegotiate the terms of the contract. Management may have more leverage than it thinks, since the customer will not want the firm to fail before its contract is completed.

Changing Discounts

There are two types of discount with which the firm is concerned: volume (or quantity) discounts and settlement discounts. Changes in a firm's discount structure tend to lead to more customer reaction than change in list price. Such discounts tend to be customer-oriented, whereas list price tends to be product-line oriented. As a method of implementing an overall price increase, cutting discounts should therefore be avoided, particularly in the emergency phase of a turn-around when it is more important than ever not to upset the firm's customers. Cutting discounts should be used only as a discretionary tactic to discourage certain classes of unprofitable customers. How we determine who these customers are will be discussed later in this chapter, but typically we are talking about large customers who demand extra-large discounts or small customers whose volume is insufficient to cover the costs of doing business with them. Legally, the firm has to offer the same terms to all customers, but clearly some discount schedules will appeal to some customer groups more than others.

In our experience, it is sometimes more important for the turnaround firm to have a competitive discount structure than for it to have a competitive list price, although this will depend on the nature of the product and the channels of distribution. Where the firm sells direct to the customer, the customer is interested in the net price paid, rather than whether the list price is high and the discount large. Where the firm sells through a distribution channel, the situation is different. In this case the discount structure influences the distributors' incentive to push the firm's products. A discount structure that is uncompetitive by only 2½ per cent of the end-user selling price on a highly differentiated product can make a big difference in the distribution channel's interest in selling it. Thus, just as reducing discounts can lead to a loss of sales volume, so increasing discounts can lead to substantially increased volume. Whether this strategy is appropriate depends on the cost/price structure discussed in Chapter 5.

Very often the greatest pressure against raising prices comes not from the customers but from the firm's own sales department. The sales manager and the salesforce are usually the last people to want a price increase since they may well believe that any price increase makes their job more difficult. (When one finds a sales department readily agreeing to a price increase, one can be practically sure that the suggested price increase is too low!) Resistance from the salesforce will probably be greater in those situations where a large portion of their remuneration is based on sales performance. Where the turnaround management team is new to the industry, it is imperative for management to listen to and evaluate the sales department's views prior to making changes; but once a decision has been made, it must then communicate and sell the need for price changes to the salesforce. A sales meeting will almost always be necessary prior to raising price. By correct presentation of the price increase to the customer, and by harder selling, the salesforce plays a key role in ensuring that volume does not drop, or that any drop is minimized, when prices increase.

The firm's own prices and those of competitors should be constantly monitored and a formal pricing review undertaken at least annually. Thus, although the turnaround manager may have increased prices within a month of arrival largely on the basis of his/her 'gut feel' for price elasticities, s/he will almost certainly have a chance to correct any mistakes and refine the pricing strategy later.

Improving the Sales Process

Before discussing ways of improving the cost-effectiveness of the salesforce, let us reiterate that increasing sales volume is often the wrong strategy to adopt in a turnaround situation. What may be needed is for the salesforce to refocus its efforts on the most profitable and cash-generative product-customer segments, rather than to go out seeking more volume from the historical product-customer base. In some situations it is even appropriate to reduce sales effort and cut selling costs. Whichever is the appropriate strategy, many of the tactics required to improve the cost-effectiveness of the selling effort are common to all situations; the difference lies only in the instructions to the salesforce and not in the tactics necessary to achieve a competent sales process. There are a number of components:

Sales Management

Sales management – which usually consists of the general sales manager or sales director and regional sales managers – plays a pivotal role in implementing an improved selling effort. It is extremely difficult to implement the necessary changes without a capable and cooperative sales management. Not surprisingly, therefore, new sales management is often required in a turnaround situation. After the finance director, the sales manager is the most frequently replaced individual in the management team. It is well known that a good salesman does not necessarily make a good sales manager, and this is particularly true in those turnaround situations where the emphasis is on focusing for profit or cash generation rather than increasing sales volume. (There will be situations, however, where the skills needed from the sales manager lie not in planning, organizing and controlling the salesforce, but actually in getting out into the field as a key account salesperson.) There are several elements of the sales manager's job which are particularly vital in a turnaround situation. These are:

- planning and controlling the selling effort so that the sales team is correctly allocated to key products and key customers
- motivating and training the salesforce
- monitoring sales performance
- evaluating and replacing salespeople where necessary
- communicating new management's marketing plan and philosophy to the salesforce.

A sales manager who has not been used to operating in this mode is unlikely to be the appropriate person to fill the position in a turnaround situation.

Targeting the Sales Effort

It is important for the company to concentrate its efforts on selected product lines and selected customers if it is to achieve a sales increase. This is achieved by planning and controlling the use of the salesforce's time. Two steps are involved:

Categorizing customers by sales potential into A/B/C customers and those not worth calling on. 'A' customers are currently large customers or customers who should be large customers, and warrant frequent calling. 'B' customers are important and profitable customers, but do not warrant the personal attention of 'A' customers. Unlike the 'A' customers, their loss would not be catastrophic. 'C' customers have still less potential, but can be profitable customers if the overheads associated with servicing them are kept in line. Thus, whereas the 'A' customer might receive weekly calls, the 'B' customer would receive monthly and the 'C' quarterly calls. Typically, this process involves the elimination of small and unprofitable accounts; these are either ignored, passed over to wholesalers for servicing, or positively discouraged from ordering by the discount structure, minimum order sizes or surcharges.

Selecting specific product lines for promotional effort: Most often, a salesperson has limited time with any one customer and cannot effectively sell more than three products in one visit. Sales managers generally like their salespeople to emphasize one major product and two minor ones during a single visit. Which products are being promoted at any one time will depend on the product–market strategy (see Chapter 10) and the season. The salesforce will usually emphasize different product lines each journey cycle.

Introduce Key Account Management

For most companies, the 80:20 rule applies when analysing customers – the majority of sales are accounted for by a few major customers. Maintaining and building relationships with these customers is of paramount importance. Key account management is the process that is usually installed to ensure these customers receive the special attention they deserve. Some key account management responsibilities may even be taken over by the turnaround manager. Ideally, key accounts will all be profitable customers, but in a turnaround it is not unusual for some major customers to be unprofitable (although the incumbent management may not know this). Stopping sales to such an account may not be the appropriate short-term response, because although not profitable, the customer is large and provides a significant contribution to overheads.

Key account management means producing a detailed plan for that account (account planning); managing the multiple relationships that may exist between supplier and customer; ensuring that good relationships are maintained; and achieving the sales and profit targets set in the account plan.

Salesforce Motivation and Training

Effective sales targeting and improved selling effort requires a considerable change in the behaviour pattern of the salesforce. To achieve the desired end, sales management must motivate and control their activities.

The personal leadership skills of the sales management team can play an important role in improving salesforce motivation; but just as important are compensation and training. A tough approach, which says, 'Increase sales or else . . .' is unlikely to work. The need for a reasonable incentive plan for the salesforce should be obvious, but it is surprising how few UK firms in a turnaround situation have an adequate salesforce incentive scheme. Certainly not all sales situations lend themselves to incentive pay schemes, but where a quick increase in sales volume is necessary as part of a recovery strategy, additional salesforce incentives can and do work wonders. We stress 'additional' here because, unlike the USA, cutting basic pay and increasing the incentive element will not usually work in the UK environment. Some managers worry about the salesforce earning 'too much'. This is a short-sighted view and certainly does not worry successful market-facing companies, whose salespeople can earn more than many of their senior managers. A good salesperson always pays for him/herself, providing s/he sells the right products to the right customer at the right price. The incentive scheme should clearly be designed in such a way as to promote the type of sales behaviour required by management.

Salesforce training can also play a big role in motivating salespeople, but can demotivate if not done well. One of us remembers when, as a turnaround manager, we announced to the salesforce, whose average length of service was almost twenty years, that they were all going on a training programme – for many the first in their working lives. The initial shock and outrage were calmed two minutes later by the introduction of the individual who was to run the training session. What a pro! Five minutes later, after a string of the dirtiest jokes, nearly all the salesforce wanted to go for training. A few of them were beyond training, but the exercise was a much-needed morale-booster at a time of uncertainty.

Monitoring Sales Performance

Simple sales control systems should be instituted at the same time as the firm's other control systems. Sales managers should be responsible for the following:

- analysis of actual product-line sales against budget on a monthly basis, although in the depth of a crisis weekly analysis is necessary (if volume and price variances can be separated, so much the better; but this assumes a reliable standard costing system, which is absent in the majority of turnaround situations)
- monitoring sales to the few key accounts, any one of which, if lost, would severely affect the firm's profit position
- implementing simple salesforce controls such as the achievement of sales targets by territory; weekly call/order reports showing daily calls and orders; the following week's call schedule, etc.

- analysis of sales trends (using moving annual totals if the firm is a seasonal business)
- monitoring the sales impact of special promotions.

Old behaviour patterns die hard, and not all can be changed by motivating salesmen to seek new targets. Changing call patterns requires very close control, since salespeople typically like to call on friendly customers (where they receive tea or coffee!), on customers who are close to home, or on customers with whom they have a good personal relationship, irrespective of whether they are ideal customers from the firm's point of view.

Communicating with the Salesforce

We have already discussed the need to communicate both within the company and outside it. The salesforce are of course key players in this process, and it is most important that they have a positive attitude to the changes that are occurring inside the company. This can be helped by open communication and dialogue between the salesforce and management. Management must give a clear indication to the salesforce that it knows what it is doing, but words alone are rarely enough in a turnaround situation: some tangible evidence of future benefits for the salesforce needs to be forthcoming as well – hence the need for salesforce motivation and training.

Evaluating and Replacing Salespeople Where Necessary

Different sales territories nearly always have different sales potential, even though salesforce boundaries may originally have been drawn with equalization of sales potential in mind. We have already discussed cutting salesforce size as a means of cost reduction, particularly when 90 per cent of the sales volume is brought in by, say, 50 per cent of the salesforce. When this situation occurs, sales territories are redrawn, and the worst performers are made redundant. However, this is not always the situation. The number and location of sales territories may be more or less correct, but the performance of several salespeople may be unacceptable. For some, this may be obvious in the first month of the recovery; for others, it becomes obvious when they fail to adapt to the new sales management style. The idea of being told whom to call on, how often, and what to say is too much for the old guard; they are not motivated by the new incentives and hate the idea of control.

Replacing salespeople can be a time-consuming activity, particularly if a large number need replacing: the process may take two to three years if the salesforce is relatively large. Recruiting and training new salespeople is, of course, a lengthy and expensive process; in the UK the problem is compounded by the legal difficulty of removing the old salespeople. If you are replacing them, you are not making them redundant, hence the firm has to show cause for dismissal, which means warning letters and often an out-of-court settlement for unfair dismissal.

Product-line Rationalization

Most turnaround situations are characterized by product-line prolifera-tion *within* the product-market segment in which the company com-petes. This is manifested in a wide range of models, sizes or colours and, in the worst situation, all three. The product line has proliferated as a result of lack of control. Detailed sales and cost figures are required to undertake product-line rationalization, and criteria must be estab-lished for screening products; but the following guidelines can be kept in mind:

- custom-made products or frequent product modification to suit the needs of individual customers is rarely profitable unless the business is set up specifically for the task
- if sales are declining and the product is losing money, cut it out or raise prices (which may have the same effect)
- eliminate immediately any products not covering variable cost
- eliminate all products where sales are below a certain minimum level

- eliminate low-profit-margin product lines requiring high capital investment to stay profitable.

The difficult decision in product-line rationalization is deciding what to do with those products which provide a healthy contribution but do not provide a profit after allocating overheads. There is no problem if overheads can be reduced by more than the amount of the contribution when the product is eliminated, but this is often not the case within a product-market segment where many fixed costs are shared jointly by a number of products. The answer to this dilemma is either to ensure that the contribution lost by cutting out one product is recouped by persuading the customer to switch to a standard product instead; or to recoup the lost contribution by way of increased sales and profit from the reduced product line. (The rationale for this is that a narrower product line enables the firm to concentrate its efforts and lower its unit costs.) In practice, firms have found both these options to work effectively.

As soon as the turnaround manager raises the issue of product-line rationalization, s/he can expect to hear the old guard (and the sales department, in particular) cry our in horror. Their argument usually goes that the firm's sales of its major-selling products are dependent on also selling products a, b, c, x, y and z! Rarely, if ever, is this a valid argument for a firm in a turnaround situation. The counter-argument hinges on the fact that there are few examples of firms having been adversely affected by not offering a full line. One may also be able to disprove the critics by demonstrating that the key customers who purchase the major-selling products do not buy the products destined for the chop. Carrying a full line may be a valid strategy for a healthy market leader; it almost never is for a firm losing money.

Cutting out a product line usually means stopping production or not stocking a product line. This implies liquidation of inventories and a reduction in debtors, possibly even the sale of machinery. Thus some cash flow may be generated in the process, although write-downs may have to be taken on inventory and sale of plant.

Improving the Cost Effectiveness of the Marketing Effort

Six major cost components may need to be examined: salesforce costs, advertising and promotion costs, sales office costs, marketing management costs, service costs and distribution costs (including both warehousing and transportation). It has already been pointed out that greater care should be taken in reducing overhead costs in these areas because they may be immediately obvious to customers. For example, a cut in service levels, even temporarily, can lead to a rapid loss of trade confidence in the company's future ability to supply, and to a loss of sales at a critical time. From a recovery point of view, the good thing about cutting marketing costs is that the time required to implement cuts is usually very short, although the same is not true of distribution costs. The danger, however, is that the lead time to increase expenditure is often much longer: for example, it is much easier and quicker to cut the size of a salesforce than to build a new one or expand an existing one.

It is beyond the scope of this book to outline the various analytical tools available for determining optimal marketing expenditure. These are well documented in the marketing literature. It is important to remember, however, that the firm's product-market strategy needs to be developed before any really drastic cutbacks are made in the marketing area. Irreparable damage may be done by wielding axes without thinking of the strategic consequences.

The key question to ask in all cases when marketing cost reductions are being contemplated is: are current operations cost effective? The severity of the turnaround crisis will influence the answer to this question, since a sizeable portion of marketing expenditure may not affect short-term sales volume. Advertising, promotion and some selling and service expenditure may be more of an investment for the future than a necessary expense to obtain sales in the short term. In some businesses (e.g., mail-order houses) the lag effect is minimal, but in others (such as capital goods and industrial projects) the time between initial marketing expenditure and the collection of sales revenues is measured in years. Where the marketing time horizon is long, there will be a temptation to cut those costs not necessary for short-term survival. Management's time horizon for the turnaround will also influence the action taken. Does management want a quick recovery, with the idea of selling the business as soon as short-term profits pick up, or are they committed to the business over the long term? There are great dangers in taking the short-term approach, and most successful recovery situations point to a balance between the short-term demands of survival and the need for longer-term actions to achieve a sustainable recovery.

From the point of view of implementation, cutting out or reducing advertising and promotion costs are the easier steps to take since they rarely involve loss of jobs. Furthermore, it is rare that an organization cannot be more effective in its advertising and promotional expenditure. Admittedly, we have to contend with Lord Leverhulme's famous dictum, 'Half of all advertising is wasted, but we don't know which half,' but some common-sense analysis of customer buying behaviour, together with some analysis of how the company is currently allocating its advertising expenditure, and a comparison of competitors' advertising expenditure based on published data, can often pinpoint potential areas for improvement. One of the most common areas for improvement in companies that have declined is to find that their advertising expenditure is spread too thinly over a large number of products; the advertising message is being drowned by competing messages from competitors' products. Unless the company can afford to spend sufficient to get above the market segment noise-level, it may be better to cut out advertising expenditure altogether for that product.

Reducing overheads associated with the sales function usually implies such actions as reducing the size of the salesforce or eliminating regional sales offices, since controls over items such as travel and entertainment expenses are rarely sufficient to make much of an impact on profitability. The main point to remember, if cuts are made here, is to ensure that the customers do not suffer while the selling effort is reorganized.

In those companies where distribution costs are significant, a substantial effort may be required to reduce both warehousing and transportation costs. The approach and problems are similar to those for reducing manufacturing overheads, except that changes to the distribution system may affect finished-goods inventory levels and hence cash-flow requirements. Inventory levels, which affect warehousing costs, also affect production costs. The point to remember is that manufacturing and distribution costs are interdependent, and that the balancing of inventory-carrying costs against production costs is a key management decision. There may be some obvious room for improvement in a recovery situation, where little analysis is required other than adopting a heuristic approach, but in most cases good cost data are required (and are often unavailable), and sufficient time must be allowed to undertake the detailed financial analysis.

Improving Operational Efficiency

The manufacturing process is concerned with fulfilling demand, and the key concerns therefore are to manufacture at the right quality for delivery on time at the right cost. In most troubled manufacturing companies, the following characteristics are observed:

- Breakdown in communications between manufacturing and the customer-facing departments of the company.
- Products are not produced on time and are often produced for stock rather than sale.
- There are no or few key performance indicators visible and the workforce are ill-informed as to required production rates, etc.
- There are problems with suppliers of raw materials, leading to a dislocated supply chain.
- There are quality issues resulting in disputed invoices on eventually delivered products.
- Maintenance is minimal and capital expenditure is too low, or non-existent.
- There is inadequate and unreliable information as to product costs or cost-drivers.
- The workforce is demotivated and would leave for another job just as soon as one was available.

- There is inadequate production planning with 'he who shouts loudest' controlling the planning process.
- Excess stocks of raw materials with inadequate provisions.
- Work in progress is overvalued because the standard costing system is based on higher-than-actual volumes.
- Procurement is neglected, with buying being undertaken by order writers who are frankly satisfied to get anything approaching that required. Raw material cost is often a high proportion of cost of sales, yet there are usually little or no management processes in place to minimize the input cost which ensures that supplies are fit for purpose and delivered on time. We find that the company is a soft customer to its suppliers.
- There are often no criteria for selecting suppliers, and the lack of internal control leads to opportunities for fraud.
- There is no framework for measuring supplier performance.
- Many people are authorized to spend the company's money through purchasing authorities.
- Plant layout is dysfunctional, resulting in poor space utilization, long lead times and high levels of inventory. This leads to poor planning of the flow of products through the factory, and thus very high materials-handling costs.
- There is an inadequate understanding of bottleneck processes and poor management of bottlenecks.
- The capability of the manufacturing process is not matched to the requirements of product design or the customer.
- Poor planning and execution of changeover processes leads to long periods of down time.
- High rework levels, due to large batch sizes and functional layout, make it difficult to pick up quality problems when they occur, and many products flow through the defective process before corrective action is taken.
- There is poor planning of requirements for tooling, contributing to excessive changeover time.
- Reactive rather than planned maintenance is the norm, contributing to high maintenance costs and long periods of down time.

- Performance measures that do exist are focused on achieving output and maximizing utilization, rather than delivering the right product at the right time.
- High rates of absenteeism are often found.

Not all of the above characteristics are present in all cases, but in our experience most are, to varying degrees. An experienced turnaround manager will know what to expect and where to look to find the tell-tale signs. Of course, if none of the above exists, this damages the prospect of a successful operational turnaround through process improvements. If this is the case, the company's problems are likely to be of a more strategic nature.

The turnaround manager usually has multiple objectives in seeking to improve manufacturing processes:

- gain control over the demand coming into the organization
- develop a formal process for the make/buy decision
- optimize the use of the company's scarce resources to deliver the orders on time
- enhance communication between the supply and demand sides of the organization
- cut the cost not only of directly purchased products but also that inflicted by late delivery and the delivery of product of inappropriate quality
- align the mode of manufacture towards the real requirements of products and customers[4] (in reality, there may be constraints to achieving this alignment due to the state of the manufacturing infrastructure)
- align operational performance measures towards what is really required, usually consistent production of the right product at the right time, rather than a focus on achieving maximum efficiency
- align the lead-time of manufacture with the requirements of the marketplace.

Options for Improvement

Regardless of the type of manufacturing process used, there are several generic steps which the turnaround manager should consider adopting. These must be prioritized so that s/he can achieve quick wins. The principal improvements are as follows:

Establish a 'master scheduling function': This requires improved understanding between the supply and demand sides of the business. It should be staffed by someone who not only understands the demands on both sides of the business but who also has the respect of the relevant parties. This is a key appointment in most turnarounds.

Establish a sales forecasting process: There are a number of ways in which demand can be forecast, depending upon the underlying demand pattern of the products or services in question. This is a difficult and inherently uncertain process, and may not yield accurate results very quickly. However, over a period of time a greater understanding of the demand patterns of the business can lead to greater accuracy in forecasting and better control over the supply chain. Clearly the manufacturing unit can only operate efficiently if it has accurate demand schedules available to it.

Establish the lead times, planned stock levels and planned service levels being offered to customers: i.e., how frequently do we want to fulfil customer orders straight away and how often do we want to raise back orders, and on which products? The requirements for planned stock levels can be set according to these parameters. If the stock levels that are required to meet the desired service levels are too high, then this is an important driver for change to cut lead times and increase flexibility in the production process.

Consider a 'service management' approach, which defines products and services which should be delivered on certain timescales at certain costs. Establish a 'contract' between the supply and demand sides of the business which is fairly negotiated between the two functions.

Undertake value engineering on major products: This is often a source of considerable cost savings in a turnaround, particularly in technology- or engineering-driven companies.

Centralize purchasing authority and make the purchasing manager accountable for all purchasing spend.

Focus attention for obtaining delivery and cost improvements on main raw materials and main suppliers.

Negotiate improved payment terms to improve cash flow, perhaps in exchange for preferred supplier status.

Move to single or dual sourcing of supply to facilitate negotiation of additional bulk discounts (taking into account cross-company spend with suppliers).

Move to consignment stocking where appropriate, thereby passing some stock risk back to the supplier and reducing the cash requirements for holding stock in the company.

Focus on buying only what is required: In many procurement departments there is too much focus on lowest purchase price, as opposed to lowest life-cycle cost. One firm in the textile sector required very small quantities of certain special fashion colours of yarn to make particular products. The yarns were available either in relatively large production quantities or in relatively small sample quantities (at a much higher unit cost). The purchasing department was buying the large production quantities at the apparently low cost, and this cost was being factored into the costs of the products. However, in reality the fashion colours quickly became obsolete and the company was left with large amounts of obsolete stock which had to be written off at the year-end. The purchasing policy was changed to purchase sample quantities of yarn at a higher cost per unit. These higher costs were factored into the product costs, and cash flow was improved through buying smaller quantities of yarn more frequently.

Adjust the planning parameters built into the manufacturing resource planning (MRP) system. These are often inappropriately set to purchase minimum batch quantities when stocks fall below a particular level. This effectively decouples the buying requirement from the actual demand for the item, and results in over-stocking and significant risks of generating obsolescence. A much better way is to generate demand for purchase items on the basis of actual forward demand, through tweaking the MRP parameters.

Examine packaging requirements and the number of moves/packs/unpacks between suppliers and company, with a view to decreasing handling and packaging costs and sharing the benefits.

In recent years the trend in supply-chain management has been towards integrated solutions and systems based on see-through processes and trading-partner alliances. While many troubled companies have not yet reached this stage of sophistication, it is unlikely they will become rehabilitated and compete effectively unless they embrace the new order. This is because at the heart of the new integrated process is the desire to take cost out by taking steps out. It would be a mistake to move to this approach in the early days of stabilization and recovery, but that does not mean that this trend can be ignored.

The objective of a supply-chain management process is to achieve a synchronized and effective response to customer requirements throughout the organization in alliance with other enterprises that form part of the total delivery mechanism from raw materials to end consumer. The goal is to break down the internal functional silos as well as the adversarial relationships which often exist with other organizations. This is not driven by a desire to be more cooperative, but to be more competitive by tackling cost-drivers. Where organizations meet, cost structures are often duplicated by the need to monitor and drive the commercial relationship, a cost that can be reduced through strategic alliances.

Optimizing the supply chain requires not only a total business focus but a willingness to work in partnership with other organizations. This demands a significant culture shift, involving more delegation, broader roles and multi-skilling, which in turn has implications for recruitment and training policies. All those who take part need to understand the concepts, their roles, and what is expected of them. Realistically, the turnaround manager is only able to adopt such processes at a very advanced stage in the turnaround process. Consequently, we do not intend to explore the concepts in any further detail in this book. The following example shows what can be achieved in twelve months.

Process Improvements at Graphic

Background

Graphic was the largest division (representing about half the turnover) of an import business. Its main activities were the design, sourcing (from third parties mainly in the Far East), and all aspects of the supply chain from the taking of an order in the UK right through to the delivery of that order to the high street stores.

Following a crisis stabilization and business planning phase, it was clear that a fundamental reorganization of the business needed to take place in order to build competitive advantage. A business review and a research exercise carried out with its customers revealed that Graphic had a very poor track record of consistent on-time delivery of quality products. The business had a credibility issue, which resulted in the customers having to add resources within their organizations to help ensure delivery, quality and design. A short review of the business revealed many internal problems and that a holistic approach was required if long-term solutions were to be achieved that would result in a competitive advantage. However, given the fact that the business was in a turnaround situation, and its resources were depleted, it was necessary to prioritize and focus on the areas that the customers were concerned about. A decision was made to focus initially on reliability and quality.

The Medicine

The first step in mobilizing the project was to gain management commitment. This was achieved by developing a vision for the organization and outlining the opportunities available to make significant improvements. Once this was established, priorities were set and a project organization structure consisting of a steering team, a project team and task groups was established.

The first task was for the project team and work groups to map the processes right through from the point of taking an order to the point of delivery to the customer. As there were several business units, this exercise was carried out for all of them. This proved very revealing, in that the business units were all using very different processes and technology for what were effectively very similar tasks. The teams then set about eliminating non-value-added and duplicated processes, and establishing best practice across each of the business units. This yielded significant benefits. However, the most substantial benefits accrued from identifying the 'critical path' across all the activities required to be performed for each order type. The identification of the critical path enabled the highlighting and consequently the prioritization of activities. Optimally sequencing these activities enabled significant reductions in lead times to be achieved. An important contributor to improving performance was the identification of highly sensitive milestones, which could have a disproportionate impact on performance – e.g., if all the resources were not available on time to meet the supplier's scheduled production slot, the result could be a delay of several weeks until production could be rescheduled. It was therefore important to establish control processes to ensure any slippage could be identified and corrected promptly.

Having identified the processes and the critical path for all order types, it was then necessary to get technology in place. Initially a bespoke network solution was developed on Microsoft Excel to achieve a speedy implementation. This enabled each merchandiser to manage and control all their orders based on the critical path outlined above. Management reports and key performance indicators (KPIs) were developed and reported to all management weekly, with trend analysis. This gave management clear and complete visibility of the status of all orders. These reports were later shared with customers, to keep them updated on status. It allowed them to plan more accurately and was a significant step forward in rebuilding customer credibility. EDI (electronic data interchange) was added and this dramatically speeded up communications with both customers and suppliers.

It was now critical to have fully competent people in place to execute the task. Profiles were developed for each position, outlining the competencies required to perform it effectively, and comprehensive skills grids were developed. All personnel were assessed by their line managers for both their inherent abilities and skills. Fundamental people issues and skills gaps were identified. Training programmes were developed and implemented. Particular attention had to be given to the development of technology skills, and resources had to be put in place for some weeks to support people during the transition. All management were trained in the principles of supply-chain management.

It was now time to establish clear accountability for the outputs from the processes. The critical path reporting gave complete visibility of where the slippages were, what the reasons were, and who was responsible. This allowed management to manage both people and issues promptly and accurately.

Management now needed to focus and align their actions with the business strategy. This was achieved through developing quarterly objectives for each business unit manager and holding them fully accountable for the outcome. This process gave clear objectivity to the evaluation process and helped eliminate what had previously been a highly political environment, where decisions were based on opinions and lobbying rather than facts. This accountability focus led to some management and merchandisers having to leave the business.

Another issue which had to be addressed was organization structure. It was clear that the Graphic business served a very diverse range of product-market segments with quite different, and often conflicting, key factors for success. Consequently a portfolio of business units managed in a generic way could not deliver the differentiation required to achieve competitive advantage. Organization structures were developed for each business unit, with the head of that unit being fully responsible for the complete supply chain for that unit and for the optimization of that supply chain. Business unit strategies were developed which focused on building the specific competencies required to deliver against the key success factors and achieve a competitive advantage in the product-market segments being served.

The next state was to build supplier and customer partnerships. A programme was started to manage the supplier portfolio strategically.

This focused on identification of the most competent suppliers, reducing their number, eliminating parties in the chain such as agents, and partnering with the suppliers to build the competencies and systems necessary to support the business-unit strategy while eliminating non-value-added activities. The building in of quality competence at source was a major part of the initial focus of the programme. Customer partnering commenced with strategic and operational planning meetings. Cross-organizational teams were set up to resolve issues, share information and identify value-enhancing opportunities. Target market information was exchanged to help facilitate the designing of relevant products. Management information was exchanged to keep all parties informed and allow better planning and reaction to events as they unfolded.

The Outcome

While many of the change initiatives outlined above are still in the process of being implemented and have not fully realized their potential, they have already resulted in a significant culture shift. The organization is now much more customer-focused, more results-oriented and accountability-driven, while at the same time supporting people in realizing their potential in a much more progressive environment. Reliability has improved from 50 per cent on time to 95 per cent on time, while the cost of quality has halved. Most significantly, the business has moved from having a credibility issue with its major customers to becoming one of their strategic suppliers.

Management Information and Performance Management

Troubled companies are often characterized by the lack of any meaningful information, or the production of information to justify internal behaviours or sustain compensation packages despite trading realities. Information relayed to external stakeholders has often been discredited as the reality gap develops and is subsequently exposed. Information for external consumption is often late, and statutory accounts are filed as close to the deadline as possible. Disputes with auditors arise, particularly on income recognition, asset valuation and provisioning policies. We see a culture of fear and denial vis-à-vis the consequences of disclosure. Consequently surprises occur, and the reliability of information is denied.

The type of information that exists is often too financial; it keeps the score but gives little indication as to the causes of performance. Management accounts are often voluminous but never referred to. Where standard costing systems are employed, the standards are way out of date, hence the true margins are difficult to establish and often overstated. If appropriate standards in line with recent performance were adopted it would be impossible for management to produce budgets which came anywhere near viability. We see cross-subsidization and illogical overhead allocations 'to preserve the core business' or justify pet projects.

It is quite common to find functional turf wars and management operating on the basis of gut feeling and unsubstantiated opinion rather than hard facts. Senior management return to their comfort zones and resist any challenge to the status quo. There is a fear that measuring things will expose problems and lead to blame being apportioned. This leads to arguments over the reliability of the information that is provided. ('It doesn't tell me what I want to hear so it must be wrong!') Perhaps most damning in a troubled company, management fatigue leads to a lack of appetite for exposing the real problems, because solving them will often require difficult decisions which upset the conventional wisdom and the status quo.

Sadly, while management deny reality and rely on information that is least troublesome to them, the workforce often understand the position and the inherent problems that need to be fixed. This can lead to a poorly motivated workforce in search of leadership.

Clearly, in such circumstances, the whole process of management information sourcing and distribution needs to be tackled. It is critical that process improvements be put in place to ensure that reliable relevant information flows quickly, because only then can sound decisions be taken. The turnaround manager needs to devise a management information system for external stakeholders which increases predictability and full disclosure even if performance is bad. The system must be able to provide that which is requested on time and accurately.

The new process must also acknowledge that people behave according to how they are measured. The key challenge for a turnaround manager is changing the behaviours and culture of the past. The new process will usually create an 'amnesty from the past' so that historical performance can be 'forgiven' and a clean break from past behaviours can be made. If this can be carried out successfully it should help in breaking down the functional turf wars and take the fear out of exposing past weaknesses. To be effective the process must be understood, and must achieve buy-in from line management, who need to be satisfied that it will provide the information to enable them to meet their objectives and give advance warning of impending barriers to that achievement.

Improved management information systems enable the people in the organization to play their part and make a contribution appropriate to their role. The improved process encourages this by:

- being transparent and available (where necessary), with different levels of access to maintain confidentiality
- developing an environment which manages on facts
- providing the ability to generate internal benchmarking and knowledge-transfer between divisions
- monitoring progress against plan and historical performance
- communicating key performance indicators to all personnel, enabling management to reward effort and success in a way that is applauded by work colleagues.

Once reliable information relevant to the turnaround plan is being produced this will enable the distribution of endless key performance indicators. The successful turnaround manager will introduce these into the business in a structured and planned way, so as to ensure firstly that the most important key success factors are measured, and secondly that the workforce understand the key performance indicators (KPIs) and what they can do to influence performance. There is a temptation to issue all information without priority, but this merely confuses managers and creates a mountain of data with little information.

Our experience is that workforces react positively and enthusiastically to readily understood KPIs, and develop an appetite for more as they gain a greater understanding of the levers that drive change and create value. The turnaround manager can use the desire of the workforce to succeed by introducing improvements in a structured way, so that the workforce who often start as sceptics become enthusiastic converts, keen to see the rewards of their contribution to the turnaround.

The goal of an improved management information system is to produce relevant information to support a performance measurement system that measures employees' contribution to the delivery of the turnaround plan. A prerequisite therefore is the development of a strategy and an action-based business plan, as discussed in Chapter 9.

The new management information process enables the regular production of reliable information to monitor performance against plan at all appropriate levels throughout the organization. Key success factors and milestones will be established for each department, and displayed there, so as to create transparency and openness of communication.

The improved management information coupled with the relevant performance measurement system will also enable the turnaround manager to develop a compensation scheme that will reward those whose performance and behaviour enhance the prospect of achieving the business plan. The turnaround manager should be aware that actual performance as presented through the improved process is often worse than originally thought, and it is therefore generally beneficial to set targets which are achievable to take this into account. The targets can, of course, be ramped up as the workforce becomes more comfortable with the new processes and their ability to influence outcomes.

The introduction of performance measurement systems is not without risk, and the turnaround manager needs to anticipate the typical barriers to successful implementation. Typical symptoms of ineffective implementation are:

People believe that the measures are not important: If this is the case, either the wrong measures have been chosen, or they have not been communicated properly. It can often take two or three launches before everyone becomes familiar with them.

Information is unreliable, particularly for non-financial measures: This occurs because of the pressure to implement new systems quickly. Open communications and a no-blame culture result in the development of acceptable information in the shortest time.

Staff believe that they do not need the measures to perform their assigned tasks: This can be the result of spending too much time collecting and reporting data rather than doing the real job. It can also be because the measures chosen are inappropriate, or their benefit and use are not understood.

Where a turnaround manager has taken the time to communicate effectively with, and enlist the involvement of, all those staff who are affected, these symptoms rarely occur.

Notes

1. For a fuller description of business process engineering, see J. Champy and M. Hammer, *Re-engineering the Corporation: A Manifesto for Business Revolution* (Harper Business, New York, 1993).

2. M. Morrow (ed.), *Activity-based Management* (Woodhead-Faulkner, 1992).

3. G. Stalk and T. Hout, *Competing Against Time* (Free Press, New York, 1992).

4. T. Hill, *Manufacturing Strategy*, second edition (Macmillan, London, 1995).

13 Implementing the Business Plan

The fact that there are many successful corporate turnarounds – some of them very swift – is evidence that implementation is not always difficult. For some people getting things done comes naturally, but most organizations, particularly those in distress, have insufficient managers and staff of this type. It is beyond the scope of this book to look at all the aspects that comprise successful implementation: there are a few good books already available on this topic.[1] We have described in Chapter 9 the process of developing a realistic yet stretching business plan. A key milestone is the presentation of the business plan and its endorsement by third parties. But there then follows a major anticlimax, and the turnaround manager needs to redirect the energy of those involved in the business planning process into making it happen. The process of developing the plan has refocused the key people and helped build the team, but now the turnaround manager needs to lead the implementation. The reality is that implementation is often boring. It is not about reappraising, discovering options, understanding markets; it is about the day-to-day, step-at-a-time implementation of all those action points that have achieved the support of the key external stakeholders. We have already discussed key aspects of implementation in Chapter 7 on leadership, and described action planning and control systems – which are key to implementation – in Chapter 9. The focus of this chapter is therefore on other selected aspects of implementation particularly relevant to the special circumstances of distressed companies.

Ingredients for Successful Implementation

Implementation starts on day one of a turnaround. The specific circumstances of a turnaround situation – time pressure, lack of reliable information, lack of resources, and the complexity of interrelated problems – do not allow for each individual initiative to be carried out in the ideal sequence of analysing, planning, implementing and monitoring. Quick wins, especially cash-effective actions, must be implemented before the draft of a business plan has even been produced.

The definition of 'day one' of a turnaround is far from easy. We have talked about the reality gap in Chapter 3, but it has to be repeated once again that the implementation of action steps does require that management recognizes the imperative for change. In order to make implementation happen, the reality gap must be closed as quickly as possible. As a rule of thumb, two to four weeks has to be sufficient. The process of closing the reality gap is often painful for incumbent management, but it is a pre-condition for successful implementation.

The style of implementation will be affected by the resources available, attitudes to change, and the severity of the crisis. Since nearly all forms of change will affect the balance of advantage between groups within the organization, and since the benefits of change may not be entirely visible to all, implementation involves both the use of power and the art of persuasion.

Implementation is all about making things happen. We believe that the four cornerstones of successful implementation are:

- accountability
- measurability
- achievable, realistic goals in terms of time, quality and costs
- clarity of output.

Accountability

The association of *one* individual with a specific task is key. Collective responsibility inevitably leads to a collective vacuum. To make one individual responsible for a specific task has a double benefit. It signals clarity to the individual and the organization, as well as allowing individuals to commit to the task and reap motivational (or even monetary) benefits.

The fact that one individual is ultimately responsible for delivering the output of a specific task does not mean that the principle of delegation cannot be applied. In fact the delegation of sub-tasks is often the only way to achieve the set goals. Also, in creative thinking processes it is always advisable to gather teams in order to foster creative solutions. However, the turnaround team or manager must be able to identify clearly with whom the responsibility resides for the delivery of an action step or an initiative comprising a series of action steps. Accountability means that one or more managers may have to be fired to demonstrate that the new culture will not tolerate failure and that people must embrace responsibility for their actions.

There is a difficult balance to be struck between firmness and fairness. People need to be encouraged to participate, to contribute, yet at the same time repeated failure cannot be tolerated, because it lets down and endangers the rest of the team. There is a role for peer pressure, and a need for everyone to know what is expected of them and what they are expected to deliver.

Measurability

Determining whether an initiative is complete demands a yardstick of some sort. This is certainly easier to achieve for quantifiable processes, such as the reduction in the levels of stock-keeping units from X to Y. Where the issue is of a more qualitative nature, measures are more difficult to establish. Motivation of the workforce or creativity in the R&D department are typical examples. But even here measures can be defined by applying creativity to the situation. For example, the participation of the workforce in a suggestion scheme or the percentage of successful R&D projects can be indirect measures of performance. More important than quantifying these measures is their trend, provided of course they have been based on a consistent definition.

Companies in a distressed situation often have the following characteristics with regard to performance measures:

- measures out of alignment with objectives of the company
- the wrong things are measured or the measures are purely financial
- performance measures are deemed to be used to expose management failures
- lack of acceptance of results.

Since a successful implementation is so dependent on the proper use of performance measures, some guidelines for their introduction and proper application may be helpful. Our advice is to:

- make performance objectives clear to everybody concerned with them
- focus on market requirements linking internal performance to key success factors in the market
- create an 'amnesty from the past' so that historical performance can be forgiven and a clean break from past behaviours can be made
- develop financial *and* non-financial measures that identify drivers of future performance
- design measures that can be directly influenced
- design a rolling data-collection and data-processing framework
- concentrate on very few performance indicators.

The pervasive approach of measuring and quantifying the processes and deliverables of an organization by way of key performance indicators (KPIs) has been extensively described in management literature.[2] As outlined below in more detail, KPIs form an integral part of the systematic implementation of turnaround initiatives. They may also describe the processes and outputs of an organization.

The turnaround management team should restrict itself to monitoring the absolute minimum number of key indicators because they need to maintain focus and clarity, and minimize the effort involved in establishing KPIs and collecting the data on a regular l

Realistic Goals

Goals must be stretching but realistic in order to keep management and staff psychologically engaged. It must be conceivable that goals can be reached by using creativity, stretching the boundaries of imagination, and extraordinary efforts. It is interesting to note how often experienced turnaround managers talk about the need to scale down the objectives people set themselves in a turnaround. Managers in distressed companies rarely have much experience of working in a performance-oriented environment, and the turnaround manager wants to avoid the psychological effect of people failing to meet objectives. The secret of implementing change is to build up a winning mentality – and that requires realistic objectives.

Clarity of Output

One of the worst things that can happen in a turnaround situation is the waste of valuable time and scarce funds by replication or misdirected effort. Therefore the output of initiatives must be clear and understood by everybody concerned. A good management discipline of written documentation of agreed action steps is most helpful, since the organization is usually overwhelmed with increasing demands and information. Templates for project plans and action steps (as set out in Chapter 9) are easily created with modern word-processing systems. What may look too prescriptive in the beginning will be successful in channelling people's efforts and focusing their minds.

Monitoring the Implementation

The Steering Committee

A successful implementation of a turnaround demands a structure in which ideas are developed, decisions are taken and responsibilities are allocated. This structure also plays a role in communications to external stakeholders. It signals to them that the turnaround efforts are under control and that the whole organization is engaged in the process.

Typically, the turnaround structure is laid over the existing hierarchical structure of the business, and conflicts may occur. The superstructure often takes the form of a steering committee of the chief executive (the turnaround manager) and those who report directly to him/her. In the early phase of the implementation, while the business plan is being developed, the steering committee ensures that targets are sufficiently stretched; only key areas of the turnaround are being tackled; and that the implementation of early action steps does not compromise the success of long-term initiatives. It has the delicate task of balancing the short-term imperatives of the business with its longer-term aspirations.

The establishment of functional and cross-functional teams is crucial to implementing the decisions of the steering committee. They are the nucleus of many, though smaller, action steps, often geared towards cost savings. People in these teams know the details of the business better than any newcomer can.

Teams can be cross-functional or functional depending on the issues the turnaround initiatives focus on. Clearly, cross-functional teams have the advantage of breaking down what may have been a highly compartmentalized organization. Good examples are initiatives that affect the supply chain of an organization. Purchasing, conversion and delivery are three activities that have a tremendous impact on how the supply chain performs. It is apparent that problems in the supply chain, which can put the company at a serious strategic disadvantage, can only be remedied if those who are concerned with these activities work closely together. Yet cross-functional teamwork is not the panacea. There are situations where a small functional team or a dedicated individual is more appropriate.

Teams of any nature do not automatically perform well: team-working, especially in its embryonic stage, is often painful and ineffective. Careful selection of team leaders and training for them can provide a solution to the problem.

The role of the steering committee in keeping a focus on the key issues cannot be over-emphasized. If it does not perform this role, efforts of the teams become channelled into activities that seem highly important from a team's perspective but are, in fact, of little significance and leverage in the overall context. Again, the steering committee has to strike a fine balance between focusing on key issues but not demotivating people who may have taken initiatives on a smaller scale.

In a later stage of the turnaround, when a business plan has been developed and the implementation of initiatives is being carried out, the steering committee adopts a slightly different role. Its membership may change, and at this stage it is often called the 'executive committee'. The executive committee has the role of monitoring the progress of key initiatives and instigating new turnaround initiatives where the need for them arises. It can also be the forum where the company gives evidence to other stakeholders or their representatives that the implementation is on track. For example, advisers of the lending banks can be invited to these meetings in order to demonstrate an open relationship with the lenders.

Finally, it is important that the structure of a steering committee supported by teams is understood and agreed by everybody in the organization, or at the very least by those who occupy key roles in the turnaround.

The Implementation Report

Successful implementation needs managerial discipline, most basically:

- adhering to agreed schedules
- agreeing action steps and recording them
- following up
- communicating what you are doing.

These four virtues are reflected in a document that we call the 'implementation report'. Regularly issued, this sets out the initial initiatives and action steps developed and set out in the turnaround plan, as well as the associated deadlines and responsibilities for them, thus building up a history of each initiative. Each action is recorded for a period of five to ten weeks, so that an audit trail becomes visible. The report also sets out the near future, i.e., the next tactical moves. It is a dynamic, living document which forces people to adhere to agreed schedules and deadlines (because of its immediate and 'public' nature), records agreed action steps, and communicates what is happening in the turnaround process. It may also summarize other important pieces of information, including, for example:

- cash position and short-term working capital levels
- other key performance indicators
- sales reports and gross margin
- a schedule of covenants
- other internal communication on specific issues, such as a progress report on a disposal of an asset.

The implementation report may serve as the agenda for management meetings supervising the turnaround progress. For an implementation report to be effective, it has to be a dynamic working document for management. It therefore demands permanent maintenance by resources which are normally scarce in a turnaround situation. If this is the case, outside help could be brought in to set up a system and procedure to collect the necessary information until the company takes over these activities and incorporates them in its normal routines to manage the business. Notwithstanding this drawback, the implementation report has proven to be a successful tool for managing the turnaround process in larger organizations, and in communicating to an array of stakeholders.

Resourcing the Implementation

Hopefully it has become clear throughout this book that a turnaround situation puts extraordinary demands on the organization and its resources. The implications of this are a narrowing and shortening of managers' horizons; physical and mental stress; and uncertainty. Furthermore, turnaround situations require different skills than the usual course of business. All this is particularly true for the implementation phase, which lies at the heart of any successful turnaround and starts, as argued earlier, on day one of a turnaround.

Given this setting, one can argue – and it has often proven true – that additional support is not only helpful but can be vital. This support can come from hiring either additional permanent staff or interim managers and consultants. The ideal specification for outside help during the implementation phase includes the following characteristics:

- strong commercial skills
- able to cope with uncertainty
- forceful implementation; down-to-earth
- creative: able to find a solution, even though this solution might be sub-optimal in an ideal world
- leads by example, re-energizing the organization
- functional and/or general management expertise
- able to handle high levels of stress.

Those characteristics reside either with practitioners specializing in corporate turnarounds, with interim managers or sometimes with consultants.

It is argued that during the first phase of a turnaround most of the groundwork has to be analytical. Future actions and their financial impact have to be founded on a solid base of facts and key indicators. In order to establish this base of confidence, key sets of financial, strategic and operational information have to be scrutinized without leaving anything to doubt. This process has been already described in more detail in Chapters 5 and 9. Turnaround consultants or practitioners have those financial, operational and strategic skills, often blended with industry expertise.

Once the business plan has been agreed, the whole emphasis of the turnaround leader and interest of the stakeholders is in implementation. In this situation, day-to-day operations need experienced and motivated functional managers, so the role of any outside help is different: it is more about relentless progress-chasing blended with people-management skills.

Employee Participation in the Change Process

In view of the responsibilities that are attached to action plans, it is important to achieve employee ownership and commitment to them. While the approach for developing the business plan will be largely top-down, the insight employees can contribute to a troubled business should not be underestimated. The turnaround manager should seek to harness this knowledge, particularly during action-plan development. However, to ensure honest and open feedback, employees must feel that there will be no retribution from challenging the status quo – no 'sacred cows'.

If employee buy-in is to be achieved in the long run, initiatives eventually have to be participative from the bottom up, with the turnaround manager acting as coach/facilitator in the process. The turnaround manager will set targets, establish and challenge working parties to achieve stretching targets, and lend much-needed experience to the process. A good example of a successful turnaround process involving significant employee participation occurred at Philips between 1989 and 1992 (see box).

Involving employees in successful project teams can be particularly effective using the concept of breakthrough projects. The crisis stabilization process may have given some managers experience of being part of a successful action-oriented project team; but it is only when it comes to implementing the business plan that the majority of the managers and staff become involved. There will invariably be lots of initiatives and lots of different project teams put to work. However, as we said in Chapter 7, top management leadership is necessary to prioritize the projects and to sustain efforts throughout the implementation phase.

Typically, initiatives where quick wins have a significant impact on cash and/or profit will take priority. However, management should not forget that project teams are most successful if they start by focusing on *breakthrough* projects, and pay attention to team-building at the start of each project.

Philips Change Process[3]

Under the name of 'Centurion', the change process started as a top-down cascade through the organization, but with the clear intention of becoming bottom-up once it had begun to generate its own momentum.

It initially involved regular meetings of the organization's top 150 managers, with geographic and functional variety, who were first given the harsh realities of the seriousness of Philips' financial health (in October 1990, Jans Timmer, President, predicted bankruptcy within two years), and then challenged to work in small groups to identify actions that would avoid this doomsday scenario and turn the business around. Working independently, the initial working groups came to the same conclusion: that the company had to take immediate action to reduce its asset base, including drastic cuts in inventory, and had to reduce its workforce by about 20 per cent, in order to match the benchmarks set by the group's leading competitors.

The initial working parties prescribed a company-wide transformation process, 'engaging employees at all levels, functions and countries in the overall task of creating and sustaining a winning culture'. This was Operation Centurion, which had the ultimate objective of developing and implementing turnaround strategies throughout the entire organization, with all 240,000 employees eventually sharing in its responsibilities. Industry benchmarks were used to establish targets for restoring global competitiveness.

Sub-groups of managers at every level of the organization met regularly (at least every three months). The groups were required to implement the decisions of their immediately senior working party, and challenged to develop solutions to specific issues within their own business or department – identified by the senior working party or by themselves through discussions of performance shortfalls against exacting criteria. A project owner or champion, milestones and KPIs were set to enable progress to be monitored at regular intervals. These sub-groups also subdivided certain issues and set challenges for working parties made up of the next level of managers down the hierarchy.

Breakthrough projects have five characteristics.[4] They involve:

- selecting an urgent initiative which grabs the attention of those involved
- breaking the initiative down to focus on achievable first-step goals
- focusing on measurable bottom-line results
- exploring what people in the organization are already willing and able to do (the no-brainers they have been wanting to do for ages)
- selecting an initiative which is achievable within the available resources of the team and within their authority.

If the project team is going to be spending a lot of time on a large, perhaps 'mission critical' initiative, it may be worthwhile to take a day out to undertake a team-building exercise at the start of the project. There is a lot of evidence, particularly in the construction and capital-goods industries, that a small investment in project team-building can bring projects in on time and on budget.

Critical Situations During Implementation

During the implementation of the turnaround plan, critical situations may occur that jeopardize the ongoing implementation or cause management to question parts – sometimes all – of the turnaround business plan. This usually occurs when company performance falls significantly behind plan and/or there is significant resistance from key personnel.

There are four principal reasons why company performance may lag behind plan:

The initiative in question addresses the wrong issue, or is inappropriate: Even though a considerable amount of operational and strategic analysis was performed by seemingly competent people, they may have made errors of judgement. If this is so, the company may face severe problems and insolvency might no longer be averted. Designing the appropriate turnaround initiatives first time right is of the utmost importance; one may not get a second chance. If there is time, management should revisit the initial analysis.

Assumptions are no longer valid: A plan is only as good as the assumptions underlying it. Assumptions which may change range from a fundamental shift of market conditions to an unexpected collapse of a major competitor. Or an initiative may have relied on the specific knowledge of a key player who has left the firm in the meantime. When underperformance has been caused by such circumstances, the assumptions behind the key initiative need to be revisited and the initiative amended accordingly.

Results are lagging behind target: Having clearly established that the expected results did not materialize, it is important to analyse the reason. Unless a reason can be identified unambiguously and corrective actions taken, it is highly dangerous to digress from the original plan. The rule of thumb should be to stick to the original plan provided that management has confidence in it and shows commitment to it. Otherwise the plan becomes diluted, and management starts to rethink and possibly 're-invent the wheel', with the inevitable distraction and loss of focus that involves. Indiscriminate and reactive changes to the plan are in danger of undermining the confidence of management and workforce.

Either management has been too optimistic in its time planning, or it is putting too few resources behind the initiative. Options may range from enhanced investment to changing operational practices, or doing nothing and being patient (see box).

Improper implementation: This is usually due to a manager failing to take action as agreed in the plan. Excuses should not be acceptable and a formal warning procedure may be appropriate in such circumstances.

Despite great management efforts throughout the implementation phase, some individuals tend to continue to resist change either overtly or covertly. The latter, covert, form of resistance is more difficult to

---

Example of Results Lagging Behind Plan

The turnaround plan of a company in the UK textile industry was intended to reposition the product range by adopting more fashionable styles and colours. Although the repositioning of the products was done with enthusiasm and support from the operations, the initial market reaction was poor and disappointing. The initiative to reposition the company and its products had seemingly failed despite extensive market research and competent internal discussions.

The fact was that these new products had to find acceptance among their customers, and only a minority of them were able to match or exceed customer expectations. The general direction of repositioning, though, was a sensible if not an immediately viable strategy; later turning out to be totally appropriate.

---

identify, can have undermining effects, and is, on balance, potentially more detrimental than overt resistance. Resistance to change usually follows from fears about job security, rewards and career expectations. The benefits of communication, discussed in Chapter 7, usually hinge on the reduction of uncertainty about the consequences of change.

Notes

1. See, for example, Tony Eccles, *Succeeding With Change: Implementing Action-driven Strategies* (McGraw-Hill, New York, 1994).
2. See, for example, R. S. Kaplan and D. P. Norton, *The Balanced Scorecard* (Harvard Business School Press, Boston, 1996).
3. London Business School, *Philips Semiconductors: Breaking with the Past, a Case Study* (March 1996).
4. For a more detailed description of breakthrough projects, see Robert H. Schaffer, *The Breakthrough Strategy* (Ballinger Publishing Co., 1988).

14 **Financial Restructuring**

In this chapter we discuss some of the fundamentals of financial restructuring. This chapter is mainly of interest to independent corporate entities that are subject to turnaround, rather than subsidiaries of parent companies, where funding is provided through inter-group arrangements.

The overall objective of financial restructuring is to achieve a debt and equity structure that enables the company to implement its turnaround plans, to meet all its ongoing liabilities as they fall due – i.e., to be solvent – and to fund the strategic redirection where appropriate. Outside the turnaround situation, the key responsibility of directors is to grow shareholder value, whereas the turnaround procedures outlined in this book are concerned with achieving stability first and restoring value second. The restructuring process goes through a critical stage where the directors have to look after the interests of, and gain the support of, their funding stakeholders first before they can return to their prime duty of growing shareholder value.

Tensions arise in this process since, to achieve the overall objective, external funding stakeholders often have to acknowledge potential and actual loss and thereby reduce their interest in the company. Debt providers, typically, may have to reduce the value in their books of the asset that the debt represented, while existing equity providers are severely diluted by the injection of new equity or, more commonly, the conversion of debt into equity.

The need for financial restructuring leads to a very real and appropriate interest in the turnaround plan by the funding stakeholders and may well lead to them presenting pre-conditions for their support. It is not uncommon for changes in management to be demanded. Management can spend as much time as they like developing a turnaround plan, but if it does not have the support of existing or new stakeholders they will not have the opportunity to implement it. The area of financial restructuring is a potential roadblock to any plan, and it is critical therefore that any restructuring proposal recognizes the best option available to the stakeholders, and clearly shows them that it is in their best interest to support the business plan and the proposed financial structure. (We have dealt with the dynamics of stakeholder management in Chapter 8.) The interests of the stakeholders and the company need to be aligned.

A refinancing is usually a two-stage process: short-term survival financing followed by longer-term financial reorganization of the capital structure. It is not uncommon to see second- and third-phase refinancing. Refinancing will generally proceed so long as it is the best alternative for the stakeholders concerned.

Short-term Survival Financing

Short-term financing ensures that there is sufficient funding in place to enable the company to produce its business plan and to develop a refinancing proposal. At this stage it is normal for the critical stakeholders to be the providers of debt. In some circumstances equity shareholders will provide the support, but this is very risky for them because their support may actually go straight to a reduction of the debt exposure.

Priority of Interest

Under UK company law, different stakeholders have different priorities of interest in the event of insolvency; thus it is vital for management to have a clear understanding of the rights of their various classes of stakeholder before entering discussions with them. Their rights are likely to affect the stance they take in any discussions. A full description of their rights is beyond the scope of this book, but the reader may find our brief overview helps in framing questions for their financial advisers – who will inevitably be involved at this stage.

Fixed-charge creditors: This class of creditor has the benefit of a specific charge or pledge over specific identified assets, and in the event of default of the terms under which credit was advanced, they may take possession of that asset and dispose of it to reduce their debt. The clearest example in a domestic situation is a mortgagor of a property. In a commercial situation fixed charges are normally available over freehold and leasehold property interests; book debts due to the company; the goodwill of the company; and fixed plant and machinery. The protection also extends to providers of finance through leasing arrangements.

Retention-of-title suppliers: These are not funding stakeholders as such, but whereas suppliers, who operate on the basis that they retain title to goods supplied until those goods are paid for, present no concern under normal trading conditions, they may cause concern during the crisis stabilization period. The rights enshrined in their agreed terms of trade may result in them having to be paid for goods supplied before other creditors in order to enable continuation of supplies.

Preferential creditors: Insolvency legislation identifies certain creditors as being preferential, which means that their entitlements are to be met out of the proceeds of sale of assets in a formal insolvency before the amounts due to subsequent creditors are settled. They rank after creditors having the benefit of fixed charges and retention of title. Preferential creditors include employees, as regards a portion of their claims on insolvency, as well as government departments as regards taxes.

Floating-charge creditors: Providers of finance have undertaken an agreement with the company under the terms of a duly registered debenture which gives them a number of very important rights in the event of default. The logic of this process, which has proved to be very successful, is that it allows banks and other lenders to lend more than they otherwise would to fund trading. It is also the instrument which gives banks substantial influence and ultimate control when the debt subject to the debenture is at risk. Creditors who have the benefit of a floating charge rank ahead of unsecured creditors. On realization of the company's assets that are not subject to a prior encumbrance, they are entitled to the net proceeds after the preferential creditors' claims have been settled in full.

Unsecured creditors: This class of creditor normally consists of trade suppliers to the business, who take a credit risk when dealing with any company. The extent of the risk is often unknown to them, and dependent on the existence of priority creditors as described above. Included within this broad category are members of the public and others who may have paid deposits to the company in anticipation of a future supply of goods. Because of the nature of the credit risk taken by the suppliers and customers in this category, the directors of companies have particular personal duties of care to them. The duties are to ensure that they do not continue to take credit where they know or should have known that there was no reasonable prospect of avoiding insolvent liquidation. In others words, directors have a duty to be careful when incurring credit, and this is particularly so during the survival or crisis-stabilization period. This can be a potent force in persuading directors to reach an accommodation with bankers. Some banks may themselves be unsecured creditors if they do not have the benefit of fixed and floating charges. We will see later that the position of the banks plays an important role in short-term refinancing.

Equity investors: This class of stakeholder includes all those funders of the business who stand to profit most from the success of the enterprise, but therefore are most at risk when the business becomes vulnerable or fails.

Short-term Refinancing

Refinancing for the short term has three key steps. The first step involves establishing the current financial position. This includes clearly understanding the current liabilities to all creditors, ranked as above, as well as establishing the current facilities that exist with all the suppliers and funders. On the positive side, it involves establishing the cash available to the company during the survival period. (We have dealt with crisis stabilization and the preparation of short-term cash flows in Chapter 6.) That cash flow will reveal what funding is required during the period that it will take to prepare a turnaround plan and agree a longer-term financial reconstruction. It is unlikely that significant headroom will be made available; consequently great care is needed in establishing the forecasts.

The second step involves establishing the company's future prospects. The board needs to form a view both collectively and individually as to whether they believe that they will be able to develop a viable turnaround plan that will gain the appropriate support of the funding stakeholders. This is a very difficult and critical stage in the short-term refinancing process. The board will not have full information, and yet they have a duty to their suppliers, and cannot expect their funders to support them if they are not confident (on the basis of their current knowledge) that a viable way forward can be found. If the board cannot reach a view that a viable financially supported plan can be produced, they should consider taking steps to start insolvency proceedings. This is a critical step for a board and they should be closely advised during this process. They should clearly document decisions made and the key considerations of the board in reaching those decisions. This is not a once-and-for-all decision but one that needs to be regularly revisited until a satisfactory restructuring is in place. The law does not require directors to avoid risk, but it does require reasonable caution in difficult times.

The final step is to request short-term support. Before discussing this area, we must stress that it is absolutely paramount that the directors conduct any such discussions with complete openness and transparency, since the consequences of a creditor or bank agreeing to support on the basis of a misrepresentation can be very severe for the directors.

Complicating factors that can adversely affect the refinancing process are the number of funding stakeholders involved, the size and complexity of the business, and the amount of short-term funding required.

The whole matter of negotiating the short-term refinancing with stakeholders was covered in Chapter 8, but some key points are worth bearing in mind:

Agree a realistic time-frame, which allows for the financial restructuring negotiations – they only start once the business plan is completed. The period required differs from situation to situation, but at least two to three months is required for the funding stakeholder to receive and consider a plan and the attached financial proposal as well as to pass it through its own credit-approval procedures and then agree the legal documentation that supports the agreement.

Restructure with existing fund providers: it is usually too time-consuming to bring in new sources of funds.

Minimize the amount required, since an early response will be necessary. We have discussed in Chapter 6 how this can be achieved, but clearly if the company can operate through the survival period without requesting new money this is the best outcome for all, unless it is achieved by the non-payment of suppliers.

Resist any request by creditors, including funding stakeholders such as banks, to improve their position unreasonably as a price for short-term support. The typical scenario is one where new money is required during the survival period but the bank or banks are unsecured or have a blemish in their existing security. Quite naturally, the banks will wish to take full security over the whole debt as the price for providing the new money, or take new security to remedy any blemishes in their existing agreements. Considering the duty of the directors to all the creditors and shareholders, a fairer outcome is to give a form of restricted security over the new money only, so that it is transparent to all that no advantage has been given in the current situation to one creditor or class of creditors over another. Even this security should not be given lightly, however, since the result will often change the balance of power and may limit the options available on the long-term financial restructuring. We have found that limiting security to a fixed charge on a discrete asset is generally wiser than the provision of a limited floating charge.

Gain an understanding of the alternatives available to the creditor whose support the company requires, before seeking that support. What is their worst-case position? What power do they have?

Once the financial position of the company has reached a stage where turnaround is being considered, all of the pressures described earlier in the book come into play, and it is not unusual for a bank to appoint investigating accountants to assess the current position and advise them. While it is important for the company to cooperate fully, and involve its bank, it is rarely in the company's interest to have an investigating accountant appointed. The company should seek to appoint its own advisors who are experienced in this work with a view to them working with management to help provide the plans and requests that are critical to achieving the support due in the survival period. Financial restructuring is an expensive business and the company can contain these costs by enabling the external stakeholders to have unfettered access to its advisors on matters of information and reports. The development of an open, transparent process should enable the funders to obtain the information they need, on which they can seek advice as appropriate.

In many cases company directors are in denial mode or do not wish to make full disclosure. In these cases it is absolutely right that the banks should insist on the appointment of investigating accountants to establish the true financial position, as a prerequisite to considering a request for short-term support. This approach, however, leads to an adversarial position which is not conducive to finding the appropriate solution and achieving sensible restructuring.

Where a number of creditors in any class are involved, it is beneficial if discussions can continue with one of those creditors only, who acts as agent for all the creditors in the class. This is harder to achieve in moratorium negotiations than in banking situations, but even here the company should seek to limit the number of advisors and principal parties involved. Not only does this save substantial costs but should also reduce the complexities that lead to disagreements.

Standstill Agreements and Moratoria

Depending on the size of the debt and the severity of the crisis, arrangements with the company's bankers are usually either managed within existing arrangements, as amended, or by a standstill or standfast agreement. These agreements are more common in a multi-banked situation than in bilateral arrangements, although where a series of bilaterals exist, the banks often come together through an inter-bank agreement among themselves, leading to a standstill agreement with the company.

Considerable time and expense are incurred in reaching these agreements and the turnaround manager can easily be diverted from the key task of operating the business by the need to deal with what is a critical issue – the continuation of adequate funding. Best practice in these circumstances is for the turnaround manager to delegate the major part of the negotiations to specific members of his/her team supported by the company's advisors.

The purpose of the standstill agreement is to record evidence arrangements as regards the terms, covenants, costs and extent of facilities during the period of the standstill. In exchange for agreeing to these, the bank or banks agree not to exercise prior rights under existing facilities. Clearly the obligation can be onerous, and it is critical that whoever is negotiating on behalf of the company has reliable information since the consequences of breach of standstill agreements can be severe for the company. As in any negotiation, the turnaround manager needs to estimate the bank's best alternative to a negotiated agreement and just beat it.

So far, we have concentrated on obtaining short-term support from the company's bankers, since banks are in the business of lending money and understand the attached risks. In certain circumstances, however, it is appropriate to seek support from major suppliers by way of a moratorium. For a moratorium to have a reasonable prospect of success it must be in the interest of the suppliers concerned for the enterprise to continue. Clear examples of this exist in the oil and gas distribution sector as well as the motor industry distribution sector. These cases are often characterized by the existence of a few major suppliers and the need for the distribution channels to remain available to them. However, as with the banks referred to earlier, for this to work, support must offer a better prospect of recovery to the supplier than the alternative available to them.

A moratorium must be negotiated openly with key suppliers, who need to be made fully aware of the facts and circumstances so that they may make a balanced decision. It is quite in order for such suppliers to be granted priority through security in exchange for support, but the observations we made earlier as regards banks apply equally here. Where a supplier is also a competitor, it is quite appropriate for the turnaround manager to request appropriate confidentiality agreements before making full disclosure of the company's financial position.

The likely outcomes of short-term refinancing are changed banking terms and/or additional short-term borrowing from existing banks. Changed banking terms will involve some or all of the following: temporary relaxation of existing covenants, extension of maturity dates, postponement of principal repayments due, and all or part of current interest payments due being rolled up into capital. Where additional short-term borrowing occurs it will typically involve higher interest payments, tighter covenants and arrangement fees.

Long-term Financial Restructuring

The short-term refinancing will have provided the company with that vital breathing space during which time the turnaround plan has been developed, and the company has begun to rebuild credibility with its key stakeholders. The crisis stabilization plan should have been implemented, and parameters for a more permanent financial restructuring plan explored. The objective of the long-term financial restructuring is to provide the company with a solvent balance sheet and an ability to implement the agreed plan whilst servicing residual or new debt. It should also restore creditor confidence, be acceptable to all stakeholders, and recognize, where appropriate, the need for management motivation.

The debt and equity stakeholders will wish to be satisfied by answers to the following questions:

- does the company have a viable future and a viable market?
- will it provide a realistic opportunity for restoring value while providing adequate returns on new monies in the meantime?

- will the banks get any new money back and increase the prospect of recovery against existing expenses?
- does the company have the right management team to implement the plan successfully?
- does the plan provide a better outcome than available alternatives even when reasonable sensitivity analysis has been applied to the financial measures?

If the answer to all of the above questions is positive, the company can expect an enthusiastic involvement from its stakeholders to find the best structure. The turnaround manager should seek to develop an atmosphere where the company and all its stakeholders are working together to obtain a solution that will enable the company to be restored to viability.

Equity stakeholders often take a different view from debt stakeholders, in that the priority for providers of debt is to recover their loans with appropriate reward for providing risk support; whereas the equity stakeholders are more willing to write off unsuccessful investments but want to retain the upside on any new money going in. This leads to a tight negotiation between the stakeholders, particularly if there is to be a swap of debt for equity by the debt provider to provide balance-sheet solvency. The debt provider would generally seek an equal ranking on converted debt to new equity injected, whereas the equity providers will want to see a discount on conversion. The negotiation will be driven by each party's perception of the value of their best alternative to the negotiated position. The company is often an interested bystander during these proceedings, which can become very frustrating.

Since financial restructuring is a lengthy, expensive and worrying process, all parties should set out to achieve a once-and-for-all solution. Unfortunately, our experience is that many refinancings require a further refinancing because the debtor banks are not prepared to take a big enough write-off at the time of the initial refinancing. However, the objective should not be lost.

Typical financial restructuring packages include:

- converting all or part of bank debt into equity or convertible loan stock

- converting unpaid or rolled-up interest into debt and/or equity
- rescheduling debt repayments, which may involve changed interest rates and changed covenants
- restructuring outstanding public debt
- restructuring outstanding preferred stock
- new borrowing
- new equity issues, usually through a rights issue or a private placement.

The financial restructuring plan starts with the financial projections of the business plan. The future cash stream is valued, and the restructuring plan attempts to allocate the value of the firm (about which, of course, there will be disagreement) across the different claimants. Factors which influence the resulting structure include:

- the existing capital structure
- the ongoing financial requirements of the business
- the current and potential values of the business
- management credibility
- the relative bargaining power of each set of claimants
- tax considerations.

Key debt renegotiation issues revolve around how much value should be given to each creditor and what type of financial instrument each creditor should receive. Senior debtors – those with priority claims – usually want cash but often have to give up some of their priority positions in order to obtain agreement. Of course, any agreement has to be better for them than the base-case insolvency option. The LEP Group provides a good example. At the end of the 1991 financial year, LEP had total borrowings of £546 million and a deficit on shareholder funds of £107 million. Due to the nature of its core freight-forwarding business, it was thought that only about £100 million would be recovered in a receivership, because the freight-forwarding business would disappear overnight. The reconstruction route was chosen, with the banks converting £180 million of debt into 85 per cent of the equity. In the event, this write-off was not enough and the company was eventually liquidated owing secured creditors £135 million (and unsecured creditors £95 million) after all the assets of the holding company had been sold.

Typical bank objectives in a restructuring are to maintain the priority of debt and convert the minimum of debt to equity. In some cases they try to ensure equity voting control. The financial restructuring of Isosceles, the Gateway Foodstores' parent company, in the early 1990s gave senior debt-holders 56 per cent of the votes with only 10 per cent of the common stock. Banks, like all stakeholders, try to maximize their return, but recognize the need for all stakeholders to agree. With the secondary-debt market in the UK just starting to grow, this is going to be increasingly difficult to achieve – particularly where the same class of debt has been purchased at different prices by the holders. Understanding a creditor's view of a potential exit will depend on the exiting cost. Within the developing secondary-debt market we now see numerous entry points at different prices in major restructurings. While the secondary-debt market provides increased liquidity, it complicates exit arrangements.

Depending on the risk profile of the restructured financing, it is not unusual for banks to trade near-term fees and margins for options to acquire shares at a pre-set price at a future date. This can of course be very satisfactory for the company, but will be the subject of discussion with the equity providers. It can also give a strong signal to the market that the banks have confidence, and this can help with other suppliers. The debt funder will often want to see asset disposals, or indeed business disposals, to reduce gearing. This is a fair request, as the bank seeks to return the relationship to one which is within their acceptable risk profile. The turnaround manager needs to resist the temptation to hold on to everything, since the company will benefit through regularized arrangements, but clear negotiations are required about what should and could be disposed of.

While the focus of financial restructuring negotiation is on the debt-holders, equity investors usually expect to end up with between 10 and 20 per cent of the company even if it is basically bust, since their support is required to vote through the new structure.

Equity investors also appreciate that their returns are dependent on the performance of management, and that a financially motivated management often succeeds better in a turnaround than a bonus management team. The ideal position is where the interests of the management team are totally aligned with the equity investors, and where management will be well rewarded for the successful turnaround. This truly recognizes the incredible effort that is needed to turn a well-thought-out plan into reality. A successful turnaround manager and his/her team deserve to have a certain percentage of equity reserved for them. At the end of the day, they are the most important of the seven key ingredients.

Where new equity comes in as part of a financial restructuring plan, in either public or private companies, the requirement is for speedy implementation of a viable plan to achieve a very profitable exit. The equity provider will therefore wish to be clear as to what the exit opportunities are, and will wish to minimize the dilution of any existing equity interest while being satisfied that the company can cope with its residual debt.

Index

Numbers in italics refer to Figures.